PARALEARNING STUDY COMPANION

www.paralearning.org

STEVE HIGGINS

First edition published April 2023

ISBN 979-8-390-16879-0 (paperback)
ISBN 979-8-390-16895-0 (hard cover)

Copyright © Steve Higgins, 2023

The right of Steve Higgins to be identified as the author of this work has been asserted by him in accordance with the Copyright, Designs and Patents Act 1988.

All rights reserved. No part of this book may be reproduced in any form or by any electronic or mechanical means, including information storage and retrieval systems, without permission in writing from the publisher or copyright holder.

Independently published by Project Weird
www.projectweird.com

PROJECT WEIRD

Exclusive Reader Offer

The 'Paralearning: Study Companion' serves as a supplementary guide to reinforce and refresh the knowledge gained from our unique online paranormal course. So before diving in, ensure you get the most out of your paranormal education by enrolling on one of our courses at paralearning.org.

To make it even more enticing, we're offering a special 40% discount on the full range of Paralearning courses. Scan the QR code below to claim your discount and start your adventure with Paralearning today.

Contents

Introduction	**13**
Quick Reference Guide	**15**
Practical Ghost Hunting	19
Demonology	29
Scientific Theory	47
Capturing and Analysing EVPs	69
Event Planning and Management	87
Practical Ghost Hunting	**103**
Determine if a Location is Haunted	105
Ruling out the Rational	123
Capture Evidence of the Haunting	133
Communicating with Ghosts and Spirits	147
Legalities of Ghost Hunting	167
Demonology	**171**
Studying Demons	173
What are Demons?	177
Possession and Attachment	181
Confirming a Demonic Presence	187
Protection Against Demons	193
Summoning Demons	199
Exorcisms	205
Scientific Theory	**215**
Energy, Fields and Frequencies	217
Instrumental Transcommunication	241
Consciousness and the Soul	257
The Anatomy of a Ghost	269
Practical Investigation	277

Capturing and Analysing EVPs — 287
Defining Electronic Voice Phenomenon — 289
The History of EVP Research — 301
Choosing the Right Equipment — 311
How to Capture EVPs — 325
Analysing EVPs — 339
EVP Classification — 365

Event Planning and Management — 373
Locations — 381
Risk Assessment — 387
Logistics — 393
Promotion and Sales — 399
On the Day — 403

Introduction

Welcome to the 'Paralearning: Study Companion', your essential guide and reference tool for the intriguing world of paranormal investigation and research. This book has been specially designed to serve as a memory aid and quick reference for those who have completed one or more of the unique courses offered by Paralearning, an online platform dedicated to providing an in-depth understanding of the science, history, and myths surrounding ghosts and the supernatural.

The courses available through paralearning.org cover a wide range of fascinating topics, including Practical Ghost Hunting and Scientific Analysis, Modern Demonology for Paranormal Investigators, Advanced Scientific Theory for Paranormal Investigators, Capturing and Analysing Electronic Voice Phenomenon, and Ghost Hunting Event Planning and Management. Each course is crafted to equip you with the practical skills and knowledge needed to excel in the field of paranormal investigation.

While the 'Paralearning: Study Companion' is a valuable resource, it is essential to remember that it is not a substitute for the comprehensive online courses offered by Paralearning. The learning platform guides users through each course, periodically refreshing and testing their knowledge of the material as they progress. Upon successful completion, users undergo a final evaluation and are awarded digital accreditation and a certificate of achievement.

This companion book is designed to complement your online course experience. It contains concise summaries, key concepts, and useful tips that will help you retain and apply the knowledge gained during your studies. However, to gain the full benefit of the Paralearning experience, we highly recommend that you complete the relevant online courses before referring to this book.

As you delve into the captivating world of paranormal investigation and research, we hope that the 'Paralearning: Study Companion' becomes an invaluable resource, both during and after your studies. May it serve as a trusted guide and a constant reminder of the fascinating journey you embarked upon with Paralearning.

Quick Reference Guide

Quick Reference Guide

This guide has been carefully designed to provide you with a concise overview of the key points and essential information from each of the five courses currently available at Paralearning. While it is not meant to serve as a starting point for your exploration of the paranormal and ghost hunting, it is an invaluable resource you can refer back to when you need to recall key facts and information quickly. Our aim is to make your learning experience more efficient, organised, and enjoyable.

The guide offers a compact and efficient tool for quick revision, presenting the most important information from each course in a digestible format, allowing you to consolidate your understanding and reinforce your memory of the course material.

It acts as a convenient resource for readers to consult when they need a refresher on particular topics or are looking for guidance on where to focus their studies, enabling you to review the material without having to retake the course. This is especially useful when you need to recall specific details or concepts.

While the Quick Reference Guide is a valuable tool, it is important to emphasise that it is not a substitute for taking our online courses or reading the full sections of the book that support those courses. The guide provides an overview of the content, but to gain a comprehensive understanding of the paranormal and become an effective ghost hunter, you must engage with the complete sections. The full sections provide in-depth explanations and practical techniques that will enrich your knowledge and skills in this fascinating field.

To get the most out of the Quick Reference Guide, we recommend using it as a supplementary resource after reading the full sections. Begin by reading the full sections to gain a solid understanding of the material, then use the guide to review and reinforce your learning. As you progress through the book, the guide will serve as a helpful reference, enabling you to navigate the content with ease and confidence.

Embrace the exciting journey into the paranormal that lies ahead. Use the Quick Reference Guide as a valuable companion, and remember that the full sections of the 'Paralearning: Study Companion' hold the key to unlocking the mysteries of the supernatural world.

Quick Reference Guide: Practical Ghost Hunting

Determine if a Location is Haunted

There are two schools of thought on whether you should research a location beforehand. Some believe that it is better to enter an investigation with no knowledge at all so that members of the group can't intentionally or subconsciously influence it. Others believe it is better to learn all you can in advance in order to better plan their ghost hunt.

Most hauntings occur on the site of a historical tragedy, whether it be a murder, a suicide, an untimely death due to illness, or an accident such as a car crash, drowning, or fatal fall. The tragedy may even pre-date the property you're researching. For this reason, in order to get the full picture, you should research the history of not only the property you are investigating but also the immediate area around the property.

The typical symptoms of a haunting are:
- A general feeling of unease
- Strange noises or voices
- Strange smells or odours
- Temperature fluctuations
- Moving objects
- Physical contact (the sensation of being touched or brushed against)
- Manifestation

Classifications of Hauntings

Hauntings and sightings of ghosts fit into one of the following categories:

- Shadow hauntings (a dark, human-like figure)
- Residual hauntings (recordings of the past that cannot be interacted with)
- Animal spirit hauntings (the spirits of animals, believed to be residual hauntings)
- Intelligent hauntings (a haunting that has an intelligent consciousness behind it that can be interacted with)
- Poltergeist hauntings (a haunting in which objects are moved)
- Demonic hauntings (haunting by a non-human, evil entity)

In order to investigate a location and prove the existence of the paranormal, it is always best to adopt the mindset of a sceptic and do everything you can to try to prove that the property is not haunted. Once you've eliminated every possible explanation for the activity you've witnessed, what you're left with will be evidence of the paranormal.

"When you have eliminated the impossible, whatever remains, however improbable, must be the truth." - Sir Arthur Conan Doyle

Occam's razor states that the simplest solution is usually the correct one. When presented with competing hypothetical answers to a problem, you should select the one that makes the fewest assumptions.

The biggest source of interference in your evidence comes from the outside world. Here are a few things you can do to reduce it as much as possible:

- Isolate the property (close all doors and windows, turn off air conditioning, cover ventilation, and eliminate draughts)
- Controlling light (where possible, black out windows to prevent light pollution)

- Passing traffic (be aware of passing traffic, trains, and aircraft)

Things commonly mistaken for the paranormal:

- Pareidolia (a phenomenon where we perceive patterns in random data)
- Electromagnetic fields (often associated with electronic devices, especially those with broadcast capability)
- Infrasound (very low-frequency vibrations that have been known to cause people to report discomfort)
- Toxins and poisoning (the physical or mental influence of carbon monoxide, formaldehyde, pesticides, and even some moulds and funguses)
- Sleep paralysis (a sleep condition that can result in visions of dark figures)

Capture Evidence of the Haunting

Your primary role as a ghost hunter is to prove the existence of the paranormal, and in order to do this, you'll need to be sure that any potential paranormal activity is logged. The two most common ways to log an investigation are to either use an audio recorder or a notebook.

You should note all paranormal and non-paranormal occurrences during the investigation so that you can later investigate these further or eliminate them from your investigation.

In order to prove that this evidence really represents paranormal activity, you'll need to make sure it is quantitative. For example, a measurable or observable physical movement or a change in atmospheric conditions.

Here are some techniques that can be used to collect measurable evidence:

- Laser grid (if anything moves in front of the grid created by the scattered beam of a laser pen, you will see a shift or discrepancy)
- Thermometer (an infrared thermometer can be used to measure the temperature of surfaces, it will not measure air temperature)
- Trigger objects (a ball, a bunch of keys, a child's toy, a marble, or any other object left stationary for a spirit to interact with)
- Camera (photographic evidence is the ultimate aim of most ghost hunts)

When photographing during a ghost hunt, any type of camera from cheap compact cameras to top-of-the-line digital SLR cameras and even smartphones are fine, but avoid using specialised camera modes like HDR and panoramic.

If you are using a smartphone during an investigation, be sure to put the phone into flight mode to avoid unexpected sounds and electromagnetic interference, which may trigger certain electronic ghost hunting devices.

- Ask the spirits to be present in your photo
- Take three photos in quick succession
- Hold your breath
- Stay still, especially in low-light environments
- Be aware of dust and particles in the air
- Maintain your equipment

Communicating with Ghosts and Spirits

Most ghost hunts involve some attempt to communicate with the spirits via a séance.

The participants of a séance should form a circle by holding hands. This focuses the energy of the participants, allowing spirits to draw on it and use it to communicate. Knowing everyone is holding hands also means you know that no one at the séance is creating any tapping noises or moving anything themselves in the dark.

If any members of the group have researched the history of the property, like names, dates, causes of death, etc., then it is best if this person sits out of séances so that they cannot intentionally or subconsciously influence it.

Calling out is when a paranormal investigator speaks aloud in an attempt to encourage any spirits that might be present to communicate with them. The classic ghost hunter's trope is, "Hello, is anybody there?" There are a few tips and best practises that should be considered when calling out.

- Encourage, don't demand (treat spirits with respect, ask if they need help or have a message)
- Say thank you (spirits have to muster up a lot of energy in order to give us these signs, so show them you are grateful for their efforts)
- Don't use jargon (don't assume that spirits understand the jargon that paranormal investigators use)
- Don't shut it down (keep the conversation flowing. Don't say things like "give us a sign that you're here, then we'll leave you alone.")

Whichever technique you are using to listen to spirits, the questions you ask will be the same. Below is a list of example questions and phrases that you can use to try to encourage the spirits to communicate with you.

If you can hear me, tap on the floor.
Can you make a noise to let us know you are here with us?
If you're here, can you show yourself to me?
How many of you are with us right now? Tap it out.
Can you make a noise?
Can you throw something?
Can you copy me? [then tap on a surface or whistle]
My name is XXX. Can you tell me your name?
Tell us who you are. Introduce yourself, please.
If there's somebody here with us now, can you walk towards us?
Are you happy for us to be here? Two taps for yes, one for no.
Can you come and talk to us?

One of the easiest ways to communicate with spirits is by asking them to **tap out their answers** and encouraging them to tap once for "no" and twice for "yes." Don't assume that spirits will understand the principles of tapping. You might need to teach them how to communicate in this way.

You should limit your questions to closed questions, that is, questions that can only be answered with "yes" or "no."

Ouija boards have been a popular part of a séance since Victorian times. In order to use one, follow these steps:

- Each participant should very gently rest one finger on the planchette
- Warm up the board by moving the planchette in a circle
- Tell the spirits how to answer by running the planchette over the markings on the board
- Call out to the spirits and attempt to make contact
- At the end of the séance, move the planchette to the word "goodbye"

Electronic Voice Phenomenon (EVP) provides another way to communicate with spirits. In order to capture EVPs, you'll need some kind of audio recording equipment. This can be anything from an old cassette deck, a reel-to-reel machine, a pocket digital audio recorder, a mobile phone, or a laptop. During an EVP session, you should:

- Try to stay as still as possible to avoid making any unnecessary noise
- Be patient and give the spirits plenty of time to make contact, but don't record too much
- When reviewing the session you'll need to use headphones rather than listening on the recording device itself
- If you do hear a voice in your recording, get a second opinion from someone by playing them the voice out of context

A **spirit box** is a popular device that rapidly scans through the AM, MW, and FM radio spectrums, emitting fleeting bursts of white noise and static that can be heard. It's said that spirits can communicate during these bursts in much the same way as on an EVP recording, but in real-time.

An **EMF meter** is one of the most popular pieces of ghost hunting equipment. They detect and alert you to fluctuations and spikes in electromagnetic flux. You are looking for evidence of a spirit either emitting an EM field or disrupting the ambient field.

EMF meters are susceptible to interference from many external factors. They can be triggered by things like mobile phones and walkie-talkies.

There are many **electronic speech-synthesis devices** on the market. They work as either random word generators or by generating random sounds, the phonics that make up words.

Supposedly, spirits can affect the random nature of these devices to form the words they are trying to say.

They monitor conditions such as temperature, pressure, humidity, and electromagnetic flux. It uses these signals as a random number generator, and this number is used to reference the database of words. The atmospheric sensors give the spirit another way to influence the random word.

A **pendulum** can be used to contact spirits. You can suggest that the spirit answer your question by swinging the pendulum back and forth to indicate "yes" or left to right to indicate "no." You can also ask for the pendulum to be moved in either a clockwise or anticlockwise motion.

When making contact with a spirit, you should aim to obtain information like names, dates, how the spirit passed, and how old they were. You should then attempt to validate this information by cross-referencing it with historical information and witness accounts.

You may also be able to obtain information that is only known to one person, such as the property owner or an eyewitness, as long as that person wasn't included in the séance. This would also be considered valid evidence.

Legalities of Ghost Hunting

The risks of a ghost hunt should always be assessed. Old properties may include dangers like low doorways, uneven floors, trip hazards, dark basements, attic spaces, and stairwells. Derelict buildings may have structurally weak floors and roofs, asbestos, and shear drops.

As most ghost hunts are conducted in the dark, all of the hazards mentioned above are greatly increased.

Whenever you are moving or walking around a property, you should always use a flashlight to avoid trips, falls, and other hazards. But it's best to keep the beam of the flashlight angled down to avoid shining it directly into people's eyes.

- Always carry a flashlight and use it whenever walking
- Avoid places where the floor or roof is obviously unsound
- Always wear suitable clothing and sensible footwear
- Never visit a property alone
- Take a first aid kit
- Always let someone know where you are going and your expected time of return
- Observe the privacy of those who live near the property

In addition to these rules, you should also observe any guidelines set by the property owner or group leaders at an event. This might include no-entry signs, instructions to keep out of certain parts of the building, or a requirement to wear a hard hat or high-visibility clothing.

It is vital to get permission before entering a property to investigate it. Without the correct permissions, it could be considered trespass, and reasonable force can be used to remove you. If you damage something while trespassing, this could be deemed a criminal offence or breaking and entering, both of which are arrestable offences.

Quick Reference Guide: Demonology

Demonology is not a supernatural ability or a gift that you are born with. It is the study of demons or demonic beliefs.

In this course, we'll be scraping away some of these conflicting and dated concepts and focusing on the modern-day demon and how demons affect you on a paranormal investigation. Traditionally, demonology required some kind of religious belief, but demons are more than the antagonists in just one religion.

Demons are rooted in various theologies and religions from around the world. As a ghost hunter, if you encounter a demon, there is no way you can know which tradition this demon originates from, which is why it is best to take a modern, multi-faith approach to demonology.

This course's approach to modern demonology will give you practical skills in identifying, communicating with, summoning, and controlling demons.

Once you have completed this course, there are a few ways you can put your new knowledge and abilities to use:
• Diagnose, understand, or put an end to strange goings-on in your own home
• Help others with their demonic issues
• Summon or provoke demons as part of a paranormal investigation

There are far too many names of demons to mention here, and the information is somewhat dated, but it can be found in the public domain and in reference books.

Demons were once considered to be exceedingly life-threatening entities, but there have actually been no recorded deaths that have been attributed to demonic possessions or hauntings ever.

Those living in houses that are said to be haunted by a demonic entity often describe a negative atmosphere and an increase in accidents and illnesses, which can lead to violent behaviour, depression, and even suicide, but the stories of these extreme outcomes are anecdotal.

Many people report bad experiences as a result of dabbling with demons because they believe they will.

If you are weak in mind and heart, then you may feel as if you have been possessed or feel discomfort after dealing with a demon.

If you have any serious doubts about demonology, then this topic isn't for you.

Demons

A demon is a non-human malevolent entity that has never been alive and has only ever existed purely as malevolent energy. This energy is intent on causing suffering to those that it haunts. Demons are deceitful and frequently lie and mix lies with truths to confuse their victims.

Some traditions say that demons may not even be from our plane of existence, instead believing them to be entities that have survived from a former universe or have found a way to cross over from a parallel universe. Demonologists call this the "infernal realm".

Demons can take any form, although usually it is a human form or sometimes animal-like forms, most often a black dog. When in human form, it's said that there is almost always something not quite right about their appearance.

Demons are believed to be the hidden cause of all of humankind's problems, including physical and mental illness, bad luck, pain, and suffering. They are much more powerful than human spirits and have abilities that humans don't possess, including telepathy, which allows them to uncover a victim's fear or worries and use this knowledge against them.

Demonic hauntings begin slowly and without violence, with activity that includes:

- Unexplained knocks and bangs
- Disturbance of electrical equipment
- Disembodied voices and whispers

A demon grows in strength by feeding on the negative energy of its victim, as it does, the paranormal activity increases and may include:

- Recurrent nightmares on a weekly or nightly basis
- Loud noises
- Growls
- Unpleasant smells
- Physical attacks on humans
- Materialisation of unknown substances
- The dematerialisation and re-materialisation of objects

Possession

Demons only prey on the weak and susceptible. They enter the body through the solar plexus, the back of the neck, the left side of the body, or by having sexual intercourse with a person. Their aim is to break down their free will and weaken them so that they can possess and control them. Eventually they will hurt their victim, and in extreme cases, they will drive them to suicide. After death, the demon is said to be able to claim the victim's soul.

The first sign for the victim is often experiencing periods of missing time or blackouts. Signs that someone is possessed include:

- Personality changes
- Inexplicable strength
- Supernatural abilities
- Knowledge of future events or other information they shouldn't know
- An ability to talk in other languages
- Producing unrecognisable voices
- Appearance of wounds and scars
- They do not blink
- They become withdrawn
- They lose interest in their usual hobbies, interests, and commitments

The easiest way to confirm whether a possession is demonic is to use a protective item without the victim's knowledge. Hold the protective item behind the head of the possessed without them knowing to see if they react.

A non-demonic type of possession is emotional possession, sometimes referred to as a temporary spirit walk-in or step-in. This non-aggressive spiritual exchange happens when someone gives a human spirit permission to use their energy and enter their body. The spirit will normally use this opportunity to share their emotions or feelings.

There are instances where people have voluntarily let demons possess them. This permissive takeover is called "perfect possession." In this situation, it is very hard, if not impossible, to exorcise the person involved.

Attachment

As well as possessing humans, demons can also attach themselves to places, vehicles, and any other object, but they most often choose objects with faces, which is why cursed dolls are so common. Attachment, sometimes called infestation, is often the early stage of possession.

Demonically infested items sometimes lay dormant for years or even generations, but may become active when they are unsettled, perhaps by being moved to a new room in the house or a new home all together, or by being sold or given to a new owner.

Attachment results in typical haunting occurrences, this might include:

- Poltergeist-like activity
- A general feeling of unease
- Sudden and unexpected deaths of pets
- Protective items are destroyed or lost
- Happenings occur in threes or sixes
- Damage to rooms or property
- Writing on walls
- Bruises or scratches on the body

Demonic hauntings are very similar to poltergeist hauntings. They both start out slowly and in a playful manner, but increase in intensity. However, with poltergeist, just as suddenly as the activity starts, it can abruptly end, whereas demonic hauntings rarely stop of their own accord.

Communications

Demons can make their presence known through Ouija boards and other methods of contacting spirits.

During a Ouija board session, demons can often be detected by mischievous behaviour, inconsistent answers, or clear lies. When asked "Is there anybody there?" the planchette may move to "no", or when asked this age, the planchette may move to the number zero on the board.

Demonic voices may be heard when using equipment to attempt to capture or hear EVPs. When reviewing the audio from a recorder or listening to responses through a spirit box. Clues that the voice is that of a demon are that it sounds gruff or deep, or animalistic growls are heard.

Protection Against Demons

When entering into an investigation or performing a séance, you should ensure that you are not troubled by negative emotions, are not tired, and that you are guilt- and stress-free.

Call upon the support of a spirit guide or guardian angel, or if you are religious, you could pray for protection or bless your surroundings.

Do not allow yourself to be alone in the presence of someone who is possessed for any length of time. Their negative energy may be infectious and drag you down, making you susceptible to possession too.

Never say a demon's name aloud. Using its name acts as an invitation and helps it grow in strength.

Avoid provoking or angering demons. Be polite when asking them questions, and thank them for their efforts.

If you are using a Ouija board, be sure to close the board after a session by moving the planchette across the board to "goodbye."

Never bring any second-hand item into your home without cleansing it first.

Burning sage, known as smudging, drives away demons and evil spirits. The technique can be used to cleanse an object, a building, or yourself.

Smudging is a form of ritual alchemy. The smoke filling the air element is said to better connect humans with the spirit world. Sage can be bought in a pre-wrapped bundle of dried herb known as smudge sticks.

Develop a 10 to 15-minute cleansing ritual that you are comfortable with and that has meaning to you. Perform it slowly, with full awareness, and in a mindful manner.

When smudging a person, have them remove metal jewellery and other distractions. Light the sage and, starting with the area above the head, pass it around the body so that the smoke surrounds them, working your way down to the feet.

This same procedure can also be used to cleanse any object. Simply move the burning sage all around it, engulfing it in the sage smoke.

To cleanse a building, walk around it with burning sage. Start at the front door, then consistently move in one direction around the building, eventually returning to your starting point. In each room, waft the smoke to fill the whole space with the sage smoke, especially dark or shadowy spaces.

Throughout this cleansing ritual, focus on what you are doing or recite an incantation that means something to you, either aloud or in your head.

Demonologists would carry protection in the form of a religious item or a defensive item that has specific meaning to them and their beliefs.

Popular protective items include:
- Jewellery such as a bracelet, necklace, or medallion (often made out of silver)
- A tattoo
- A sacred item
- An amulet of protection or a charm
- Anything else that makes you feel safe and secure

Protective items often include symbols like the Celtic triple knot, a pentacle, runic symbols, or the evil eye. They may also include crystals or semi-precious stones, including:

- Amber
- Amethyst
- Black onyx
- Chrysoberyl (specifically protects against possession)
- Jade
- Peridot (specifically wards off demons)
- Ruby
- Tourmaline

Iron is also thought to repel demons.

Salt is believed to repel demons. It can be worn in a pouch in the form of rock crystals or used to draw a circle on the floor to make a safe area that demons cannot enter.

A house can be protected using a terracotta demon bowl that is inscribed with incantations and buried in the foundations of the house or placed in windows or entrance halls.

Summoning Demons

You should perform invocations responsibly due to a demon's tendency to attach itself to or follow those who summon it. To increase your chances of summoning a demon, do the following:

- Set the mood. It's best to hold your ritual in low light
- Make sure you're comfortable, as making contact with a demon can take time and patience
- Remove all distractions, like phones
- Make sure you are mentally prepared and alert
- Attempt between 3 and 4am, this is the witching hour (the high noon of the demonic day)

Paranormal investigators believe that in order for a demon to manifest, it needs to draw on all of its energy, but in a light environment, a demon doesn't always have enough energy to overpower surrounding energy fields and become visible.

Demons are unpredictable by nature, so you should avoid angering or antagonising them, not because they might hurt you but in order to ensure they cooperate with you. Be sure to treat the demon with honesty and respect.

Call out encouragement to any demons that can hear you to come forward. Don't make demands or command the demon. You should only make requests.

If a demon has previously identified itself to you, then use its name, as a demon's name holds power and is usually taken as an invitation by the demon. You should recite words or incantations that are meaningful to you. You could try phrases like:

- I invite the forces of darkness to bestow their infernal power upon me and show me you're here
- Come forward, forces of darkness, and greet me
- I invoke thee [the demon's name]

- Come forth and answer to your name
- Come forward, [demon's name], where I can see you
- I summon you into visible form before me

Once a demon makes its presence known:

- Tell it exactly why you have summoned it
- Ask if they need help or have a message
- Ask it to show you a sign that they are with you
- Give it encouragement
- Thank it for its efforts if they do something that you've asked them to do

Be sure not to shut the session down prematurely by saying things like, "Give us a sign that you're here, and then we'll leave you alone."

Try to establish a more meaningful conversation with the demon using questions and phrases like:

- If you can hear me, tap on the floor
- Can you make a noise to let us know you are here with us?
- If you're here, can you show yourself to me?
- Can you throw something?
- Can you copy me? [then tap on a surface or whistle]
- My name is XXX. Can you tell me your name?
- Tell us who you are. Introduce yourself, please
- If there's somebody here with us now, can you walk towards us?
- Are you happy for us to be here? Two taps for yes, one for no
- Can you come and talk to us?

Once your session with the demon comes to an end, you should do all you can to ensure that the demon is not still present in that location. This might include:

- Closing the Ouija board correctly
- Asking that the demon return to where it came from
- Performing a cleansing ritual
- Performing an exorcism

Exorcisms

An exorcism is a ritual that aims to remove demons and negative energies from a place, object, or person. Exorcisms are not limited to just one religion. Anyone can perform an exorcism by building on their own belief system and drawing on their own spiritual energy.

When performing an exorcism, you should aim for a ritual that is positive and compassionate. It should not be as dramatic as the inaccurate rituals portrayed in movies and the media.

Once you have completed the ritual, do not stir things up again. Don't acknowledge the demon, don't talk to it, and don't attempt to contact it in order to see if it is still present. This can be taken as an invitation and permission to remain.

Ridding a Location of a Demon

To exorcise a location:
- Ensure that you are in a fit emotional and physical state
- Start by cleaning, decluttering, and smudging the building
- Open the curtains or blinds and let the light in
- Confidently command the demon to leave and never return
- Avoid using an angry, aggressive, or confrontational tone
- Let the demon know that you mean it no harm
- Call upon your spirit guide or guardian angel to help push the demon out
- Use the name of the demon you are trying to banish

After the ritual:
- Cleanse the property again with sage
- Draw protective symbols around the home
- Encircle the house with salt

Ridding a Person of a Demon

Exorcising a person is a lot more serious than ridding a house of demons. If you don't practice the ritual with compassion, respect, and sensitivity, then you could end up making things worse. An exorcism should never be violent or aggressive in any way.

The three most important things to establish before continuing are:
- Does the victim truly need to be exorcised?
- Do you categorically have their explicit and direct consent?
- Is the person mentally stable enough to go through this ritual?

To exorcise a person:
- Ensure that you are in a fit emotional and physical state
- Cleanse the person using sage
- Confidently command the demon to leave its victim's body
- Avoid using an angry, aggressive, or confrontational tone
- Use the name of the demon you are trying to banish

You might want to try some of these example incantations:
- I call upon you, [the demon's name]. Obey my commands and leave this person
- I command you to return to the infernal realm. You are no longer welcome in this place
- This person is protected from all evil. No negative entity may remain here

Ridding an Object of a Demon

Do not give away or throw away an item that's possessed.

The best way to deal with an object with a demonic attachment is to burn it:
- Light a fire, either outdoors or in a fireplace
- Carefully throw the object in and let it burn

- Do not extinguish the fire, wait for it to naturally burn out
- Allow the ashes to cool down and pour salt into the ashes
- Place the salt and ashes in a container and bury them

If you want to keep the object, then try placing it on a stone instead and allowing it to absorb the negative energy. You can then dig a hole, place the stone in it, pour salt over it, and then bury the stone. The best place to bury an object or ashes is at a crossroads.

Another method for items that can't be burned is to throw them into a fast-moving living body of salt water, like a river or an ocean.

Quick Reference Guide: Scientific Theory

This course is aimed at established paranormal investigators and assumes you already have a working knowledge of subjects such as electronic voice phenomena, stone tape theory, spiritual energy, and the various methods of communicating with spirits.

The course will help you build on these basic principles to give you a better understanding of the areas of physics and Earth science that determine the behaviour and perception of hauntings while adding clarity to many of the scientific buzzwords that are often bandied around within the paranormal community.

The aim of the course is to help you use provable and repeatable scientific principles to debunk or explain hauntings in order to make the evidence you collect more robust and compelling.

The modules in this course will cover many advanced topics, including lessons on the electromagnetic spectrum, which will help you gain a better understanding of how differing frequencies of energy relate to experiences of the paranormal in different ways.

The course also covers the principles that govern instrumental transcommunication, especially how they affect audible voice phenomena, electronic voice phenomena, and visual forms of spirit contact. There are also lessons on how to analyse any audio captured electronically by examining the waveform, taking into account amplitude, wavelength, and frequency.

Of course, no one knows what happens to us after we die, and the true nature of what consciousness is remains illusive to scientists, but there are some leading theories and promising research in this field that we will discuss in this course, some of which will take us on a journey into the realms of quantum physics. Learn how subatomic particles and the unified field theory might result in psychic energy that cannot be destroyed after death or perhaps even a shared "quantum consciousness," which gives us all our life force.

We'll look at the anatomy of a ghost and attempt to answer the question, "What are ghosts made of?" By looking at some of the leading theories, we can start to form an idea of how a ghost can be captured on camera or detected with an electronic ghost hunting gadget.

The course will end with a look at the scientific aims of a modern paranormal investigator. These aims are more about collecting and evaluating evidence than more spiritual aims, which might involve the clearing of spirits. We'll also attempt to clear up some common misconceptions and outdated beliefs about the paranormal.

Energy, Fields & Frequencies

The term energy, when used in relation to the paranormal, refers to positive and negative "vibes." Some people radiate positive energy, and others negative energy. This is a metaphor and bears no resemblance to "energy" in the scientific sense of the word. It's just people appropriating technical terms for emotional states. When we get a "vibe" from someone, we're simply forming an emotional reaction to that person.

It's also said that a location or haunting case can have a lot of energy. Again, this isn't energy in the scientific sense but instead refers to the level of activity.

The scientific term energy is a measure of work or potential. Work is when a force causes any form of movement or state change. If a human knocks on a surface, this is a transfer of energy. The potential energy stored in our cells is converted to mechanical movement. When it comes to ghosts, we need to question how something without a solid form can transfer its energy into sound, bearing in mind that it doesn't have potential energy stored in cells like we do.

Theoretically, negative energy can exist in the universe. However, we've never encountered it, and how likely it is that negative energy actually exists in our universe is still unknown. The term is a concept used in physics to explain the nature of certain fields, most frequently when talking about attraction.

The universe is very good at balancing itself out. For example, magnets have two poles, and electricity flows between the negative and positive poles. Negative energy is simply the exact opposite of ordinary energy and would move in the opposite direction from its momentum and accelerate in the opposite direction of an applied force.

The electromagnetic spectrum is made up of various types of radiation, including visible light, x-rays, radio waves, and even the heat generated by things like your oven. Only a very small portion of the EM spectrum is visible to the human eye in the form of white and coloured light. On either side of visible light are infrared and ultraviolet.

An electromagnetic field meter, or EMF meter, alerts you when it detects an electromagnetic field from 50 to 20,000 Hz. The device gives instant feedback via a digital display or LED indicators. There is no exact scientific understanding of how spirits can communicate using an EMF meter, but there are two major schools of thought within the paranormal community.

1. Ghosts can cause a spike or fluctuation in this ambient field in order to bring it up to a level that the device can detect. The ambient EM field is a field that is created by wiring and electrical devices. Otherwise, there would be no ambient field for spirits to manipulate in remote outdoor or isolated locations.

2. Ghosts create and emit their own EM field, in a similar way that the human brain uses tiny electronic impulses to control our bodies. It's believed that this synaptic energy can live on as a disembodied consciousness after death, and it is this that EMF meters can detect. However, EMF meters can't detect brainwaves as they cycle at 12.5 to 30 Hz, lower than the 50 Hz minimum threshold of an EMF meter.

EMF meters were originally used to try to rule out the possibility that artificial EM fields could actually be causing people to experience certain haunting phenomena. This is because strong electromagnetic fields can induce strange experiences in people exposed to them.

The visible light spectrum is the range of electromagnetic radiation that a typical human eye can detect. Light travels in straight lines at approximately 300,000,000 meters per second. It travels in waves that can pass through a vacuum.

Cameras are capable of capturing wavelengths of light wider than the visible spectrum. They can capture both near infrared and ultraviolet light, which are invisible to the human eye. Camera manufacturers include a filter to prevent this unwanted light from being captured.

Night vision video cameras use an infrared illuminator. This frequency of light is just outside the visible spectrum of the human eye, but it can be picked up by the camera's sensor and appears in monochrome, either with a greenish tint or in black and white. This is because the camera cannot see visible light, it is only sensitive to IR light.

Full-spectrum cameras are cameras that have had their filter removed and can see the full light spectrum, including light in the infrared and ultraviolet frequencies that the human eye can't see. When a full-spectrum camera is paired with an infrared light source, it too can act as a night vision camera, capturing images in a pink-purple hue. However, a full-spectrum camera will still be able to see visible light and colours alongside the IR-illuminated images.

Infrared is a measure of the heat radiated by an object with a temperature above absolute zero. The loss of energy as electromagnetic waves. The warmer the object, the more infrared it emits. A thermal imaging camera gives a visual representation of this otherwise invisible infrared energy emitted by objects.

The temperature of objects is indicated with colours. Hot areas show as shades of yellow, orange, and red, depending on how hot it is. Very hot areas will appear white. Cold areas will show as shades of blue, with very cold areas being black. This type of camera can be useful during an investigation as sudden drops in temperature and cold spots are commonly reported phenomena in haunting cases.

While air does emit IR, thermal cameras are tuned to ignore the frequency range at which air emits IR waves. This means they can't be used to measure air temperatures. They can only read the temperature of the object it is pointed at. A point-and-click infrared thermometer works in the same way.

Radio noise is something that crops up often in the field of paranormal research. It is most commonly encountered when using a Spirit Box, which scans through the AM, MW, and FM radio spectrums. The belief is that spirits can re-arrange the snatches or radio broadcasts, as well as the noise between the frequencies, to communicate with the device's user.

Some investigators take this a step further and use white noise to try to capture examples of Electronic Voice Phenomena (EVP) based on the theory that spirits can reorganise radio noise to form words. This is done by playing back a pre-recorded sample of white noise, by recording near a source of noise, or by using a white noise signal generator to artificially produce noise. Some EVP experts use audio editing software to remove the white noise in order to analyse the audio, leaving only the more sustained sound in the recording, which could include spirit voices.

Humans create a magnetic field and emit EM radiation, but they are very weak. The body's internal magnetic field is generated by the extraordinary amount of internal electrical activity, which is produced in several different types of cells. Nerve impulses are electrical energy signals, and like all electricity, they create energy fields in the visible and ultraviolet spectrums but are too weak to be seen with the naked eye.

Like all objects, human bodies emit thermal radiation that is dependent on their temperature. Most of the radiation emitted by the human body is in the infrared region.

In a circuit, an electrical current flows between the negative and positive poles. Where there is no circuit or flowing current, we have static electricity. Static electricity is used in devices that radiate their own static field. They're called REM-Pods, or radiating electromagnetism pods. The REM-Pod radiates its own static EM field and can detect a difference in field strength when a conductive material enters its EM field.

Instrumental Transcommunication

ITC, or Instrumental Transcommunication, refers to all forms of spirit communication using any kind of electrical instrument, such as electronic voice phenomenon (EVP), but it isn't limited to audio devices. ITC encompasses any communication between the living and spirits through any electronic device.

ITC also covers visual forms of communication, normally conducted with the use of a television or video camera feedback loop where a picture recursively appears within itself or simply by observing patterns in static.

Modern-day devices include spirit boxes, electronic speech synthesis devices (like the Ovilus and Echovox), digital audio recorders, and EMF meters. These are just a few of the most commonly used electronic devices in the ITC field, but the list doesn't end here. Over the years, there have been reports of just about every type of electrical device being used to communicate with spirits.

You'll often be required to analyse audio recorded during ITC sessions in order to determine if any spirit voices or audible phenomena have been captured in the recording. Proper analysis of the audio requires you to understand some of the important parts of a waveform:

Peak - the highest point above the rest position
Trough - the lowest point below the rest position
Amplitude - the maximum displacement of a wave from its rest position
Wavelength - distance covered by a full cycle of the wave, usually measured from peak to peak or trough to trough

Another important property of a wave is its frequency. This is what determines the pitch. We either hear the sound as low-pitched or high-pitched. It is measured in Hertz (Hz) as the number of waves passing a point each second. The amplitude of a sound wave determines its volume.

Ultrasound waves have a frequency that is outside the upper limit of human hearing. Microphones, including those in smartphones and digital audio recorders, are designed specifically to pick up the frequency range that roughly matches the range that the human ear can hear. This means that if you are using a digital audio recorder to try to capture EVPs, you know that the device isn't going to pick up any sounds that you can't hear with your own ears.

So, if there is an EVP in your audio recording, then you know it must have been created in one of two ways:

1. The sound was audible at the time of recording and was extremely quiet. It must have been either very close to the microphone or closer to the microphone than you were, or the device is more sensitive to low-level noise than your ear.

2. The sound was not audible at the time but has made its way into the recording via a form of electrical interference, which affects either the device's circuitry or storage medium.

Ultrasound detectors are used during paranormal investigations to obtain a baseline reading of ultrasound at the location, but they are also used as a means of capturing EVPs at a higher frequency than we can normally hear or capture using a recording device.

Infrasound is a very low-frequency sound that falls below the human range of hearing and is the cause of many mistaken reports of paranormal activity. Low-frequency vibrations have been known to cause people to report discomfort in the form of disorientation, feeling panicked, and an increased heart rate and blood pressure.

Kinect **SLS (Structured Light Sensor) cameras** work by projecting their own invisible, infrared, structured grid of laser dots over a wide field of view. The camera's sensor is able to calculate the distance between these infrared dots in order to build a three-dimensional model of its view. If something moves within its field of view, there will be a change in the distance between the dots, which the camera recognises as movement. Everything the camera sees is displayed in real time on a screen, and any figures it detects are highlighted by overlaying a bright green stick figure.

The problem with SLS cameras for ghost hunting is that they are designed to do something else. The software is looking for a human form. It expects to see one or more players in its field of view. The software's algorithms have been trained by developers to detect people standing in front of the camera. The device doesn't have algorithms included in the software to detect ghosts.

An **oscilloscope** is a type of electronic test instrument that displays a real-time visual representation of an electrical signal. Investigators often connect allegedly haunted items to an oscilloscope in one of two ways:

1. The ground clip is connected to a grounded contact, and the probe is clipped on to the item itself.

2. Both clips are placed on opposite sides of the item in the hopes that an electrical current might flow across the object.

You can also use an oscilloscope with an artificial signal generator. This is the equivalent of using white noise in an EVP experiment. It gives the spirits the raw waves that they can then hopefully manipulate in some way.

If a spirit does become responsive, you may be able to ask it to change the shape of the waveform, increase or decrease its frequency, or completely drop the amplitude and "flat line" the scope.

Audible Voice Phenomena also known as **Direct Voice Phenomena** are audible, disembodied voices that are heard during paranormal investigations, séances, or at haunted locations and are spoken directly to the investigator or witness. A DVP is similar to an EVP, but no audio or electrical equipment is used, and they are heard live.

Consciousness and the Soul

The possibility that some form of consciousness persists after our bodies die and decay into their constituent atoms faces one huge, insuperable obstacle: the laws of physics underlying everyday life are completely understood, and there's no way within those laws to allow for the information stored in our brains to persist after we die. However, some argue that consciousness, like all forms of energy, can't be destroyed and therefore lives on outside of the body when someone dies.

Our awareness of a physical universe is just a perception. When we die, there is an infinite existence beyond the physical universe in the form of energy. When a person temporarily dies, their conscious energy is released into the universe, only to return to the body's cells if the person is revived and brought back to life. This explains how people have near-death experiences.

Robert Lanza: "We are all the ephemeral forms of a consciousness greater than ourselves." He claims that the mind of every human being is instantly connected to each other, "a part of every mind existing in space and time." This is called quantum consciousness, or the quantum mind, based on the quantum field theory.

If our souls can live outside the body as some form of mental energy, then there's the potential for the living to pick up on the energy of the dead in the form of ghosts or spirits.

Roger Penrose: "If the patient dies, it's possible that this quantum information can exist outside the body, perhaps indefinitely, as a soul."

Quantum field theory states that there is one field for each type of particle. This means all of the photons in the universe are part of one field. This is true for every other type of subatomic particle. In the quantum consciousness model, there is one uniform field of consciousness that exists throughout the universe and cannot be destroyed.

All consciousness that has ever existed and will ever exist is present in the universe right now. Sir Penrose says that he believes consciousness to be packets of information stored at a subatomic level. The scientist believes that this mental energy is stored in microtubules within the cells of our brains. These are quantum devices where information comes together into an instantaneous calculation, called "quantum coherence."

Those who oppose the theory do so on the basis that if "spirit particles" or mental energy exist, then we should be able to detect it, which we haven't. Professor Brian Cox recently stated that if some kind of spiritual energy existed, the Large Hadron Collider (LHC) should have detected it.

If "spirit particles" can't be detected, then they can't interact with other particles and exert their influence on the human brain in order to give rise to consciousness. If ghosts are manifestations of this type of energy, then they wouldn't be able to interact with their surroundings. Poltergeist activity wouldn't be possible, ghosts wouldn't reflect light and would therefore not be visible to the naked eye, and they would also be unable to manipulate the air in order to produce the sound waves required for speech.

Others believe that we're not able to detect this energy due to the weird properties of quantum mechanics, an odd principle known as the observer effect, which can be demonstrated using the double-slit experiment. The outcome of this weird experiment changes depending on whether we observe or measure the results.

The experiment involves firing single electrons at a panel with two parallel slits in it. Although there is only one particle each time, over time, an interference pattern builds up on a second panel. It is consistent with the pattern we'd expect to see if a stream of electrons was passing through both slits simultaneously and interfering with itself.

However, when scientists put a detector behind the slits to try to establish which slit the electron had passed through, it forces the particle to pass through one specific slit, not both. When this happens, the interference pattern vanishes.

The microtubules in our brain may be capable of changing their state in response to these peculiar quantum events. They could even enter a superposition state themselves, like the particles in the double-slit experiment.

All this brings us back to our mythical spirit particles, which we now know must exist as a unified field like other types of particles. If this fundamental field of unified mental energy exists and can interact with our brain chemistry but can't be measured because of superpositioning and the observer effect, then this could explain why we can't detect, photograph, or otherwise measure ghosts or paranormal activity.

Some researchers think that the soul weighs exactly 21 grams and that it can be detected escaping the body after death. This figure was calculated back in 1907 by Duncan MacDougall, who converted a hospital bed into weighing scales so that he could measure the change in weight of a patient at the moment of their death.

MacDougall's experiment has since been heavily criticised due to its small sample size. He only managed to obtain permission to test his theory on six dying people. His scales were inaccurate, and his data varied dramatically. He failed to consistently pinpoint the exact time of death, and the time taken for the weight loss to occur ranged from an immediate drop in weight to a drop over several minutes.

The Anatomy of a Ghost

If people are able to sense the presence of a ghost, detect them with ghost hunting gadgets, or even see an apparition, then there must be something measurable and tangible that creates them.

There's a belief within the paranormal world that some ghosts are intelligent and capable of interacting with their surroundings. Then there are residual hauntings, which are said to be merely past events being replayed.

Residual hauntings are thought to be an imprint of energy that has been left behind by someone. The energy used by the body and the brain in resisting death can be so immense that those events can be replayed. The phenomenon is known as "stone tape theory." As residual hauntings represent nothing more than a reflection of the past, they don't have a physical presence as they don't interact with their surroundings.

If ghosts can't interact with the physical world around them, then it is impossible to see one or interact with one in any way. They wouldn't be able to interact with the air, light, and other forms of electromagnetic energy around them. Light would not be able to hit a non-physical spirit and bounce off, which would mean they're not visible to the human eye. They would not be able to interact with the air around them, making speech and sound impossible.

When it comes to intelligent hauntings, it's a little different. These types of hauntings are the classic "ghost", they can reportedly move objects, push or touch people, slam doors, and even throw objects across a room. So clearly, when they manifest, there is some kind of physical force behind them.

The law of conservation of energy states that energy cannot be destroyed or created. So, if a poltergeist pushes, throws, or breaks something, then energy has been created, which is a violation of the law of conservation of energy.

Another form of energy transfer is when light reflects off of an object and is converted into electrical impulses by our eyes before being passed along the optic nerve to your brain, which interprets them as a vision of the object. This process relies on the fact that an object can reflect light. If it couldn't, then the light would pass straight through it and it would be invisible.

Sound also requires a physical form. For a ghost to be able to speak or make a sound, it needs a physical form so that it can create the vibrations in the air required to transmit sound.

The only possible plausible explanation is that ghosts can change states. Whether this change occurs at will or is the result of environmental or atmospheric conditions is unknown.

One of the easiest and therefore most common ways to communicate with spirits is by asking them to tap out their answers by encouraging them to tap once for "yes" and twice for "no." According to Dr. Barrie Colvin, these unexplained sounds could not be made by any means other than as a result of paranormal activity.

Colvin analysed the audio recordings of several poltergeist cases and found that the sounds shared similar acoustic qualities to those of an earthquake. He found that similar artificially produced noises appeared similar but lacked sound signatures, which cannot be reproduced.

You must have experienced that phenomenon when you've sat at home and suddenly something on a shelf falls off for no reason. There are plenty of reasons why this might happen. The object could have been perched precariously in the first place, or a draught could cause it to fall over.

Items can also fall off of a piece of furniture over time due to tiny forces generated from within the home. Even a sudden change in air pressure due to opening a door or window could cause an object to topple over.

There are also plenty of external sources that can cause vibrations, like road works outside the house, heavy traffic passing by, an earthquake, low-flying aircraft, or a gust of wind through an open window.

Another factor that can make something fall is gravity and how it affects an object as it changes state. A towel, for example, is placed on a towel rail in the bathroom. It can be hanging over the rail quite happily, then all of a sudden it slips and lands in a heap on the floor. The towel drying over time could also change how gravity affects it. If one side of the towel is wet, it will be heavier. As it dries, it will get lighter and change the balance of the towel.

It's a little harder to find a rational cause when an object appears to have been thrown across the room, but there are non-paranormal ways to explain this too. When something falls, usually it hits the floor and stays roughly where it landed, but there's a chance it might hit something on the way down and get deflected, land on something, roll, bounce, or a combination of all of these actions. In this case, the landing position and orientation can be very hard to predict.

Practical Investigation

Firm believers in the paranormal tend to take a dim view of skeptics. They often deem them to be close-minded and pedantic, but a skeptic would view a believer in the same way. It's not that either group is close-minded. It's just that they've both already formed an opinion on the paranormal and will therefore, in most cases, only consider evidence that supports their stance.

Believers often say that skeptics make irrational and endless demands for more and more evidence and that they feel like the skeptic is judging them, but if you are trying to convince that skeptic that ghosts exist, then you have opened yourself up to judgement and scrutiny, and you need to provide evidence in order to convince that person. If you turn the tables, a believer would require an equal amount of evidence to convince them that ghosts don't exist.

If every investigator was able to carry out an experiment, get the same result every time, and rule out anything that may be interfering with the experiment, then this would be irrefutable evidence that couldn't be debunked. The fact that different, independent investigators could repeat the same results would satisfy the peer review requirement. This is simply the scientific method.

Ghost sightings generally aren't repeatable. There are many spooky stories of the ghosts of soldiers walking through a castle at night or of a lady in grey who appears in a church on the anniversary of her death. If these stories were true, then any skeptic could be taken to that castle at night or to the church on the correct date, and they should be able to see the ghost, but they don't and can't.

Strange mists are often caught on camera and could be ghosts, or they could be the photographer's breath lit by the camera's flash or a lens flare. One photo proves nothing unless it can be repeated and the possibility of things like lens flares are removed. Why, in

200 years of photography, has no one ever found a haunted location where the spirit of someone can always be caught on camera sitting in the chair they died in?

Similarly, no psychic medium has ever been able to prove that they are able to contact the dead, despite the One Million Dollar Paranormal Challenge, set up by James Randi to pay out a cash prize to anyone who can demonstrate supernatural abilities.

What we do know about the paranormal is that people report seeing, hearing, being touched by, or otherwise sensing a ghostly presence in just about any location at any time of day or night. Yet modern ghost hunters ignore their own senses and embark on investigations in darkened buildings while arming themselves with an array of elaborate ghost hunting gadgets. Most commonly, devices like EMF meters are used.

Traditionally, ghost hunters were armed with nothing more than a notebook to jot down their findings, and their senses were their first and most important method of spiritual detection. Today, a digital audio recorder is more commonly used.

The Society for Psychical Research guidelines state that electronic ghost-hunting devices are not an effective way of investigating a haunting. Instead, they advise using nothing more than a few simple tools when investigating the paranormal that mimic the human senses:
- Notebook
- Wristwatch
- A camera
- An audio recorder

A digital thermometer might also be a useful tool, as it allows us to obtain an accurate measure of the ambient air temperature at a location, confirming the existence of "cold spots," which are often felt by witnesses of hauntings.

You've probably been told by many people that messing with the occult is extremely dangerous and potentially even life-threatening, but the average number of people who die as a result of occult-related activities each year is zero.

There are some deaths that are very loosely linked to the occult, including the odd, bodged, forced exorcisms performed by people who get carried away. There are also examples of murders and mass suicides driven by occult groups. These deaths aren't really the result of dabbling in the paranormal, they're just deaths at the hands of a deluded member of an ill-informed cult.

There is one occult field that historically has been very dangerous to dabble in, and that's witchcraft. The 16th to 18th centuries were a pretty dangerous time to be a witch. In Europe alone, it's estimated that up to 60,000 women and men were tried and executed as witches.

Many within the paranormal field think that deaths as a result of meddling with the occult are often disguised as other, more common causes of death. It's said that demons and certain types of hauntings can drive people to depression and exhaustion, which can eventually lead to accidents due to lapses in concentration or even suicide.

The occult accounts for fewer deaths each year than riding a rollercoaster does. That accounts for around four deaths a year in the US alone. And, sadly, around 70 children die every year from choking on a hotdog, making hotdogs statistically more dangerous than the occult.

Perhaps the most commonly believed misconception when it comes to the law is that certain aspects of the paranormal are banned or illegal. For example, it is often said that Ouija boards are illegal to sell or use in some countries.

Ouija boards have a reputation of being an extremely dangerous occult tool, especially in the United Kingdom, but despite the fear that surrounds them, no ban has ever been imposed on the sale or use of Ouija boards. Today, they are easy to get hold of on Amazon and eBay, as well as at specialist online retailers.

The myth that Ouija boards are illegal is most prevalent in the UK. This is probably based on the church's attempts to ban all occult practices. The church feels the same way about other forms of divination, including tarot cards, palm reading, and many of the activities you might perform as part of a paranormal investigation.

Although spirit boards themselves aren't banned, there was a law passed in Britain in 1951 that did affect their use as part of the Fraudulent Mediums Act. This act prohibited the use of any device used by mediums to intentionally con those who seek out their services in England and Wales. The act was replaced in 2008 by new Consumer Protection Regulations, which offer similar protection to the public.

Quick Reference Guide: Capturing and Analysing EVPs

Defining Electronic Voice Phenomenon

Electronic Voice Phenomenon (EVP) is the sound of disembodied human-like voices of unknown origin that are heard through electronic devices. It is a form of Instrumental Transcommunication (ITC). They are usually heard in the form of sounds imprinted on an audio recording or through radio noise.

The term "ITC" isn't limited to audio devices and encompasses any communication between the living and spirits or any other supernatural entity through any electronic device.

The quality of EVPs varies from sounds like groans, whispers, and growls to clear, human-like voices. At their best, an EVP can be a recognisable voice that gives an intelligent or direct response. Sometimes amplification, noise filtering, or enhancement is used in order to hear the voices.

Paranormal investigators generally believe that EVPs are produced by the spirits of the dead communicating with us.

Electronic Voice Phenomenon shouldn't be confused with Direct Voice Phenomenon (DVP). DVP is sometimes also referred to as an AVP, or Audible Voice Phenomena. DVPs are disembodied voices that are heard aloud during paranormal investigations, séances, or at a haunted location without the need for any electrical equipment.

Residual Hauntings: No intelligent spirit is responsible for the voice

Intelligent Hauntings: The source of the voice has an awareness or consciousness that can understand your questions and reply with relevant responses

Spirits don't have physical bodies or vocal cords, but they seem to sometimes be able to move objects. Therefore, they must at times be able to take a physical or partially physical form, which means they should also have the ability to vibrate the air around them in order to make sounds.

When it comes to EVPs, the voice isn't actually heard out loud, so it could be that the voice is imprinted in the recording using a kind of psychic energy or manufactured electrical interference.

It is possible that the source of EVPs isn't spirits but that the sound is coming from a parallel universe. There's growing support for the many-worlds interpretation, which suggests that there are one or more, perhaps an infinite number, of complete universes co-existing with us on a plane we are not aware of.

EVPs could even be coming from another time, perhaps due to the focused energy of ghost hunters in the past at a location.

Another theory is that EVPs are not coming from a spirit or another being at all but are audible imprints of the experimenter's own mental thoughts that are subconsciously projected and recorded on the audio device.

Scalar waves are a proposed type of exotic wave that some paranormal investigators think could be responsible for carrying EVPs because they can be captured by devices even when electromagnetically shielded in a Faraday pouch, and scalar waves are thought to be able to pass through solid objects.

The History of EVP Research

1910
Father Roberto Landell de Mour, a Brazilian Catholic priest and inventor, used a device that allowed two-way communication with spirits based on radio technology.

1920
American inventor Thomas Edison fuelled the possibility that technology could be used to communicate with spirits. In an interview, he said he was proposing giving investigators a more scientific approach to spiritualism than the other more "crude methods" employed at the time, but died in 1931 having never completed the device.

1932
Reverend Charles Drayton Thomas, a member of the Society for Psychical Research, captured a spirit voice in a recording while investigating the validity of a well-known medium of the time, Gladys Osborne Leonard.

1940s
In 1941, Attila von Szalay used one of the first commercially available home recording devices to capture EVPs on a blank record. He worked with psychologist Raymond Bayless and became one of the first to experiment with a reel-to-reel tape recorder.

1952
Agostino Gemelli inadvertently captured a voice while attempting to record the sounds of Gregorian chants in Milan with Father Pellegrino Ernetti. They were experiencing technical issues with the microphone, causing Gemelli to look to the heavens and ask his dead father for help. When they reviewed the tape, they heard a voice that Gemelli recognised as his dead father.

1959
Friedrich Jürgenson caught unexplained voices on tape while trying to record bird song in woodland. Later in his research, Jürgenson became the first to combine the technique of recording EVPs with the earlier method of radio contact in order to improve his results. Jürgenson went on to write two books on the subject of EVP, 'Voices from the Universe' and 'Voice Transmissions with the Deceased'.

1965
Konstantin Raudive initially worked with Juergenson to capture EVPs. In one of these early experiments, Raudive heard multiple voices in various languages, one of which translated as "Go to sleep, Margaret." He took this as a reference to someone of the same name he knew who had recently passed. He later captured the voice of his mother using his childhood name.

Raudive used several methods of recording EVPs. Each method was carried out in strict laboratory conditions and asked volunteers to interpret the voice to avoid bias. His methods included using:
- a normal microphone connected to a tape recorder
- a standard radio that was not tuned to any station
- a modified radio with a germanium diode fitted

1972
The American Association of Electronic Voice Phenomena was founded by Sarah Estep. It later became known as the Association Transcommunication (ATransC) and survives to this day.

1974
Marcello Bacci started giving public performances in Italy of his method of spirit communication, in which he used an old military radio and later a larger vacuum tube radio set. Audience members were given the chance to hear the voices of their deceased loved ones.

1976
Des Vereins für Transkommunikations-Forschung (the German Association for Transcommunication Research) was founded.

1976
Sarah Estep began her research after reading about the work of Friedrich Jürgenson and Konstantin Raudive using a reel-to-reel tape recorder. She popularised the first widely accepted A, B, and C EVP classification system.

1982
George Meek and William O'Neil used a similar germanium diode to Raudive's to develop their Spiricom, a radio-based device that made two-way communication with the dead possible.

Choosing the Right Equipment

A digital audio recorder can be used to log entire investigations. When you start recording, speak out loud the current time, the location you are in, and who is present. Note verbally any non-paranormal sounds that are heard during the investigation, like coughs, sneezes, and movements, so you can rule them out when you review the audio.

Recordings on analogue devices, such as a cassette recorder or reel-to-reel tape machines, may contain more unwanted noise in the form of unwanted hisses, pops, and rumbling.

Recordings on digital audio recorders tend to be clearer and have less background noise. These are recordings made on devices like handheld audio recorders and dictaphones, the audio recording app built into your mobile phone or tablet, or audio recording software on a laptop.

You can also use a computer or laptop to capture EVPs using audio software like Audacity or Adobe Audition. If a sound is captured that you didn't hear aloud, then it will show as a peak in the waveform.

In addition to your recorder itself, you may also want to invest in an external omnidirectional microphone. These can easily be connected to a computer or laptop, and some models of handheld audio recorders have a standard 3.5mm microphone jack so you can plug one in.

Spirit boxes rapidly scan through the AM, MW, and FM radio spectrums, and as they do, fleeting bursts of white noise and static can be heard. It's believed that spirits are able to change or influence these bursts of audio in order to form sounds, words, or even sentences.

Some paranormal researchers put their spirit box inside a small bag that acts as a Faraday cage and filters out radio broadcasts.

The GeoPort and GeoBox are a type of spirit box that monitors three different types of input: EMF, vibrational waves, and radio frequency. The original GeoBox uses analogue components, while the newer GeoPort has digital components.

The audio processing in the Geo devices drastically reduces the level of the characteristic radio noise produced by spirit boxes, making it easier to hear any voices.

A laser can be used to send an audio signal to a light-sensitive receiver, and as the laser beam passes through the air, paranormal researchers theorise that spirits may be able to manipulate or interfere with the light's waveform in order to change the sound being transmitted or even add a sound of their own into the stream, like a voice.

The Phone Experiment involves placing a phone in a location and monitoring any sounds heard via a phone call in real time. A similar experiment can be carried out with a pair of walkie-talkies. You could also experiment with transmitting trigger sounds through the walkie-talkies and the phone line.

How to Capture EVPs

You can experiment with recording EVPs anywhere, not just at an allegedly haunted location but also in controlled environments. Even if your home isn't haunted, you can still invite spirits to communicate with you there, including those of a particular person, such as a deceased loved one, with whom you wish to make contact.

When setting up your audio recorder or recording app on a mobile phone, avoid any 'noise reduction,' 'low cut,' or 'auto gain' features. Set it to record at the highest possible recording quality. This is usually in WAV PCM format rather than the heavily compressed MP3 format. If you can use a sample rate of at least 44,100 Hz, always choose the high-quality (HQ) or 'lossless' setting, or, if available on your device, extra high quality (XHQ) or super high quality (SHQ).

Experiment with the microphone sensitivity settings where available to determine what works best with your specific recorder. It might also be a good idea to use a windshield or muffler to reduce unwanted noise. Ensuring you are using new batteries and freshly charged equipment will also ensure there is no reduction in the quality of the recording.

An external omnidirectional microphone can be easily connected to a computer or laptop for better-quality recordings. Some models of handheld audio recorders will also have a standard 3.5mm microphone jack, so you can plug one in.

Ensure the environment is free of background noise - things like heating, AC, fans, and any other loud mechanical devices. Close windows and internal and external doors, and limit the number of people in the building or room. Place your recorder on a flat, solid surface away from other electrical devices to avoid unwanted interference, especially any device that transmits a radio signal of any kind.

Holding a device is a common cause of unwanted sounds. Do not place the recorder inside anything, such as a box, pouch, or your pocket. Get comfortable and avoid moving around during the session to limit unwanted noise.

Upon pressing record, leave a five to 10-second pause at the beginning to allow the recorder to adjust its levels to the baseline noise level. If you're using a tape recorder, then remember that the cassettes have a seven to 10-second buffer at the beginning that can't be recorded on, so allow for this.

Whenever you start recording, introduce the session by speaking out loud the date, time, location, and number of people present. This will make it easier to keep track of recordings when you review the audio later.

Verbally note any non-paranormal noises you hear while recording. For example, if you cough, sneeze, clear your throat, move slightly, or your stomach rumbles, say out loud "that was me" so that there is no doubt later.

How long you record for is really up to you, but a good duration for a session would be around 10 to 20 minutes.

Passive EVP Sessions
A passive EVP session is one in which the investigators conducting the experiment are not actively asking questions or encouraging the spirits to interact.

Active EVP Sessions
An active EVP session is when investigators are actively making attempts to communicate during the session. This normally involves asking a question out loud, such as "Is there anybody here?"

Burst Session
A burst session involves recording two or three minutes of audio before reviewing it straight away, then moving on to the next recording.

Realtime Session
A real-time, or "listen-live session," is where the investigator monitors the audio being captured in real-time. The easiest and most common way to conduct a real-time EVP session is by simply plugging a pair of headphones into your audio recorder and monitoring the sound as it is recorded.

With both burst and real-time sessions, the idea is to listen to EVPs as they occur. This allows investigators to follow up on any words or phrases they hear in order to continue the conversation.

Unless you are conducting a passive EVP session, you'll need to ask any spirits that might be present questions. This is called "calling out" or "asking out." It involves speaking aloud in an attempt to encourage any spirits to come forward, talk to you, and answer your questions in your recordings.

1. Leave a gap
After each question, remain silent and leave a space to allow the spirit time to answer.

2. Encourage, don't demand
Be polite and respectful. Don't make demands of the spirits, and thank them for taking the time to communicate with you.

3. Make your questions relevant
When calling out to spirits, remember that they are unlikely to be from your time.

Based on the theory that spirits can reorganise radio noise to form words, some EVP researchers use a white noise source to give spirits a base of raw sound to use to form words. This is done by playing back a pre-recorded sample of white noise or by recording near a source of static noise.

The drawback to using this technique is that the white noise contaminates the recording, making it hard to analyse the audio. However, audio editing software like Adobe Audition or Audacity can be used to filter out white noise.

Some research uses the "ghost tone" instead of white noise. This is a low, constant sound. It can't be heard with the human ear and is too low to play from most devices, but a low-frequency subwoofer can be used.

Analysing EVPs

Review and analyse your recordings using a good-quality external speaker or over-ear headphones. A better approach is to transfer the audio to your computer to allow you to review the audio in greater detail.

Transferring audio from an analogue recording device such as an old tape recorder or an early dictaphone might lead to unwanted noise in the transferred audio.

Listen to the audio from start to finish. You might hear unexpected voices in parts of the recording where you weren't expecting responses.

If you hear anything, either make a note of the time in the recording and what you think the voice is saying, or isolate the specific piece of audio and save it as a separate file.

Auditory pareidolia is by far the strongest argument against the credibility of EVPs. This is the tendency for the human brain to perceive a familiar or meaningful sound or word in random noise, which in reality isn't paranormal at all.

Understanding or interpreting what an EVP is saying is subjective. As the listener, you may be influenced by the question that was asked prior to the EVP or by your knowledge of the location you were investigating. You are likely to simply hear what you expect to hear.

Other causes of sounds often misinterpreted as EVPs include ambient sounds, atmospheric electrical interference, radio interference, faulty equipment, sounds caused by the recording device being moved or handled, or the sounds of the inner workings of the recorder itself.

Remove subjectivity by listening to the clip out-of-context and by asking other people to listen to it, ideally a group who are not interested in the paranormal or familiar with EVP research. Do not tell them what you believe the voice is saying.

A researcher may choose to enhance their audio in order to make the words heard clearer or to filter out background noises.

The problem with doing this is that if you are intentionally manipulating the audio to make it sound more like the words you think it sounds like, then what you're left with is your ideal interpretation of your own subjective perception of what that EVP should sound like, not a true representation of what it sounded like at the time it was captured.

In order to enhance your audio, you'll need some audio editing software like Audacity, Adobe Audition, or Goldwave. With some practice and experimentation, you can use this software to filter out just the extraneous sounds, leaving you with a more accurate representation of the captured sound, or simply amplify the audio in order to enable you to hear any potential EVPs more clearly.

In the spirit of keeping your audio as true to the source recording as possible, limit yourself to just one or two enhancements. Try to find filters and enhancements that work for you and stick to them.

In the case of EVP recordings, there's often a low or even negative signal-to-noise ratio, which means that the signal power is lower than the noise power. This can make it hard for noise reduction tools to enhance the audio, as they will not be able to tell the difference between the noise and your suspected EVP.

Some audio editing software allows you to switch to a 'Spectral Frequency Display' view rather than the standard waveform. This view can be very useful for identifying and removing or enhancing noise in your recordings.

Amplification can be used to increase the volume of your clip. Be sure not to amplify your clip too heavily, as over-amplification will cause it to become distorted.

Most software has some basic noise reduction tools. This might be called simply 'noise reduction', but also look out for restoration, hiss removal, hum removal, and vocal enhancer.

In some applications, the noise reduction tool requires you to select a sample of noise for best results. You should try to pick a part of the recording where the noise is similar to the background sounds heard throughout the clip and at the point where the sound of interest is heard.

In order to properly analyse an EVP session that you've recorded, be familiar with the parts of the wave:

Peak - the highest point above the rest position (the red line through the centre of the wave)
Trough - the lowest point below the rest position
Amplitude - the maximum displacement of the wave from its rest position
Wavelength - distance covered by a full cycle of the wave, usually measured from peak to peak or trough to trough

Another important property of a wave is its frequency, measured in Hertz (Hz), which determines whether the sound we hear is low-pitched or high-pitched. The amplitude of a sound wave determines its volume.

Capturing voices that are outside the normal human hearing range of 20 Hz to 20,000 Hz is difficult and requires specialist equipment.

Microphones, like the ones you'd find in a smartphone, camera, or digital audio recorder, are designed to capture what the human ear can hear. Anything beyond this is just unnecessary data, especially in the case of digital audio, where keeping file sizes low is important.

If there is an EVP in your audio recording, then you know it must have been created in one of three ways:

1. The sound was audible at the time of recording and was extremely quiet.

2. The sound was not audible at the time but has made its way into the recording via a form of electrical interference.

3. The sound was somehow imprinted onto the recording via some kind of currently not-understood supernatural method.

A very high-frequency sound, those over 20,000 Hz, is called ultrasound and falls outside the upper limit for human hearing. To capture ultrasound, you will need some specialist equipment, like a bat detector, which can be tuned to pick up frequencies from 15,000 Hz to 130,000 Hz.

Very low-frequency sounds are called infrasound and fall between 0.1 and 20 Hz. These sounds are below the human range of hearing. Infrasound is very hard to record, but there are purpose-built infrasound mics available.

EVP Classification

EVPs can be split into two types:
Type 1 - **Transformative**: Manipulation of dissimilar sounds
Type 2 - **Opportunistic**: Selective use of existing voices

Type 1 EVPs are sounds made up of background noise or sounds that have been transformed to a pitch in the range of the human voice. This would cover most EVPs, including those captured on audio recorders.

Type 2 EVPs are new words or sentences made up from words or word parts of existing human voices. This would cover EVPs captured using a device that has voices being input into it, such as a spirit box.

These two types are divided into subclasses and labeled either A, B, or C, or 1, 2, 3, or 4, with A or 1 being the best quality or less objective.

The exact meaning of the A to C or 1 to 4 categorisation depends on the scale you are using. The two most commonly used systems today are the AA-EVP System and the KM System.

The AA-EVP System

Class A
EVP is a message that can be heard without headphones, and people can generally agree on its content.

Class B
EVP requires headphones to distinguish message content, and not everyone will agree on the message.

Class C
EVP requires headphones, often needs amplification and filtering, and will seldom even be heard by others.

The KM System

Class 1: Interactive
Spirit voice is a direct response to a human statement, question, action, activity, or spirit voices respond to each other.

Class 2: Non-interactive
Voice is a general statement and not a direct response to a statement, question, action, or activity, by humans.

Class 3: Non-speech
Spirit voice is a sound other than the spoken word (growls, screams, humming, etc.)

Class 4: Null/valueless
The EVP contains nothing of value in understanding the spirit realm or spirit psychology (words are unintelligible.)

Quick Reference Guide: Event Planning and Management

The key to hosting a successful paranormal event is to meticulously plan how the event should unfold. The benefits of having such a plan include:

- Efficient movement of people and equipment
- A reduction in the likelihood of issues that could result in additional costs due to damage and cleaning activities
- The ability to respond to unexpected occurrences
- Securing long-term loyalty from clients and staff and generating repeat bookings
- Reduction in liability arising from accidents and injuries and related insurance costs

In order to plan your event, you'll need to develop a few essential skills that every event planner relies upon, including the following:

- Ability to work in a team or independently
- Interpersonal and social skills
- Analytical ability
- Communication skills
- High organisational skills
- Good time management
- Ability to work to deadlines
- Able to pay attention to details
- Negotiating skills
- Ability to deal with pressure situations
- Problem-solving skills
- Creativity
- Marketing and public relations

When planning an event, you should always ask why, who, when, where, and what. Throughout the course, we will attempt to answer these questions in relation to a paranormal event, but here's a quick overview of those five important questions:

- Why am I putting on the event?
- Who do I want to come to the event?
- When is the best time to stage the event?
- Where is the best place to stage the event?
- What concept or idea will best serve the purposes of the event?

Not all paranormal events are the same, and customers will be looking for different things. The most common types of events include:

- A ghost walks on public land
- A ghost walks at a private venue
- Ghost hunts

Location

One of the most important things to consider when planning a paranormal event is the location. If you are planning on having 20 or more people attend, then you will have to consider your venues carefully.

Before choosing the location for the event, you should carefully consider the exact specification of space required for the particular event, taking the following into consideration:

- The size of the venue
- The location of toilets
- Ease of access
- Where to put signs to direct people to specific locations throughout the venue
- How would rooms be accessed, at all times or at specific times only?
- Providing information about the rules for using facilities at the venue
- The number of reports of ghost sightings or paranormal activity

Based on these factors, you'll need to create a shortlist and evaluate each location based on the following:

- Permission to display branding and signage
- Physical state
- Capacity
- Control of lighting
- Available amenities
- Accessibility
- Out-of-hours access

The venue will usually be able to provide you with guidelines in regards to promotional activities that can be carried out at the venue.

Once you have decided on a location and researched its haunted history, you should always try to obtain written evidence of the venue's availability to avoid booking conflicts.

Finding a suitable venue is only half the battle. Once you've chosen your location, do your research. You need to make sure that it has a suitable haunted history and that your guests are likely to experience some kind of paranormal activity, although this can never be guaranteed due to the nature of the paranormal.

As well as getting the facts on hauntings, you should also research the history of the location, including details such as:

- When it was built
- What it's been used for over the years
- Notable residents
- Events of interest such as fires, murders, or ancient battles

When holding your first event at a new location, you should always hold a staging night. This should be done with a group of staff, friends, or volunteers of approximately the same size as the group that will attend the real event.

An important part of planning any event is doing all you can to avoid accidents and injuries, and with paranormal events there are significantly more risks, such as darkness and the dangers of derelict buildings. These dangers should be taken into consideration when planning an event, and as many risks as possible should be eliminated.

A risk assessment is a document that lists in detail anything that could cause harm to people, so that you can weigh up whether you have taken enough precautions or should do more to prevent harm. Its main objective is to determine the measures required to avoid incidents and accidents.

The four main steps to ensure that your risk assessment is carried out correctly are:

- Identify the hazards
- Decide who might be harmed and how
- Evaluate the risks and decide on control measures
- Record your findings and implement them

In order to control the risk, you need to work out the best method of handling it. The following methods, which are referred to as the 'hierarchy of controls', guide you on how to eliminate or reduce the risk:

Elimination: by removing the hazard entirely through new design or implementing a new process

Substitution: by replacing hazardous materials or methods with less hazardous alternatives

Engineering: by isolating, enclosing or containing the hazard or through design improvements

Administrative: by ensuring guests are familiar with safety guidelines and that staff and volunteers are trained effectively

Personal protective equipment (PPE): by making sure that appropriate safety equipment, such as gloves, hats, sunscreen, etc. are available

Due to the varying nature of events and venues, it is impossible to foresee all potential hazards. Below are some examples of common hazards:

- Trip hazards such as cables running across a floor, loose flooring, or carpet
- Falls and drops, check for any sheer drops, steps that aren't clearly visible
- Collision risk with vehicles and guests/staff on the event site
- Certain activities cannot be offered due to weather conditions
- Extreme weather effects on guests and personnel such as heat exhaustion, heat stroke, fainting and sunburn

Logistics

The key to successfully staffing an event is assigning the right person to the right job. Of course, when it comes to paranormal events, the more experience the staff members have with ghost hunting, the better, as this will allow them to inject their own personality and experience into the event.

The ratio of staff to guests at an event should be identified early in the planning process based on the risk assessment. Every event is different, and as such, we would not recommend applying a formula to assess the number of personnel needed.

Budgeting for an event is important, and one of the biggest costs you'll need to budget for to put on a ghost hunting event is paranormal kit and gadgets. Most people attending your event won't have their own equipment, but using the gadgets of the trade is something they will expect to experience.

When preparing your event budget, you should consider the following:

- A balance sheet showing a list of all expenses relating to accommodation, transportation, catering services, marketing, etc.
- Sufficient funds must be available to pay for all expenses, and a separate account must be opened for accrued expenses during the event.
- Estimate costs using records of budgets for similar events held previously.
- Make budget provisions for licenses and insurance for all potential liabilities, such as cancellation, postponement, or a fire.
- Have some emergency funds available to take care of unexpected expenses.

A document containing details of all expenses should be prepared. Take into account all your costs so that you don't end up with nasty surprises along the way. This may include:

- Creating a website
- Venue hire
- Publicity and promotion
- Purchase of ghost hunting equipment
- Spare batteries
- Decorations/branding
- Audio-visual equipment hire
- Refreshments
- Transport
- Phone bills, postage, and other admin
- Insurance
- First aid equipment
- Fees for licenses and permissions
- Hire of a photographer or videographer

However well prepared you are, accidents do happen. For this reason, if you're running an event for members of the public, then you must have public liability insurance and professional indemnity insurance.

Public liability insurance covers legal costs up to £5 million relating to:
- Injuries
- Loss of life
- Loss or damage to property
- Damage to the venue

It does not cover your staff or volunteers. You may also want to investigate employers' liability insurance, which protects staff, short-term staff, casual workers, contractors, and volunteers.

Professional indemnity insurance covers you against claims from clients who allege that the advice or services you provided them caused them loss, damage, or suffering.

Paranormal events almost always take place in the evening, this is mainly due to the fact that it is dark in the evening, which adds to the atmosphere. When planning an event, be aware of the time of year, as summer days may be much longer and daylight will last much longer into the evening.

Start planning your event well in advance. Producing early publicity gives you an opportunity to appeal for volunteers.

Promotion and Sales

It is best to promote your event to an existing audience on social media. You may also need a website if you don't have one already.

If you don't have a following already, paying to promote your event on social media can be effective. You can also manually target those who you think might be interested in the event.

It is best to get publicity out early, even if this means that it can't include all the final details of the event.

A few tried and tested ways to promote your event include:
- Offer early bird tickets
- Run a competition
- Offer group discounts

In order to sell tickets for your events, you'll also need to not only find a suitable site to sell them through, but you'll have to decide on the price for your event tickets. You should ask:

- Will you sell the same ticket to everyone or offer discounted early bird tickets and VIP tickets with extra perks?
- How many of each type of ticket will you sell?
- How will you process payments, monitor your ticket sales, and stay connected to the buyers?

For small and medium-sized event organisers, self-service ticketing sites are the most efficient and affordable way to sell tickets for events. These sites let you create events and sell event tickets on your own.

You can also use tools that enable you to create a website or turn your existing website into an event ticket shop. A final option is to sell tickets at the door, but the downside of this is that you don't have a clear idea of the number of guests in advance.

On the Day

In the days leading up to the event, you'll need to run through the day in detail:

- Where will everybody be on the day?
- What will each person be responsible for doing?
- Are all the jobs covered, or do you need to do a last-minute ring round to fill some gaps?
- Have you set up all the admin (forms and paperwork) that will be needed on the day? e.g., guest lists, photo consent forms, etc.
- How will equipment and volunteers get to and from the venue?
- Will you be able to take hired equipment directly to and from the event, or will it need to be stored?
- What will happen if it rains?
- Do you have enough time, materials, and people for setting up and clearing away?

Most event organisers use a '**schedule of events**' to ensure the event runs smoothly. This document takes into account activities such as the arrival of guests, transportation plans, hospitality arrangements, security, information about the venue, clean-up procedures, and equipment set-up procedures.

Remember that if you are using an event photographer or videographer, you should put up signs informing people that their image may be captured in photographic or video form.

The welcome or orientation is the time to let guests know what they can expect over the evening and to run through important safety information in order to keep them safe.

While you may want to tell guests about the venue's history, you may want to avoid telling them too much about its haunted past. This means that if a guest does unearth some information like a name or date during a vigil, it's less likely that they've been influenced by what they've heard.

Things to tell your guests at the orientation:
- This is a genuine investigation of the paranormal
- Mention anything they see, hear, feel, or experience at the time
- Guests should respect each other's beliefs
- Safety in the dark and use of a flashlight
- Rules for photography and filming
- Fire and evacuation procedures
- No smoking policy
- Acceptable behaviour
- The running order of the event

Activities

You will not be able to run a ghost hunt with more than a few people without having a few extra expert helpers to teach guests the way of paranormal investigation, guide guests through the venue, and help guests interpret their findings.

When it comes to equipment for events, the most common items are:
- Ouija boards
- Thermometers
- Electromagnetic field meters
- Electronic speech synthesis devices
- Spirit boxes
- Trigger objects

Many events start out with a group vigil before breaking out into smaller teams for individual vigils. They should ideally be conducted in silence, so you should make sure there is a good separation between groups.

These vigils usually consist of a few staple paranormal activities:
- Calling out to spirits
- Ouija boards
- EMF meters and other gadgets
- Table tipping
- Lone vigils

It's best to perform these vigils or séances in darkness because it helps set the mood and is also said to help the spirits around you manifest. The participants of the séance should either stand or sit around a table. You should make sure your guests are comfortable, as movement or fidgeting may be wrongly attributed to paranormal activity in the dark.

The guests should then hold hands to form a circle. This is done for protection, to focus the energy, and so your guests know that no one at the séance is creating any tapping noises or moving anything themselves in the dark.

Call out to the spirits and look for responses through either a ghost hunting gadget, a Ouija board, through tapping, or by using a trigger object.

One of the easiest and therefore most common ways to communicate with spirits is by asking them to tap out their answers by encouraging them to tap once for "yes" and twice for "no."

There are a few tips and best practices that should be observed when calling out:
- Encourage, don't demand
- Say thank you
- Don't use jargon
- Don't shut it down

Whichever technique you are using to listen to spirits, the questions you ask will be the same. Here are some example questions and phrases:

If you can hear me, tap on the floor.
Can you make a noise to let us know you are here with us?
If you're here, can you show yourself to me?
How many of you are with us right now? Tap it out.
Can you make a noise?
Can you throw something?
Can you copy me? [then tap on a surface or whistle]
My name is XXX. Can you tell me your name?
Tell us who you are. Introduce yourself, please.
If there's somebody here with us now, can you walk towards us?
Are you happy for us to be here? Two taps for yes, one for no.
Can you come and talk to us?

Ouija Board
- Facilitators should not get involved with the ouija board themselves
- Members of the group should rest one finger very gently on the glass or planchette
- You might want to start off the conversation with any spirits that might be present, but after giving a few example questions and statements, encourage the group to take over
- Once the planchette starts moving, you can suggest that the group start asking more specific questions

Electromagnetic Field Meters
- An EMF meter can be used to communicate with spirits, you should encourage the spirits to try to trigger the lights on the device
- EMF meters are susceptible to interference from many external factors, they can be triggered by things like mobile phones and walkie-talkies

Electronic Speech Synthesis
- Encourage the spirits to provide you with answers to your questions rather than just letting the device run of its own accord
- Only intelligent answers are likely to be the result of spirit interaction

Spirit Boxes
- Ask the spirits questions, and then listen for their answers within the white noise

Trigger Objects
- Encourage spirits to move, throw, or otherwise manipulate the trigger object

End the night by asking your guests about their experiences and asking them to give feedback on the event, which should be noted.

It is your responsibility to return the location to its original condition.

It's a good idea to gather your staff and volunteers before they leave for a brief discussion about the event. Remember to thank them.

Practical Ghost Hunting

Determine if a Location is Haunted

There are two schools of thought when it comes to doing background research on a location before you visit and investigate it: should you do your research upfront or not?

Some believe that it is better to go in with no knowledge at all. This means that if you uncover a name, date, or other significant piece of information during your investigation, you know that you haven't been influenced by information you've already read about the location.

Others, often those who are less spiritual or don't include séances in their investigations, prefer to find out as much as possible about the property and its alleged hauntings. This approach gives you the opportunity to consider the type of haunting and activity experienced there and shape your investigation around it. For example, if disembodied voices are frequently heard, you may wish to set up audio recorders around the location.

Either way, it's wise to consider a property's likelihood of being haunted before you invest your time and energy in investigating it. [SPOILER — IT'S NOT HAUNTED] Sometimes claims of a haunting can be easily discredited without even visiting the property, especially when there is a potential financial gain for the owner to claim it's haunted. If a 16th-century inn suddenly gains attention [OR SIMPLY ATTENTION TO THE PERSON CLAIMING A HAUNTING] as a haunted pub after new owners have taken over, this could be an attempt to attract more customers. You should try to establish whether the stories date back further than the current owners and whether there is a history of hauntings in the area. This logic can be applied to most property types and haunting cases.

According to records of the most haunted locations worldwide, castles account for the biggest number of hauntings by property type. Given that there is a much smaller number of castles than residential houses, it means that, statistically, a castle is very likely to be haunted. The list of most haunted property types is also dominated by the likes of hospitals, hotels, pubs, cemeteries, and prisons.

[handwritten: LOL NO →]

However, the second highest number of hauntings are reported in normal residential homes. Of the ten most haunted houses in the world, six were built before 1900. The average age of the twenty houses considered to be the most haunted in the world is 200 years old.

[handwritten: SHOCKER →]
[handwritten: THAT IS NOT THAT OLD FFS]

From this data, we can deduce that the older a property, the more likely it is to be haunted. This seems logical, as in most types of hauntings, there needs to be some history at the property in order for paranormal activity to occur.

[handwritten: AGAIN, LOL NO →]
[handwritten: ARE YOU FUCKING SHITTING ME? THERE IS NO LOGIC IN THIS "LOGIC."]

Most hauntings occur on the site of a historical tragedy, whether it be a murder, a suicide, an untimely death due to illness, or an accident such as a car crash, drowning, or fatal fall. The tragedy may even predate the property. For this reason, in order to get the full picture, you should research the history of not only the property you are investigating but also the immediate area around the property and the former uses of the land.

[handwritten: WHEN RECORDS FAIL TO GIVE YOU A DEATH FOR THE HOUSE, BLAME THE "HAUNTED LAND" INSTEAD. CLASSIC.]

Newly built houses and buildings are much less likely to be haunted. However, a new home that has a recent tragic or harrowing past could still have its share of attached experiences, whether they are genuinely paranormal in this case or just a knowledge of past events that make the residents feel on edge. It is up to you to decide. Some investigators believe that a spirit is able to attach itself to an object. If this is the case and that object has been brought into a property, then this could cause residents to experience haunting phenomena. The source of a haunting may also predate the property. Perhaps the property is built on a former battlefield, a plague pit, or an ancient burial ground.

[handwritten: EVERY INCH OF THE PLANET HAS SEEN DEATH, SO BY THAT "LOGIC", THE ENTIRE PLANET IS HAUNTED.]

[handwritten: BECAUSE THEY'RE LIARS]

[handwritten: AKA - EVERYWHERE ON EARTH]

By finding out who owned or lived in the property before the current owners, you might be able to answer some of these questions. If you can, contact the former owners and people who have lived in the area for many years and ask them if they have witnessed anything strange or unusual taking place at the property.

AND IF THEY SAY NO, JUST IGNORE THEM FOR THE SAKE OF YOUR INSANE BELIEF

This sort of historical information can usually be found at the local reference library, town hall, or local historical society. You may be able to find out some of the history of the local area online or in local interest books. There are plenty of websites that detail local history and offer old maps of areas.

You may even be able to establish the name and identity of the person who is alleged to haunt the location. If you're able to find out these details, then you can use this information to validate any contact you might establish with their spirit as part of your investigation. *OR YOU CAN USE IT TO TWIST A FABULOUS NARRATIVE TO PEDDLE THIS WANK*

If this is how you intend to use the information, then it is often best to keep the details of names, dates, causes of death, etc. to one person in the group. This person should sit out of séances so they cannot intentionally or subconsciously influence them. The information obtained from the séance can then be quickly verified on site by the person entrusted with the information.

LOL! DON'T LET THE PERSON WITH INFO SIT IN ON A GROUP OF MUPPETS ASKING THIN AIR SOME QUESTIONS

LMAO BY WHOM? HOW? HOW DOES ONE "VERIFY" THIS BOLLOCKS? 2ND OPINION SPIRITS?

The Symptoms of a Haunting

When interviewing someone who has witnessed paranormal activity at a property or when trying to establish whether the goings on at a property are paranormal or not, you should consider whether the reports fall within the <u>normal types</u> of activities associated with a haunting.

(WHICH WERE ESTABLISHED WHEN/HOW/BY WHOM? A "NORMAL HAUNTING" IS A BUNCH OF LIES

OF COURSE NOT — THEN SHIT COULDN'T BE TWISTED TO SUIT THE STORY

Of course, these rules aren't hard and fast, but they are a good guide when trying to decide whether someone's claims of the paranormal really are <u>proof</u> of something out of the ordinary.

THERE IS NEVER PROOF

Remember that people may experience certain happenings that they attribute to the haunting. These happenings might not be in line with your personal beliefs, but their story and claims should be respected. If something felt real to the witness, then no matter what the actual cause, it was a real experience from their point of view.

Listening to someone's claims in a non-judgemental, open-minded way will allow you to plan your investigation and help you identify any non-paranormal explanation for some of the claims.

A General Feeling of Unease

This can present itself in many different ways. Witnesses may report feeling like they are being watched or picking up on a negative vibe or atmosphere. They may also feel emotionally drained, upset, or even depressed while in a certain room, part of the property, or the property as a whole.

An open-minded investigation of the property will shed light on these claims. You should ask yourself whether the property is overlooked, which could result in the witness feeling exposed and watched. Is it oppressive, dark, or enclosed? This could lead to negative feelings or emotions.

Does the witness have a history of depression or a current reason to be in this state of mind, such as a recent family death?

Strange Noises or Voices

Noises such as knocking, banging, footsteps, slamming, scratching, or the sound of objects being dropped or moved are very common in paranormal cases. Reports of disembodied voices, whispering, crying, sobbing, laughing, and screaming are also common, as are guttural moans and growls.

Before conducting a full paranormal investigation, you should spend some time in the property, ideally in the daytime and when it is being used for its normal purpose. For example, if you're investigating a home, you should visit when the family is home. The children may be playing upstairs, the central heating might be on, and the kitchen could be in use.

Observing the house in this way will give you an understanding of the normal sounds you can expect to hear in the house, allowing you to eliminate these sounds from your investigation later. This could be things like the heating turning on and off, pipes expanding, creaky floorboards, or electronic devices creating noise.

The same technique can be applied to any type of building. It would be a good idea to observe an office building while it is in use, allowing you to hear the elevators and various pieces of office equipment in action. In a castle surrounded by tourists, you'll get a feel for how sound travels and echoes around the thick stone walls.

Strange Smells or Odours

Often, haunted locations are said to have unusual smells. These can sometimes be unpleasant stenches or odours, but are more often the scent of perfumes, flowers, cigarette smoke, or food, which are thought to be linked to the spirit that is haunting the property.

Bear in mind that smells can drift in through open windows, ventilation, and even the foundation of a property if there is damage to the property's structure or drainage. You should do all you can to eliminate these causes from your investigation. This can be achieved by simply closing windows, temporarily covering air vents, or turning off ventilation or air conditioning units.

Temperature Fluctuations

It's believed that unexplained cold spots are a sign that a spirit is present or even close to manifesting in a physical form. You should be aware of not only cold spots in a location but also unexplained hot or warm areas, as these too might indicate a supernatural presence.

Before an investigation, you should take baseline temperature readings throughout the property. But be aware that the temperature will naturally change according to the time of day and depending on how many people are in the room. But getting an understanding of how the temperature varies throughout the property will tell you if some rooms are likely to be naturally hotter or colder.

You should also take note of any potential sources of draughts, like windows or ventilation, and warmth radiated from pipes, boilers, or heating ducts.

Moving Objects

Another common sign of a haunting is when objects move of their own accord, usually unseen by those living in, working in, or visiting the location. This can include jewellery or personal belongings, everyday items like dinner plates or mugs, or, in extreme cases, a piece of furniture sliding across the floor. This type of paranormal activity may also manifest itself through doors opening, closing, or slamming on their own, or electrical sockets or lights turning themselves on or off.

Objects or belongings may also disappear completely only to reappear days, weeks, or even months later, either in the exact same spot they vanished from or in an unusual location.

Immediately before an investigation, it's a good idea to take as many photographs or as much video of the property as possible.

This way, if you suspect something has moved, you'll be able to check your photos or video to determine if there has been any movement.

Be aware that draughts and vibrations can cause objects to move and doors to close. Vibrations can be caused by machinery as well as household appliances such as washing machines and gym equipment. External factors may also cause vibrations in a property, such as heavy traffic passing by.

Physical Contact

Some witnesses of the paranormal experience the sensation of being touched or brushed against. This could also include the feeling of someone's breath on their skin or hair. In rare occasions, reports of physical contact are much more extreme and have included reports of flicking, pinching, slapping, punching, or pushing.

During a paranormal investigation, the group should be encouraged to make themselves aware of their surroundings. Involuntary swaying while standing could result in one of the team members brushing against or nudging another, especially in the dark.

Apparitions

An apparition is said to be the physical manifestation of a spirit or ghost. This is very rare but results in sightings of ghostly figures, unexplained shadows, or moving shapes in the corner of the eye. Usually, these shapes or shadows take human or human-like form.

On rare occasions, these manifestations have been caught on camera or video and witnessed by multiple people at once.

Possible non-paranormal causes for seeing manifestations could be shadows caused by unaccounted-for light sources, such as camera screens.

Classification of Haunting

As with any field of interest, paranormal researchers like to label and categorise hauntings. This can be useful in order to group together similar cases, allowing you to more easily spot trends in findings and reported phenomena.

However, the truth is that we can't categorically identify any supernatural entity and say for certain that it is a ghost, spirit, elemental, poltergeist, demon, or anything else. In fact, after hundreds of years of paranormal research, no one has ever even been able to prove for certain that any supernatural entities exist at all.

What the commonly used terms on the next few pages actually define is the characteristic of certain types of hauntings, no matter what the paranormal cause of the haunting is. So really, when we use these terms, we're talking about specific types of cases, not any specific type of entity or cause for that case.

These terms refer to instances in which witnesses report seeing a shadow out of the corner of the eye through to what they believe to be a full-blown demonic haunting with malevolent intent.

Hauntings and sightings of ghosts often fit into one of the following categories:
- Shadow hauntings
- Residual hauntings
- Animal spirit hauntings
- Intelligent hauntings
- Poltergeist hauntings

- Demonic hauntings

Let's take a look at these six types of hauntings in depth.

Shadow Hauntings

Shadow hauntings are a very common type of haunting that many of us will have experienced. Perhaps you've woken up suddenly in the night and seen a dark figure standing over the foot of your bed. Those who have experienced this type of haunting call the figures either shadow people or shadow creatures.

These aren't believed to be ghosts or spirits as such. They're more like a feeling that you're being watched or that someone is in the room with you. It's often a shadowy mass or figure seen in your peripheral vision, in a fleeting glance, or out of the corner of your eye.

These apparitions, which are said to be able to pass through walls, are sometimes described as a hooded figure in black, dark mists, or humanoid forms. They have no facial features and vary in size from that of a child to an adult, but paranormal researchers believe they are not the spirits of humans.

A shadow haunting can also occur in the form of unidentified shadows. This can be a normal-looking shadow of a human in a room when there is no one present to cast that shadow. It can also occur as a drop in the output of a light, as if being blocked by an unseen mass.

Parapsychologists believe that sightings of shadow people are an example of pareidolia, our subconscious tendency to turn random patterns into identifiable objects, such as 'the man on the moon' or, in this case, someone in the shadows. This is why they are more frequently seen in peripheral vision and seem to disappear when looked at directly.

Other common causes for this might be the headlights from traffic passing outside a property, creating an unusual shadow, or insects or pets passing in front of a light source or window. Eliminate these causes by closing curtains or blinds to stop outside influence and by being aware of the whereabouts of animals.

The biggest problem with this categorisation of a ghost is that a shadow figure could also be a residual haunting or even an apparition associated with an intelligent haunting. Shadows have also been linked to poltergeist cases, and of course, a dark mass is common in demonic cases.

Residual Hauntings

Residual haunting describes a common experience in which a witness experiences something unexplained that doesn't feel like it has any intelligence or intent behind it. It's almost like becoming aware of a person or an event that took place at that location in the past. For this reason, residual hauntings are sometimes called place memories.

Residual hauntings are described as being like an imprint of energy or emotion that has been left behind by someone who suffered a tragic, premature death, usually a murder, suicide, or execution. Reports of these events being replayed are said to coincide with the anniversary of the event, when atmospheric conditions are similar, or when someone is susceptible to or in tune with that energy.

The phenomenon is known as "stone tape theory" due to the controversial and disputed belief that energy is captured and stored like a video recording in the surrounding bricks, woodwork, stone, and possibly even the soil. Those who support this unscientific theory claim that when the conditions are right, these materials release this unknown form of energy, and you see the event occur in exactly the same position as it did years ago. Haunted buildings typically tend to be older buildings that are likely to be constructed of more stone, wood, and natural elements than some modern buildings.

As residual hauntings represent nothing more than a reflection of the past, you can't communicate with them. The visions seen are not aware of their surroundings. They cannot interact with you and are not aware of your presence. They are benign and non-threatening.

A residual haunting can be a vision, but it can also be the sound of footsteps or other noises being replayed from the past. It can also be a sense of foreboding in a particular room or location where something traumatic has occurred.

Occurrences classified as residual hauntings often seem to take place in a manner that is unrelated to the present-day setting. This is why residual hauntings are said to pass through doorways that have since been bricked up and even walk up long-gone flights of stairs. There are reports of apparitions walking with only the upper parts of their legs or bodies visible due to a change in the level of the ground over the years. They may also be seen to float above the ground.

It's not known whether these events replay for everyone or just those who are open to these types of energies or who have psychic abilities.

A residual haunting is perhaps the most robust of these categorisations as it has some distinct characteristics, such as the fact that it repeats and is non-interactive. However, there's nothing to say that an intelligent haunting might also be stuck in some kind of loop, which would make it appear like a residual haunting.

Animal Spirit Hauntings

Most accounts of hauntings from eyewitnesses revolve around dark, shadowy figures that take vaguely human form. For instance, they might appear as grey ladies, monks, or soldiers, but as animals are so woven into our lives and human history, they also sometimes appear as ghosts.

There are famous reports of the ghost of a monkey at Carew Castle in Wales, and even the Tower of London is haunted by the ghost of a bear.

One of the animals most commonly seen as ghosts are horses. They are often seen on the sites of battlefields, pulling ghostly carriages or even with a headless horseman on their back. In some cases, the horse and the rider died together, but this is not always the case.

The reason horses are so commonly seen as ghosts could be because they're just one of a handful of animals to have achieved a level of sentience that makes them capable of manifesting in the physical realm from beyond the grave. A 2016 study found that horses are more emotional than many other animals. Researchers found that horses react differently to seeing photographs of happy and angry human facial expressions.

Primates are also high on the list of emotive animals, which could explain the Carew Castle monkey ghost. Of course, monkeys are pretty rare in towns and cities, so it's unlikely we'd see large quantities of ghost primates.

The ghosts of animals could be a result of the stone tape theory, but it may not be the emotions or psychic energy of the animals that's been recorded by the physical materials around the haunting. It could be a human's emotional response to an animal that has been captured that goes on to create animal apparitions.

In the case of the long-dead soldiers riding apparitions of their trusty steeds across former battlefields, it may be human psychic energy that is binding the vision of a horse to the location. After all, the ghost soldiers are able to conjure up a supernatural reconstruction of their own clothing. Clothes are clearly not sentient or alive in any sense.

It's not too much of a stretch of the imagination, as there are tales of ghostly horses complete with carriages. And it's not just wooden carriages that exist as ghosts. Stories of ghost trains and even ghost ships are common. These were never living things, so in order for them to exist, we must agree that it is human consciousness that is manifesting these inanimate, soulless objects.

Intelligent Hauntings

Intelligent hauntings, also known as interactive hauntings, are what most people consider to be a traditional or classic "ghost."

It's believed that in this type of haunting, a spirit manifests or communicates in some way with intent as the result of an intelligent consciousness. This can include disembodied voices, responsive knocks and bangs, as well as leaving a sign such as a significant or meaningful object, or moving objects in such a way as to communicate a message, desire, or course of action.

A common belief relating to intelligent hauntings is that the spirit requires help from the living world or has a message to deliver to those they have left behind. It's said that the spirit might not know they have passed, often have unfinished business, and may need help passing on.

An intelligent haunting can be a shadow figure, an animal spirit, a poltergeist, or a demon, which once again shows that categorising hauntings is more about the activity than trying to identify any specific type of supernatural entity. Put simply, if the activity seems to have intelligence behind it, no matter what that activity is, it can be considered to be an intelligent haunting.

Since intelligent hauntings are said to be able to move objects in order to communicate, it could be very easy to confuse this type of haunting with a poltergeist. It gets much more complicated if you believe that ghosts have a personality or intent. In the world of the living, we get good and bad people, so the same must be true of ghosts. If a ghost is evil, how can you tell it apart from a mischievous poltergeist or even a demon, especially when poltergeist and demonic activity do seem to have intelligence behind them?

Poltergeist Hauntings

The term poltergeist is German in origin. It first found its way into the English vocabulary in the 1830s and literally translates as "noisy ghost." The term is formed from the German words "poltern," meaning "to make sound," and "geist," meaning "ghost."

Although "noisy ghost" is generally accepted in common vernacular, it's not quite as simple as this. Geist can also mean "spirit," so "noisy spirit" would also be acceptable.

The German verb poltern does mean "to make sound", but it can also mean "to knock", "to rumble," and "to rattle." So sometimes the term is translated as "rumble ghost," "loud spirit," or "knocking spirit."

These verbs all have traits that are common in poltergeist hauntings: furniture rumbles, door handles rattle, knocks, and rapping are heard. We also categorise objects being moved or thrown as poltergeist activity. This would normally result in some kind of noise and would "make sound".

Making the distinction between a ghost and a poltergeist is very difficult, especially since the commonly held beliefs about how these two entities behave overlap so much. It's said that ghosts rattle chains, knock as a method of communication, and trigger objects are commonly used on ghost hunts to encourage entities to move them. So, how exactly is a poltergeist any different from a regular ghost or spirit?

What the term poltergeist really defines is any case that is characterised by the violent movement of furniture or objects, foul smells, spontaneous outbreaks of fire, turning lights or appliances on or off, and by making screams and other loud noises. On rare occasions, it's been reported that poltergeist cases can include victims feeling as if they've been pushed, hit, bitten, or scratched.

Again, these are all traits that can be attributed to any paranormal investigation, once again proving that the label applies more to the activity in the haunting than its cause. Despite this fairly obvious realisation, it's still commonly stated as a fact that poltergeist cases tend to be focused around one person, most often a child or a young woman, an epileptic, or a hysterical subject.

Paranormal researchers also tell us that the activity usually begins suddenly, slowly at first, and in a playful manner, but then increases in intensity, gradually becoming more and more malicious. This activity is said to abruptly end and never be repeated. However, this conflicts with the countless examples of witnesses reporting spontaneous poltergeist activity like stones being thrown, a beer glass being pushed off a bar in a pub, or unexplained knocks and bangs.

Demonic Hauntings

Demonic hauntings are rare but can be very terrifying experiences for those who witness them. Again, there is no way to know for sure if you're dealing with a supernatural entity, let alone whether it's a ghost, poltergeist, or demon.

A demonic haunting has a lot of similarities with intelligent hauntings. The only real difference is the witness's or investigator's interpretation of the haunting's intent, which in this case they deem to be more negative and threatening. It also comes down to belief in the cause of the haunting. While ghosts and spirits are believed to be the result of deceased human spirits, believers in demons claim that they were never humans, have never been alive, and have only ever existed purely as malevolent entities that are intent on causing suffering to those that they haunt.

It's said that they aim to break down their victim's free will and weaken them so that they can possess and control them. This may involve victims feeling as if the demon has attached itself to them or even possessed them. It is also claimed that demons can attach themselves to objects such as dolls and children's toys.

Those who have reported being haunted by demons rarely see them, but historic descriptions of demons tell us they are hideous, grotesque, or evil-looking.

Many of the characteristics of a demonic haunting match those of a poltergeist. As mentioned, the belief is that the difference is that the activity is carried out by non-human, more malevolent entities, but the truth is that there is no way to tell the difference. However, like poltergeist hauntings, activity often starts out slowly and non-menacing, but as the demon grows in strength, paranormal activity increases, which can result in full apparitions, unpleasant smells, and even the victim feeling as if they've been physically attacked.

Demons are considered to be pure evil and are prevalent in many religions, including Judaism, Christianity, Islam, and Hinduism. In fact, the Catholic Church recently announced that the demand for exorcisms is on the rise, but only a limited number of priests could perform the ritual because the texts were written in Latin. To meet this new wave of demand, the church has been distributing its guidelines on exorcism in English, meaning that the ritual will be accessible to more priests.

Victims of demonic hauntings often claim that they feel they have been tricked or deceived by what they perceive to be a demon. This has led to the belief that demons will try to trick their victims into thinking that they have left them while they quietly wait for an opportunity to take advantage of them when they are weak and at their most vulnerable.

Another thing that further blurs the line between these categorisations of hauntings is the claim that demons can take on an angelic form or the appearance and characteristics of a child. If this is true, then any type of haunting could be a demon pretending to be something else.

Ruling out the Rational

In order to investigate a location and prove the existence of the paranormal, it is always best to adopt the mindset of a sceptic and do everything you can to try to prove that the property is not haunted. Once you've eliminated every possible explanation for the activity you've witnessed, what you're left with will be evidence of the paranormal.

As a court aims to prove its case by removing all reasonable doubt, you should do the same. This is the only way your findings will be taken seriously. Sir Arthur Conan Doyle wrote, "When you have eliminated the impossible, whatever remains, however improbable, must be the truth."

You must remain rational, which is where the problem-solving principle of Occam's razor should be observed. The principle states that the simplest solution is usually the correct one. When presented with competing hypothetical answers to a problem, you should select the one that makes the fewest assumptions.

For example, if a loud noise is heard in a house next to a busy road, you could assume that a bomb was detonated in the area. But the most likely explanation is that a car has backfired. Occam's Razor isn't an irrefutable principle of logic, as there will be times when a bang will in fact be a bomb. Following the principle helps keep investigators grounded.

Apply the principle of Occam's razor to the symptoms of a haunting that we discussed previously. If there is a strange smell or odour in a property, is this most likely to be caused by a haunting or the result of cleaning chemicals, scents drifting in through an open window, problems with the drains, an overflowing bin, or pets?

Of course, a non-paranormal smell is the most likely cause and the one that fits Occam's razor, but if all of these everyday smells can be eliminated from your investigation, then whatever remains, however improbable, must be the truth, i.e., the smell is the result of paranormal activity.

Sometimes it helps to forget that the location you're in is said to be haunted. If you heard a knock coming from the wall at home, would your first thought be that it was a ghost, or would you just put it down to your plumbing?

Eliminate External Influences

The biggest source of interference in your evidence comes from the outside world. Unfortunately, this is also the hardest thing to protect against. External influences can be anything from the wind rattling around the property to passing pedestrians, traffic, trains, aircraft, and even the local wildlife.

All these things can introduce unexplained sounds into your investigation, but there's also the risk of light in the form of car headlights or the sun striking objects in the property at odd angles and causing reflections. The smell of car fumes, cigarette smoke, local farms, or flowers could also drift in through an open window or ventilation.

In rare cases, earthquakes, tremors, and extreme weather may cause vibrations within a property. Vibration may also be caused by passing traffic (especially heavy plant,) road works, nearby construction sites, and underground services such as metro networks. The sound of neighbours moving around their house, talking, or their televisions may also affect your results, especially if you are investigating an attached house or an individual room or floor in a shared building.

In most cases, it's impossible to completely block out this external influence, but below are a few things you can do to reduce the impact of the outside world as much as possible. If anything does occur during an investigation that is the result of outside influences, you should make a note of it. If using audio or video recording, explain what the sound was as it occurred so that when you review the recording, you'll know what the sound was. Even if the source of the sound is obvious at the time, it's easy to forget what the cause of the sound was when you listen back, and noises may sound very different in audio recordings.

Isolate the Property

This includes closing all doors and windows and, if possible, turning off air conditioning units and covering ventilation. Even with the windows and doors closed, draughts could still be an issue. If you're able to, you should seal draughts with tape or use draught excluders and close curtains to reduce the draught further. These precautions will also reduce some of the noise from the outside world.

Controlling Light

As previously mentioned, drawing the curtains will also help to reduce light pollution, but where possible, you should also try to blackout the windows by covering them.

Passing Traffic

While you can't prevent this, you can make sure you're aware of movement outside. Most airports aren't active 24 hours a day. You can check the published departure and arrival information so you are aware if there will be any flights going over the property during your investigation. Trains can be harder to predict as they may run late. Extra services may be laid on, and maintenance trains might be using the tracks once other services have stopped for the day. Of course, passenger train services are published on railway timetables, but you can also find the times of freight trains online.

Things Commonly Mistaken for the Paranormal

There are a few non-paranormal explanations for some of the most common paranormal occurrences. Of course, these explanations won't explain away all claims of the paranormal, but they will help you filter out claims that might be untrue or exaggerated.

You should bear these common causes in mind when reviewing your evidence and deciding the credibility of a witness' story.

1. Pareidolia

Pareidolia is a psychological phenomenon where we perceive patterns in random data. The word is derived from the Greek words "para", meaning something faulty, wrong, or instead of, and the noun "eidolon", meaning image, form, or shape.

The most famous examples of this are the image of a man on the surface of the moon, shapes in the clouds, and even the image of Jesus on a piece of toast or the Shroud of Turin. This principle can explain some photographs of ghosts. The human eye sees a face or human form in the abstract elements of a photo. This can also happen with the naked eye, when someone sees a shadow as a human shape.

The best way to check if this is really a paranormal photo or nothing more than pareidolia is to try to recreate it. It might be that a face in a photo is nothing more than an unusual shadow, creases in a curtain, or a defect or indentation in a wall. If you can easily recreate the phenomenon, then it's almost certainly not paranormal, and you'll probably be able to deduce what is creating the odd image.

Our tendency to spot shapes and, more specifically, faces in random patterns is said to date back to early humans, when spotting the face of a potential threat from a distance or in poor visibility was an important survival instinct.

The term pareidolia can also be applied to audio. Many believe they have heard "back-masking" in music. It can be heard when records are played backwards. Conspiracy theorists believe the words and phrases that are heard have been intentionally recorded backwards and hidden on the records, but in most cases, it is nothing more than the human brain trying to find order in chaos.

Some of the most memorable examples of this are in songs by the Beatles. Many fans claim to have heard "Paul is dead" in "Strawberry Fields Forever." While some believe this is a reference to the fate of Paul McCartney, in reality, it is nothing more than noise. This form of audio pareidolia can influence paranormal researchers too. Often, the sounds in EVP recordings can be mistaken for spirit voices.

EVP, or Electronic Voice Phenomenon, is a technique that uses analogue or digital audio recorders to try to capture communications with spirits. If you hear something in a recording that sounds like a word or phrase, you should be aware that pareidolia might be responsible for your hearing this.

Often, a paranormal researcher will hear a word or phrase they were expecting to hear. For example, if the researcher knows the spirit in a haunted location is called Fred, they might call out to the spirits and ask, "What is your name?" and hear the reply, "Fred."

The best way to prove or disprove this evidence is to ask someone who is not connected to the investigation and has no knowledge of the spirit's name to review it. When playing the audio to them, remove the context, i.e., the bit where you ask the question. If they are unable to pick out the name Fred, then it is almost certainly audio pareidolia.

There will be more on the nature of EVPs and how to capture them later in the book in the "communicating with ghosts or spirits" chapter.

2. Electromagnetic fields

Electromagnetic fields are most often associated with electronic devices, especially those with broadcast capability, but there are also naturally occurring EM fields. When field strength is high or aggressively fluctuating, it can affect the temporal lobes of the brain. This can cause symptoms ranging from seeing light anomalies to feeling a perception of a presence or sensations of being touched.

Michael Persinger, a Canadian neuroscientist, is known for his research into the phenomenon and has even recreated the effects in his lab. He uses a specially designed helmet, which uses weak pulsed magnetic fields to induce the feelings in volunteers. According to his findings, someone exposed to these kinds of fields for just 15 minutes can start to feel like there's an invisible presence in the room.

This could explain reports of hauntings in locations where there is an erratic or strong electromagnetic field. The best way to validate a haunting is to ensure that there are no constant or erratic fields in or around the property using an EMF meter. If you find that the location has high or changeable field strengths, you should bear in mind that people in the building may be susceptible to these fields and use other methods other than human senses to validate the claims.

For example, you may want to discredit light anomalies seen with the naked eye and instead rely on evidence captured on camera, which shouldn't be affected by low-level EM fields.

3. Infrasound

Infrasound is a very low-frequency sound that is below the human range of hearing, and it too is a cause of mistaken reports of paranormal activity. These low-frequency vibrations have been known to cause people to report discomfort in the form of disorientation, feeling panicked, and an increased heart rate and blood pressure.

In extreme cases, infrasound has been attributed to feelings of depression, a general feeling of unease, as well as the vision of apparitions.

Scientists researching the low-frequency noise created by wind turbines and traffic noise discovered the effects of infrasound on humans. They found a link between infrasound and the sensations often described as getting chills down the spine.

As specialist audio equipment is required to detect infrasound, it can be hard to eliminate this from your investigation. However, keeping doors and windows closed will help to keep these frequencies out of the building. It should also be noted that some machinery and even fans can produce the low frequencies associated with infrasound. This is another reason why care should be taken to turn off any electrical equipment that could interfere with your investigation.

4. Toxins and poisoning

You should already know the dangers of carbon monoxide. With just mild, short-term exposure, you might experience headaches, nausea, vomiting, and fatigue. It's even said to cause aural and visual hallucinations. A faulty boiler, gas fire, or other gas appliances can result in a carbon monoxide leak.

It goes without saying that experiencing these symptoms regularly in the same location will lead to a feeling of unease and unhappiness there. Of course, these are all feelings and symptoms that are often associated with a haunting.

So, you should do all you can to try to eliminate carbon monoxide poisoning from your investigation. If you find yourself investigating a property where someone has reported a haunting that fits the description of carbon monoxide poisoning, then a sensible line of investigation would be to take a carbon monoxide detector along with you.

Similar symptoms can also be caused by poisoning from other toxins, including formaldehyde, pesticides, and even some moulds and funguses that might be growing in a damp room.

Some moulds reproduce by releasing tiny spores into the air. They are so small that they have to be magnified hundreds of times before we can even see them.

About one in five people is allergic to mould spores, but even those who aren't allergic may be at risk, as some species of mould contain a toxic compound called mycotoxins. These toxins can cause symptoms including headaches, fatigue, coughing, and sneezing and are very dangerous for asthma sufferers, young children, and the elderly. Some moulds and fungi can trigger significant mental or neurological symptoms.

5. Sleep paralysis

Sleep paralysis is a phenomenon that can explain some sightings of shadowy figures and apparitions.

Sleep paralysis is when our body suddenly snaps out of deep sleep. During REM (Rapid Eye Movement) sleep, we start to dream, and to stop us from physically acting out those dreams, our body releases a neurotransmitter called glycine. This triggers nerve receptors in our muscles in order to stop them moving while in this phase of deep sleep. Essentially, we are paralysed, but the chemical normally wears off by the time we wake up.

If you suddenly become conscious while dreaming, perhaps due to a nightmare or a loud noise, you may find your body is still in its paralysed state. It can be terrifying, and to make it all the more scary, those who suffer from sleep paralysis have reported seeing everything from ghosts to mysterious black figures near their beds.

Many report that breathing is difficult and describe the sensation as feeling as if someone or something is applying pressure to their chest or even holding them down. In some cultures, it is believed that sleep paralysis is a demon that sits on a person's chest if they have neglected prayer or other duties.

Of course, this doesn't explain all cases of dark figures or apparitions, but where stories involve seeing these visions from bed during disturbed sleep, more investigation may be required to prove that this is a genuine paranormal incident.

Capture Evidence of the Haunting

Your primary role as a ghost hunter is to validate claims of the paranormal, and in order to do this, you'll need to be sure that any potential paranormal evidence is logged. This will also help you discredit anything that may not be a result of the paranormal.

The most common ways to log an investigation are to either use an audio recorder, a video camera, or a notebook. While notebooks are great, they can't be seen in the dark, which can be a problem during an investigation. An audio recorder is a good option for making a record of everything that occurs, as is a video camera, which has the added benefit of being able to capture any visual evidence too.

If using audio to log the investigation, you should ensure that the recorder is running continuously. Audio files are relatively small compared to a modern memory card's capacity, which means you can easily record several hours of audio.

When you start recording either audio or video, say the time out loud. This will then give you a timeframe for the whole recording. When recording audio only and moving around the property you're investigating, describe your movement out loud, for example, "We're moving into the living room."

It's also a good idea to note in the recording how many people are present in each situation. This means if a sound is captured in the recording, you'll know if you were in a room alone or not. This will tell you if the sound could have been caused by someone else present.

You should also note verbally any non-paranormal sounds that are heard during the investigation. This includes sounds from outside the property, people moving, objects being dropped, coughs, sneezes, and stomach rumbles. You might think you'll remember these sounds when you listen back, but things can often sound quite different when captured by the recorder.

Having a running commentary in the recording will enable you to eliminate these sounds from your investigation, leaving only the unexplained sounds to be investigated.

If you're using a notebook instead of an audio recorder, then you should observe this same method of logging anything strange that happens, as well as any sounds heard. Jot down a brief description of the occurrence along with a timestamp.

Collecting Quantitative Data

Now that we've ruled out rational explanations for any paranormal occurrences, eliminated external influences, and identified the things most commonly mistaken for the paranormal, what we're left with is possible evidence of the paranormal.

In order to prove that this evidence really represents paranormal activity, you'll need to make sure it is measurable empirical evidence. This is data where a quantitative change can actually be observed. For example, a measurable or observable physical movement or an increase or decrease in atmospheric conditions.

Empirical evidence wouldn't include any evidence that is subjective, such as the use of Ouija boards or other communications, although we will look at how this type of subjective evidence is useful and can be validated later.

We will continue by looking at a few techniques that can be used to collect measurable evidence.

Laser Grid

In recent years, green lasers have become inexpensive and easy to get hold of in the form of laser pointers. The human eye is much more sensitive to green light, so the light from these kinds of lasers appears to be much brighter than that emitted from more conventional red laser pens.

A lot of green laser pointers come with a simple filter that scatters the light into multiple beams, creating a grid-like pattern of dots. Many ghost hunters use this pattern to look for motion during paranormal investigations.

The technique was first seen in the US paranormal show, 'Ghost Hunters International.' The idea is that the dots scatter across the walls, floor, and ceiling, and if anything moves in front of the laser, you will see a shift or discrepancy in the grid.

You may think it's easier to just turn on the lights or use a camera in night mode if you want to see movement in the room, and of course this is a valid option, but the nature of the laser light means it's not susceptible to dust particles in the air in the same way as infrared night vision is. Dust, insects, and other artefacts can pass through the beams without creating orbs or other light anomalies.

In order to obtain quantitative evidence using this method, you'll need to capture the laser grid using a video camera. Seeing movement in the grid isn't considered quantitative unless you have an actual record of the movement in the form of video. Otherwise, it's just word of mouth and anecdotal.

Lasers produce a highly focused and energetic beam of light, which can reflect and bounce around unpredictably, so you should take care not to move the laser around in front of the camera as refractions in the lens could cause light flares. It's best to mount the laser to a camera tripod so it's fixed and there's no unnecessary movement.

The one downside to using a commercially available laser pen for this task is that they are only designed to be used for short periods as a pointer. The diode that produces the light gets very hot, and there is no cooling system built in, so you'll need to give it a chance to cool down after about two or three minutes of continuous operation.

Failure to allow the laser to cool can result in permanent damage to the device but can also cause temporary fluctuations and irregularities in its output, which can be seen as a twinkling effect across the grid, giving you false positives of ghostly movement.

Thermometer

The easiest way to record the temperature fluctuations associated with hauntings is to use a thermometer. The most common type used in ghost hunting is a basic infrared thermometer gun. These point-and-click thermometers don't require any contact with the object they're measuring the temperature of. You simply point the device and press the trigger.

Unlike regular glass or mercury thermometers, infrared thermometers don't measure air temperatures. They only measure the surface temperature of the object they are pointing at. Therefore, if someone reports feeling cold, an infrared thermometer won't give you an accurate reading of the temperature around the person.

Another pitfall of infrared thermometers is that they are unreliable at a distance. This is because most commercially available infrared thermometers have a distance-to-sight ratio of 12:1. This means that if you are holding the gun 12cm from an object, then the target area that the gun is looking at is 1cm in diameter. As you move the gun further away, the size of the target area increases. When the device is at a distance of 12 metres from an object, the gun is measuring the temperature within a circle 1 metre in diameter. The reading on the digital display will effectively give you an average of the temperature within the whole target area.

It should also be noted that turning the gun's laser on or off doesn't change the field of view, as sometimes stated. The red laser is included only for aiming purposes.

Another, more expensive option is a thermal imaging camera. Instead of capturing visible light, these cameras can see the heat being radiated by an object, or the lack thereof. This gives you an indication of the temperature of everything within the camera's field of view.

The temperature of objects is indicated with colours. Hot areas show as shades of yellow, orange, and red, depending on how hot it is. Very hot areas will appear white. Cold areas will show as shades of blue, with very cold areas being black.

Thermal imaging cameras are able to record, which means there is less need to log temperature changes. As you're unlikely to be using the device continuously throughout the investigation, you'll need to make sure that the date and time are set correctly on the device to give you an accurate time reference on the video files.

It should also be noted that, like the point-and-click infrared thermometer, thermal imaging cameras don't measure air temperature. They are also susceptible to reflection. This means that if you point the camera at a shiny or reflective surface in front of you, you may see your own heat being reflected back at the camera.

A better solution is to use a digital thermometer, which gives you an accurate, real-time indication of the current air temperature. When using this type of thermometer, you should take care not to place it near the source of any potential draughts, like windows or ventilation, or warmth radiated from pipes, boilers, or heating ducts.

This type of thermometer is often built into other ghost hunting devices, such as EMF meters and static detectors. Some of these paranormal multi-tools will log the temperature changes and save the data on a memory card with a timestamp. If you don't have access to one of these devices, then be sure to log any significant temperature changes in the way previously discussed in the section on "logging evidence." A significant change would be a sudden change of five degrees or more in either direction.

Camera

Capturing photographic evidence is the ultimate aim of most ghost hunts, so having the right camera is important. The most suitable camera for an investigation depends on your expertise as a photographer and your budget, as the cost of good cameras ranges dramatically. You can use anything from a cheap compact camera to top-of-the-range digital SLR cameras. Even a modern phone's camera is easily good enough to use during a paranormal investigation. Some people find it easier to capture a ghost on a traditional film camera rather than a digital camera or smartphone.

Spirit photography is a field of photography that aims to capture images of ghosts or apparitions in the shot. The principles are very old, dating back to the early 19th century, and as cameras have got better and more advanced, so have the photos of spirits.

As a paranormal investigator, you should take care to ensure your photos are taken with as little chance of capturing light anomalies or random noise as possible. The simple steps below will help you take photos of spirits, which can hopefully be corroborated by avoiding some of the mistakes that amateur ghost hunters make.

No matter which camera you use, the main thing you should be aware of is its quirks, which could give you false positives on a hunt and reveal a spirit that isn't really there. For example, with older film cameras, it's easy to catch a "ghost" on camera if you forget to wind the camera forward after each photograph you take.

This simple mistake will result in double exposure. This is when one image is superimposed on another, often with an eerie transparent quality.

Another thing to look out for with older cameras is light leaks if there are defects in the camera's body or if the film itself is old or has been stored in poor conditions. Light could leak onto the film and expose areas of it, giving you streaks or patches of light.

When shooting in the dark on film, it's best to use a film with a high speed, measured in ISO, but in doing so, you will find that your pictures can appear grainier, which can introduce odd shapes and elements into your photographs.

The issue of grainy photos in low light isn't just a problem with film but is also apparent on photos taken on digital cameras and smartphones. As technology improves, low-light photography is getting better and better.

There are plenty of quirks to look out for with digital photography too, whether you're using a digital SLR camera, compact digital camera, or smartphone. If you're snapping a photo of a fast-moving object, due to the way the camera's sensor (CCD) captures the light, you may find chunks of the object are missing or even in the wrong place. This is most apparent when taking a photo of something like a fan or propeller.

Using camera modes like HDR (High Dynamic Range) and panoramic can also increase your chances of catching an anomaly on camera. These settings should be avoided. Both of these options involve the camera automatically taking multiple photos. This means that between photos, objects can move and appear distorted or semi-transparent. In the case of panoramic photos, multiple images are stitched together horizontally. In the case of HRD photography, two or more images of different exposures are captured and laid on top of each other by the camera.

If you are using a smartphone during an investigation, be sure to put the phone into flight mode to avoid unexpected sounds and electromagnetic interference, which may trigger certain electronic ghost hunting devices.

Ask the spirits to be present in your photo

Let's say you walk into your living room at home. All of your family is sitting on the sofa, and you take out your camera and point it at the wall and say, "Smile." None of your family members had time to stand up, walk across the room, and pose for your photo.

If, however, you'd walked into the room, asked your family to pose for a photo, given them a chance to run their fingers through their hair, and gotten in line, you'd get a much better result, and the same applies for the spirit world.

You're more likely to capture a ghost on camera if you let the spirits know your intentions. When taking photos, call out to the spirits, let them know what you are doing, and ask them to show themselves in your photographs if they can. There will be more on calling out to spirits in the next chapter.

You could also try taking selfies. If a spirit has attached itself to you or is following you, you might find that a selfie is a good way to capture a spirit that is lurking over your shoulder.

Take three photos in quick succession

When taking photos, keep the camera still and take at least three photos as quickly as your camera will allow you to. Some cameras have burst mode, which is perfect for this.

If you're lucky enough to have caught an apparition or spirit on camera, that's great, but a single photo doesn't tell you much. If you can capture multiple photos, this will give you a timeline of events. If an anomaly appears in just one of the photos taken at the same angle and under the same conditions, then you know it's not just something in the photo that, due to the angle, looks like a ghost.

If, however, the object is in all of the photos, then it could be something non-paranormal like someone's shadow or pareidolia. If you can eliminate these causes, then what you are left with could be paranormal. If the anomaly you've captured appears to move between photos, this gives you an indication of the object's speed and direction of travel.

You should also try taking photos in each location with and without a flash. Sometimes a flash can bounce in unexpected ways and cause strange tricks of light. On the other hand, using a flash could give you a bright, even shot that will neutralise anomalies as a result of rogue artificial light or natural light through a window.

Tips and pointers

Hold your breath. In cold environments, your breath will condense as you breathe out and may be visible as a ghostly mist in front of the camera, especially when using a flash. So breathe in and hold it while you take your photos.

Stay still. When taking photos in the dark or low light, the camera compensates by keeping the shutter open for longer. This means that if you move the camera, your images will be blurred. Use a tripod where possible.

Be aware of dust. Particles in the air passing by the camera's lens closer than the subject will appear out of focus, and when caught in the camera's flash, they may also be more illuminated than the subject or backdrop. This is a common cause of "orbs." Being aware of your surroundings and using the techniques above, you should be able to determine whether a glowing spot in a photo is dust or something more.

Maintain your equipment. Checking your camera before a ghost hunt is a good idea. This may avoid dirt on the lens or the DSLR's mirror (behind the lens), which could be mistaken for strange spots in photographs.

Trigger objects

A trigger object can be anything from balls, a bunch of keys, a child's toy, or a marble. The idea is to leave these objects in a haunted location during an investigation in the hope that they might be moved through paranormal means.

In order to obtain quantitative data using a trigger object, you'll need to be able to measure any movement of the object. This can be done by placing the object on a sheet of paper and drawing around it. It's then easy to see if the object has moved. It may also be a good idea to point a static camera at the object in the hope of capturing the movement in a video.

You should always make sure that trigger objects are placed on solid, flat surfaces, ideally in a location where people won't need to walk past them, as the weight of passing footsteps might produce vibrations that cause the object to move. Draughts may also move trigger objects, as well as vibrations from passing heavy traffic.

If you know a little about the history of the haunting, then you can select a trigger object that is relevant to the location and therefore more likely to appeal to the spirits haunting it. For example, if there is said to be the ghost of a child at the location, you may wish to use a ball, a marble, or a cuddly toy. If smugglers or pirates haunt the location, then a coin might be more appropriate.

Working in the dark

Paranormal investigators are known for hunting ghosts in the dark, but there's a very good reason why they should be searching for spooks in the light too.

Ghost hunters give various explanations as to why they prefer to ghost hunt in the dark, but there are countless reports of ghost sightings not only in the dead of night but also in broad daylight and in lit buildings.

Of course, darkness helps set the mood and is appropriate for a public ghost hunt. It's the paranormal equivalent of lighting a candle for a romantic meal - it sets the mood. However, if you're conducting a scientific investigation, the darkness isn't required and may actually hinder your research.

One reason that ghost hunters investigate in the dark is because they tend to have more free time in the evenings and are only able to investigate locations at night when they are closed to the public. This is, of course, a valid reason for investigating at night, but it doesn't explain why they also turn the lights off at the location.

One commonly stated reason for not turning the lights on and avoiding sunlight is that the darkness heightens our other senses and makes it easier to spot spooks. This isn't a very logical statement. The darkness might heighten your other senses, but it also completely takes away what is arguably your most valuable sense: sight.

If you are looking for evidence, your eyes are a great tool. Not only do you stand a better chance of seeing a ghostly apparition or poltergeist activity with the lights on, you can also use your eyes to validate or debunk happenings.

At the very least, you should conduct an initial walk around the location with the lights on. This will allow you to properly check the state of every room. You'll have an idea of which doors were open and closed if you hear a slam. If something is thrown, you might remember where that object came from, having seen it in the light.

Another reason some ghost hunters prefer to work in the dark is because they believe it's easier for a ghost to manifest in the dark. It's thought that after death, the soul continues to live on outside of the body as a form of spiritual energy. This is why ghost hunters often use electromagnetic field metres to detect what they think might be the early stages of ghostly manifestation.

It's claimed that in order for a spirit to become a ghost or figure, it needs to draw on all of its energy to become physical, or at least visible, but in a light environment, it's drowned out by surrounding energy fields, like the solar radiation from the Sun that ionises our atmosphere. Occasionally, a spirit will be strong enough to overcome this obstacle and manifest during the day, but generally, it's thought to be more difficult.

This theory could be true, but like any theory about the paranormal, it needs to be tested by doing investigations in well-lit locations as well as in the darkness. The only way to determine whether paranormal activity is more rife in the darkness is to compare it to levels in the light.

Investigating in the darkness is also not an appropriate approach for all hauntings. Where reported activity exclusively takes place at a specific time of day in broad daylight or in well-lit workplaces or homes, then the haunting should be investigated at the same time of day or in the same conditions.

If the ghost of a lady in white has been seen roaming around a castle by tourists in the daytime, then why would you even consider trying to observe that same apparition yourself in anything other than the original conditions, broad daylight?

One particular method employed on ghost hunts suggests that light might actually increase paranormal activity. Some investigators experiment with a device called an EM pump, which pumps electromagnetic energy out into a location in the hopes that spirits can draw on that energy and use it to manifest or communicate.

The obvious fact that is being overlooked here is that light is a form of electromagnetic energy too. Turning a light on is a much more efficient way of pumping EM into a room, especially since most EM pumps are battery-powered and capable of pumping out just a few microwatts of power, while a standard incandescent electric light could be supplying up to 100 watts.

Plus, there's the massive amounts of electromagnetic energy that the Sun radiates to Earth during the day.

The biggest problem with ghost hunting in the dark is that while our eyes are an invaluable tool in the light, in the darkness they can be unreliable. Our eyes can play tricks on us in the dark. You may think you've seen something that's not really there in our hyper-sensitive state as our eyes struggle to compensate for the low light. Our eyes strain to see in the darkness, and the brain tries to make sense of what it's seeing by forming familiar shapes and patterns, and it's at times like these when you are most likely to see something that isn't really there.

Communicating with Ghosts and Spirits

Most ghost hunts involve some attempt to communicate with the spirits that haunt the location. In this chapter, we'll look at various ways that you can talk to spirits, but first, we'll look at an overview of how to conduct a séance, as the techniques that follow are most frequently used during séances.

It's not strictly necessary to hold a séance in darkness, but the unavoidable truth is that most are. Of course, there are downsides to this, as previously mentioned.

However, for the purpose of a séance, it does help set the mood. As well as turning out the lights, you can also set the mood by burning incense, but avoid burning sage, as this is often used for spiritual protection and is believed to drive spirits away.

The participants of the séance should either stand or sit around a table. You should make sure you are comfortable, as movement or fidgeting may be wrongly attributed to paranormal activity in the dark. Participants should then hold hands to form a circle. This is done to focus the energy of the participants, allowing spirits to draw on it and use it to communicate. Knowing everyone is holding hands also means you know that no one at the séance is creating any tapping noises or moving anything themselves in the dark.

At this point, you can start asking the spirits questions. If one of your group is a medium, then they will have their own way of communicating with spirits. Others are likely to communicate by calling out to the spirits while looking for a response through either a ghost hunting gadget, a Ouija board, through tapping, or by using a trigger object. The next few pages will look into these methods.

Remember that if any members of the group have researched the history of the property, like names, dates, causes of death, etc., then it is best if this person sits out of séances so that they cannot intentionally or subconsciously influence it. It's useful to have them on hand at a séance so they can quickly verify the information that comes through against the information obtained from the property's background research.

How to Call Out to Spirits

Calling out is when a paranormal investigator speaks aloud in an attempt to encourage any spirits that might be present to communicate with them. The classic ghost hunter's trope is, "Hello, is anybody there?" There are a few tips and best practises that should be observed when calling out.

1. Know your audience

The most common mistake people make is calling out to the spooks at a location by saying, "If there are any spirits here, can you give us a sign?" The issue with this is that it's often said that spirits carry on about their daily lives without knowing they're dead, so they might not identify with the label "spirit".

A better way to call out is to give whatever you are calling out to the respect of treating them like a person. Perhaps say something like, "I'm speaking to anyone who can hear my voice. If we've left you out of our circle or you're outside of this room, then come towards us."

But this leads to another problem. How will they find their way? As previously discussed, a lot of ghost hunts are carried out in the dark, and there's no reason to assume that when someone dies, they develop night vision as a ghost.

Some people believe that spirits see us as a glowing beacon of energy in the darkness and can be drawn towards us, but the truth is that no one knows this for sure. So, it's better to hedge your bets and assume that whoever you are talking to can't see you in the dark and say something like, "It might seem a bit strange, all of us standing here in the dark. If you can't see us, then follow the sound of my voice and come towards us. We're all very friendly."

But of course, the chance that a spirit who doesn't realise they're deceased would be happy walking towards a group of strangers in the dark seems just as unlikely as the chance that a living human being would be comfortable enough to do the same.

To make them feel safer and more welcome, you might consider turning your torch on for a moment and scanning it around the room to show the spirit where you are, who you are, and who is with you.

Since we don't really know who we're dealing with and what being a ghost is like, it could be that they can see in the dark and that they're ready and waiting to interact with us when called, but by being clear and inclusive, you increase your chances of getting a reaction.

2. Encourage, don't demand

You need to get the spirits on your side. If you're on a ghost hunt, then you're probably in the spirit's former home or a place that means something to that person, so treat them with respect. Tell them you're not there to mock them, that you want to communicate.

Chances are, you're not the first paranormal investigator on their patch. They might already feel like a performing monkey. If spirits truly do exist, then it's unlikely that they're going to be happy existing in spirit form for no purpose other than to amuse you.

So, instead of demanding they perform for you, ask the spirits if they need help or have a message. Ask them to show a sign that they are with you so that you can talk to them, perhaps even to help them move on.

3. Say thank you

Ghosts are usually only able to give very subtle clues to the fact that they are present. They might use our energy to communicate through a Ouija board, knock over an object, tap on a hard surface, or whisper in someone's ear. It's unusual to hear a loud noise, a clear voice, or see an object deliberately being moved for any sustained period of time.

Therefore, we can assume that spirits have to muster up a lot of energy in order to give us these signs. So, you should thank the spirits for their efforts if they do something that you've asked them to do. Give them encouragement. Let them know that what they've shown you is great, but ask them to do a little more if they can.

4. Don't use jargon

Don't assume that spirits understand the jargon that paranormal investigators use. A lot of ghost hunters talk about their equipment and gadgets when calling out. Often they'll say things like "try to affect the EMF meter" or "can you make the lights flash on the REM-Pod?"

Even if a ghost did understand what an EMF detector was, it's unlikely they'd actually understand how they can affect its circuitry or sensors, but the belief is that a spirit's energy can trigger these devices. So, if you want the lights on your ghost hunting gadget to blink, it's much better to say something like, "Can you move towards the lights on the floor?" or wherever your equipment happens to be.

5. Don't shut it down

If you are able to make contact with a spirit, be sure not to shut the conversation down prematurely. You almost need to think of it like a sales pitch. You've got to keep the conversation flowing and don't give the spirits any chance to leave.

One common mistake is to say things like, "Give us a sign that you're here, and then we'll leave you alone." To be true to your word, if the spirit does give you a sign, then you're going to have to pack up and end your investigation. Otherwise, you'll have lied, and the spirit is unlikely to trust you again or do as you ask.

Similarly, don't use phrases like "don't you want to talk to us anymore?" Because you're giving the spirits the chance to say goodbye.

6. Configuration

When holding a vigil as part of an investigation, you should think about how you present yourself and your team and set up your equipment. It might seem quite natural to stand in a circle around the edges of the room with the equipment on the floor in the middle, but this could be counterproductive. This set up might make any intelligent entities feel like circus performers taking to the stage, surrounded by an audience. No one, living or dead, would want to walk into a room full of strangers and be asked to step into the middle and perform. Instead, try to mingle and act normally. Maybe place the equipment near the doors or around the edges of the room rather than in the middle.

Whichever technique you are using to listen to spirits, the questions you ask will be the same. Below is a list of example questions and phrases that you can use to try to encourage the spirits to communicate with you. You shouldn't copy these exactly, as it is better to be yourself and talk in a natural and open way as you normally would.

If you can hear me, tap on the floor.
Can you make a noise to let us know you are here with us?
If you're here, can you show yourself to me?
How many of you are with us right now? Tap it out.
Can you make a noise?
Can you throw something?
Can you copy me? [then tap on a surface or whistle]
My name is XXX. Can you tell me your name?
Tell us who you are. Introduce yourself, please.
If there's somebody here with us now, can you walk towards us?
Are you happy for us to be here? Two taps for yes, one for no.
Can you come and talk to us?

Knock Once for No, Twice for Yes

One of the easiest and therefore most common ways to communicate with spirits is to encourage them to answer you by tapping once for "no" and twice for "yes."

Don't assume that spirits will understand the principles of tapping. You might need to teach them how to communicate in this way. It's important to frequently remind any spirits present that they should knock in order to communicate, as often spirits drift in and out of séances and vigils.

Make it clear what you are asking of them. You should limit your questions to closed questions, that is, questions that can only be answered with "yes" or "no", such as:
Did you die here?
Are you male?
Are you stuck in this place?

It's the easiest way to communicate with a spirit, as it doesn't require the use of a Ouija board, a spirit box, or any other equipment. You can also ask the spirits to tap out how many of them are present. Or you can write down the letters of the alphabet and run your finger over the letters, asking the spirit to tap to indicate the letter you're pointing at in order to spell out a word, sentence, or date.

The origins of knocking ghosts

The first recorded case of rapping as a way of communicating with ghosts dates back to New York in 1848. Two sisters, Kate and Margaret Fox, were just 12 and 15 years old when they moved with their family to a new house in an area that was known as Hydesville.

The girls soon came to the conclusion that their house was haunted after experiencing frequent, unexplained sounds that they described as being like knocking.

One night, Kate asked the spirit to copy her when she snapped her fingers, and it's reported that the spirit obliged. She then asked the ghost to tap out the ages of her and her sister, which it again got right. From this point on, the girls developed the technique of responding to questions or indicating a letter of the alphabet with taps.

Over the next few weeks, the girls determined that the spirit they were talking to, "Mr. Splitfoot," was the ghost of a market trader named Charles B. Rosna. They believed he'd been murdered five years earlier and buried in the cellar.

The events gave birth to modern spiritualism when Kate and Margaret's older sister, Leah, started to promote them as mediums. They became famous as well-known mediums and as some of the first spiritualists to publicly display their skills.

However, in 1888, Margaret and Kate confessed that their tapping had been a hoax and publicly demonstrated their methods, but by this time it was already common practice in séances and spiritualism around the world.

Ouija Board

Ouija boards, also known as spirit boards, talking boards, or séance boards, have been a popular part of séances since Victorian times. Ouija boards are usually wooden. They have the letters of the alphabet marked on them, the numbers zero to nine, and the words "yes," no," and "goodbye." There's also often a sun and moon symbol.

From a skeptic's point of view, a Ouija board is nothing more than a perfect demonstration of the ideomotor effect. Ouija boards work on the basis of this subconscious behaviour. It's the same principle that makes dowsing rods swing, and it manifests itself in the subtle subconscious movement of the planchette as it spells out the words the participants of the séance are willing it to.

You can use a Ouija board on your own, but you may find it hard to get any response from the spirits, so it's best to find at least one other person to practise with, and ideally a total of three or four people.

You don't actually need an expensive board. You can make your own by writing the letters A to Z on slips of paper and spreading them out on a table. Then place a glass in the middle of the table.

Next, you'll each need to place one finger on the glass or planchette. The planchette is the wooden pointer, which will slide around the board. You should very gently rest your finger on the planchette - so gently, in fact, that it is barely touching it.

Some people recommend moving the planchette around the board to "warm it up," and while this may not be necessary as the spirits themselves are capable of getting the planchette moving, it is good practise to familiarise the spirits as well as the participants with the board.

First, move the planchette around the board in a clockwise circle. You can do this by sliding the planchette with your finger. This is OK at this stage. Then call out to the spirits, saying something like, "If there's anyone here who wishes to make contact, you can talk to us through this board. You can answer our questions with 'yes' or 'no'." Move the planchette over the "yes" or "no" to demonstrate as you say this.

Then continue, "You can also spell out words," move the planchette across the alphabet, "using the letters A to Z. There's also number zero to nine," and again, move the planchette over the numbers. After this, move the planchette to the centre of the board. From this point on, you should not intentionally move the planchette.

Now it's time to start a conversation with any spirits that might be present. Don't be scared to start with a cliché, ask aloud, "Is there anybody there?" If the planchette doesn't move straight away, don't give up. Sometimes it can take a while for the spirits to come through. Ask again, "If there's someone there who wants to communicate with us, can you move the planchette to 'yes?'"

Keep asking the spirit to show itself in this manner. Encourage the spirit to use the combined energy of all of the participants to move the planchette.

After a while, you should see the planchette move across the board, hopefully towards "yes." Be sure to follow the movement with your finger and don't remove your finger from the planchette. If you ask, "Is anyone there" and the planchette moves to "no", then you've probably encountered a mischievous spirit or possibly even a demon.

Once the planchette starts moving, you can begin to ask more specific questions. It's best to start with simple questions to try to establish who you are talking to. These are the questions we covered previously in the section on "how to call out to spirits."

While asking questions, always be polite, say please, and thank the spirit when it answers. All spirits are different. Some will move the planchette slowly, others much quicker. Spirits may also come and go during a séance. If the planchette is moving slowly or infrequently, don't give up and remain patient.

At the end of the séance, it's advised to close the board by moving the planchette to the word "goodbye." You should physically slide the planchette across the board to "goodbye." This will ensure that any spirits that have been called forward won't follow you after the session.

Over the years, Ouija boards have gained an unfair reputation for being dangerous, but the boards themselves aren't evil or dangerous. Using one is no more dangerous than any other method of spirit communication, such as responsive knocking or intelligent communication through a ghost hunting device.

Part of the reason why we have the perception that Ouija boards are so dangerous is due to their use in popular culture. Countless movies feature them, such as the 1973 horror film 'The Exorcist.' Often the boards burst into flames, glasses fly off of them smashing against the wall, or players become possessed by demons.

Another factor that clouds our judgement when it comes to the use of Ouija boards is the dim view that many religions hold in regards to them. Religious denominations have criticised Ouija boards for generations, with one group saying, "The Ouija board is far from harmless, as it is a form of divination (seeking information from supernatural sources)."

Religions generally tend to deem all forms of the occult to be sinful. They're not singling out Ouija boards as being dangerous as such. They feel the same way about tarot cards, palm reading, and many of the other activities you might perform as part of a paranormal investigation.

While some think that Ouija boards are a portal directly to the underworld, in reality, there is no danger, and there is not one documented case of someone being harmed that can be directly attributed to a Ouija board.

Having said all of this, people have had bad experiences as a result of using a Ouija board because they believe they will. Suggestible people may feel as if they have been possessed or feel discomfort upon returning to a part of the house where they have used a Ouija board. Of course, this is all in your mind, but the fact that it's all in your mind doesn't make it any less scary.

So, if you have any serious doubts about using a Ouija board, don't use it. Similarly, if it is against your religious beliefs, then stay clear as it may cause feelings of guilt and conflict. If you are nervous or unsure about using a Ouija board, there are a few things you can do to protect yourself.

Digital Audio Recorder

Another common way to communicate with spirits is by capturing ghostly dialogue in the form of Electronic Voice Phenomena (EVP). In order to capture EVPs, you'll need some kind of audio recording equipment. This can be anything from an old cassette deck, a reel-to-reel machine, a pocket digital audio recorder, a laptop, or a mobile phone. To increase the quality of your EVPs, you may also want to use an external omnidirectional microphone.

As with making an audio log of your investigation, when recording EVPs you should start by speaking the date, time, location, and number of people present out loud. You should also note verbally any sounds that are heard during the séance so that you can eliminate them from your investigation when you later review the audio.

You should also try to stay as still as possible to avoid making any unnecessary noise. Not only could these be mistaken for paranormal contact in the recording, but you could also drown out genuine EVPs.

You should call out to the spirits and encourage them to come forward, talk to you, and answer your questions. Use the same method of calling out as we discussed earlier in this chapter. Be sure to leave plenty of time after each question to allow the spirit time to answer. You may not hear anything at the time, but when reviewing the audio, where EVPs could be present, you'll be able to hear the spirit answering your question.

Be patient and give the spirits plenty of time to make contact, but don't record too much. Remember, you're going to have to review this audio after the investigation, so it's best to keep EVP sessions to around five to ten minutes. You can also try real-time EVPs, where you ask a question and then review the recording straight away during the investigation.

When reviewing the session, you'll need to use headphones rather than the small and inadequate speakers in the recording device itself. However, the best way to review the audio is to transfer it to a computer, which allows you to review the audio in greater detail. You can use free audio editing software like Audacity to boost the audio level and hear responses more clearly.

If you do hear a voice in your recording, there are a few things you should do to validate this evidence, as what you're hearing could all be down to a weird quirk of the brain. Pareidolia is our subconscious tendency to perceive a familiar or meaningful vision or sound in random patterns or noise. There is more on auditory pareidolia in the section on EVP research later in the book.

Spirit Box

A spirit box is a popular paranormal device that rapidly scans through the AM, MW, and FM radio spectrums. As it does, fleeting bursts of white noise and static can be heard. Spirit boxes usually have various settings that allow you to tweak which bands the device scans through and how much of each frequency step you hear. This usually ranges from a hundredth of a second up to a second.

The idea of using what is essentially a modified radio to pick up the voices of the dead divides the paranormal community, with many thinking it is a valid way to communicate with spirits, while others think it is nothing more than our psychological tendency to hear what we want to hear within random radio noise.

Unless you are in a cave or well-shielded building, you will almost certainly hear fragments of speech and music from radio stations. Although this might include words, what you are listening for are meaningful words and intelligent responses to your questions.

Just like with electronic voice phenomenon, you should call out to the spirits and ask them questions, and then listen for their answers within the noise of the spirit box, ideally a response that spans across several steps of the frequency scan.

Some paranormal researchers prefer to put their spirit box inside a small bag that acts as a Faraday cage. This filters out the entire electromagnetic spectrum, which means that radio broadcasts don't make it to the device. In this case, it is much more likely that any voice that is heard is a result of paranormal contact.

As with other forms of audio communication, you should bear in mind that audio pareidolia may be playing a part in what you're hearing. Recording the audio and asking for a second opinion in the same way as mentioned previously in relation to EVPs will help validate this evidence.

Electromagnetic Field Meter

An electromagnetic field meter, or EMF meter, is one of the most popular pieces of ghost hunting equipment. They are simple to use, often consisting of nothing more than an on/off switch. They detect and alert you to fluctuations and spikes in electromagnetic flux from 50 to 1,000 Hz. The device gives instant feedback via a digital display or LED indicators, usually five.

The belief within the paranormal community is that ghosts either emit an EM field or disrupt the ambient field. This is based on the fact that the human brain uses tiny electronic impulses, and it's this synaptic energy of a disembodied spirit that EMF meters can detect.

An EMF meter can be used to communicate with spirits during a séance. As with the previous methods of spirit communication, you should call out to the spirits. When using an EMF metre, you should encourage the spirits to come forward and try to trigger the lights on the meter to show that they are present or to indicate an answer to a question.

A compass is a cheap yet effective alternative to an electronic EMF meter. A compass can detect fluctuations in the electromagnetic field in just the same way as an EMF meter. Just look for erratic movements of the needle.

EMF meters are very susceptible to interference from many external factors. They can be triggered by things like mobile phones and walkie-talkies, so this should be accounted for when investigating. Phones should be turned off and results discredited if a radio is being used. EMF meters are also prone to interference from things that might be beyond your control, like radio transmissions, and interference from sources in neighbouring properties, like baby monitors and even fluorescent lights.

An EMF meter's susceptibility to false positives, combined with any lack of scientific backing as to how a spirit could produce or manipulate electromagnetic fields, make these sorts of devices a poor choice for any serious investigator.

If EMF meters are so flawed, then why are they so widely used on ghost hunts? Well, the original reason for taking an electromagnetic detecting device along on a paranormal investigation has been lost.

EMF meters were originally used to try to rule out the possibility that artificial EM fields could actually be causing people to experience certain haunting phenomena, as previously mentioned in the "things commonly mistaken for the paranormal" section.

Using an EMF meter will allow you to detect high-level EM fields. If they are present, then you might want to disregard the haunting phenomenon that's been experienced, which is similar to that caused by exposure to high levels of EM.

Electronic Speech Synthesis

There are many electronic speech synthesis devices on the market, but they tend to be quite expensive. However, there are cheaper versions available as apps for smartphones. They work as either random word generators or by generating random sounds, the phonics that make up words. Supposedly, spirits can affect the random nature of these devices to form the words they are trying to say.

Most devices of this type use atmospheric sensors to generate their random output. They monitor conditions such as temperature, pressure, humidity, and electromagnetic flux. It uses these signals as a random number generator, and this number is in turn used to reference a database of words. The atmospheric sensors give the spirits another way to influence the random word.

The belief behind these devices is that intelligent spirits can manipulate the atmospheric conditions in order to affect the random nature of the app. This would essentially mean increasing or decreasing the temperature, humidity, or pressure in a room, or affecting the electromagnetic field. This change would be detected by the device's sensors and then used to reference a list of words or sounds.

Of course, there's no scientific understanding of how a spirit could manipulate atmospheric conditions or know how much it would need to manipulate a certain measure in order to choose the word or sound it intended to pick from the list stored in the device's software.

This means that it's very likely that the words produced by these sorts of tools are purely random. Therefore, you should try to encourage the spirits to provide you with specific answers to your questions rather than just letting the device run of its own accord. Call out to the spirits and ask questions in order to elicit a direct and meaningful response from them.

You should discredit any words that aren't relevant to your questions. Only intelligent answers are likely to be the result of spirit interaction. If you can encourage a spirit to repeat an answer, this further rules out the possibility of the word coming through randomly.

Although you should discredit seemingly irrelevant responses, do not ignore them completely. You should take note of how many responses serve as intelligent answers to your questions and how many don't. If the success rate is poor, then it means the technique probably isn't working, and it's purely coincidental that the very occasional word does seem to fit your question.

Pendulum

Some trigger objects can be used to communicate with spirits, most commonly a pendulum. In order to contact spirits using this method, you need to allow the pendulum to hang while holding the other end between two fingers. Then, using the techniques previously discussed, call out to the spirits and encourage them to interact with the pendulum.

You can suggest that the spirit try moving the pendulum in order to answer your questions. Encourage it to swing the pendulum back and forth to indicate "yes" or left to right to indicate "no." You can also ask for the pendulum to be moved in either a clockwise or anticlockwise motion.

Another cheap and easy-to-obtain trigger object that can be used to communicate is a candle. In this case, the spirit can manipulate the flame. You should again call out to the spirits and encourage them to answer your questions by making the flame increase or decrease in intensity. You can also ask the spirits to make the flame flicker or blow it out all together. Make sure that this method of communication is carried out away from draughts and that the property owner allows naked flames.

With both of these methods, it's a good idea to use a static camera on a tripod so that you can review the footage and determine exactly how much the pendulum swings or the flame changes in response to your questions.

Validate Contact with the Spirit

When communicating with spirits through any of the methods discussed in this chapter, your main aim should be to obtain some evidence of contact with the spirit world. You can then attempt to validate this information to establish its authenticity.

You should aim to obtain information like names, dates, how the spirits passed, and how old they were. If you have chosen to do your background research on the property, you can now refer back to this in order to prove or disprove your evidence by establishing whether those names and dates match the recorded history of the property or the area.

If you didn't research the location in advance, now is the time to do your research in order to enter the investigation without being influenced.

You should try to obtain evidence from those who currently live or work in the property, as well as from former residents or people who have lived in the area for many years. Where possible, try to find out about the building's history and the local area. What was the land used for before the current property was built?

This sort of information can usually be found at the local reference library, town hall, or historical society. You may be able to find out some of the history of the local area online or in local interest books.

Remember that testimonies from eyewitnesses and locals may not always be accurate. They may include an element of exaggeration, hearsay, or anecdotal evidence. But if many witness accounts are similar, then this could corroborate the claims.

You should be wary of any information that comes through in a séance if any members of the group had access to information about the property before the séance. While it is sometimes useful to go into an investigation armed with knowledge, during a séance there is a chance that someone could intentionally or subconsciously influence the results, especially when using a Ouija board.

If a name, date, or another piece of information comes through during the séance that no one at the séance knew about in advance but can be verified using old documents relating to the property, then this is deemed to be strong evidence of the paranormal.

You may also be able to obtain information that is only known to one person, such as the property owner or an eyewitness. As long as that person wasn't included in the séance, then this would also be considered valid evidence.

Legalities of Ghost Hunting

Ghost hunting may not be an extreme sport and seems like a relatively tame past time, but there are risks that should be assessed.

Most paranormal researchers investigate old properties, which may contain hazards like low doorways, uneven floors, and plenty of things you could trip over, not to mention dark basements, attic spaces, and stairwells.

Other popular locations include derelict buildings, which can be extremely dangerous places. There are many hazards, such as structurally weak floors and roofs, asbestos, and shear drops.

Caves and underground locations such as cellars and wartime bunkers are also frequently investigated. Underground spaces come with their own dangers and should be visited with great care and appropriate preparation. In places, the roof can be extremely unstable, and it is easy to get lost in the maze of passages.

As most ghost hunts are conducted in the dark, all of these hazards are greatly increased.

We've already established that there are plenty of pieces of ghost hunting equipment that can be used during an investigation, but one essential piece of kit that isn't optional is a flashlight. You should buy the best flashlight you can. A bright, long-reaching flashlight is invaluable if investigating large areas or open spaces.

It may also be useful to find a flashlight that has different brightness settings. Sometimes a very bright flashlight can be an irritant if turned on suddenly in the dark during an investigation, as the eyes of those taking part in the investigation may have grown accustomed to the dark.

Whenever you are moving or walking around a property, you should always use a flashlight to avoid trips, falls, and other hazards. But it's best to keep the beam of the flashlight angled down to avoid shining it directly into people's eyes.

Below are a few basic safety rules that you should follow when investigating a property. In addition to these rules, you should also observe any guidelines set by the property owner or group leaders at an event. This might include no-entry signs, instructions to keep out of certain parts of the building, or a requirement to wear a hard hat or high-visibility clothing.

- Always carry a flashlight and use it whenever walking
- Avoid places where the floor or roof is obviously unsound
- Always wear suitable clothing and sensible footwear
- Never visit a property alone
- Take a first aid kit
- Always let someone know where you are going and your expected time of return
- Observe the privacy of those who live near the property

Obtaining Permissions

Most ghost hunts you embark on will either be organised events at locations you've been invited to or at locations open to the public. However, you may be tempted to investigate abandoned or derelict buildings, including houses, asylums, or hospitals. It is vital to get permission before setting foot in these or any properties.

Without seeking the correct permissions, your presence on the land will be deemed trespassing. As trespass is a civil matter, not a criminal offence, the police are unlikely to get involved. But the property's owner, caretaker, or security guard can use reasonable force to remove you.

However, it is a criminal offence to cause damage by getting onto land or into a building. This could be deemed to be aggravated trespass, criminal damage, or even breaking and entering, all of which could put you at risk of a criminal conviction.

When properties are closed to the public, it's often for a very valid reason. Even when properties look safe, they may have many dangers, including structurally rotten floorboards, asbestos, shear drops, or the risk of collapse.

Demonology

Studying Demons

Demonology is not a supernatural ability or a gift that you are born with. It is the study of demons or demonic beliefs.

Demonology isn't a subject that can be studied at university; it's not a recognised profession, and the title has little or no credibility outside of the church. However, if you take the time to study and reach a high level of understanding of demons and demonic beliefs, then this would qualify you as an expert in demonology. By studying demonology, you will, by the very nature of the title, become a demonologist. Don't worry, this doesn't mean you need to start dressing in black and wearing a crucifix.

The study of demons dates back centuries and can be found in many cultures and civilisations, often rooted in religion and cultural mythology. Digging into all of these various cultures and theologies reveals similar tales, which boil down to the idea of malevolent entities that are driven to destroy the positive aspects of the world around them.

Stripping away some of the myth around these entities will help you gain a clearer and more practical understanding of what demons are. In all cases, you'll find that demons are said to do all they can to drive away love and happiness in order to destroy lives.

So, it doesn't really matter where the demons come from or what a person's beliefs may say about them; the aim of this book is to help you tell the difference between a demon and a regular spirit, based on current theories, trends, and beliefs in the paranormal community. It will help you identify demons on a ghost hunt, deal with a demonic presence that may be haunting your home, or even help you summon a demon, should you wish to do so.

Traditionally, demonology required some kind of religious belief because demons are woven into theology. In the case of

Christianity, demons are servants of the Devil; they are biblical characters. But, with similar characters spread across all religions and cultures, clearly demons are more than the antagonists in just one religion.

This means that you don't need any religious beliefs to study the nature, behaviour and control of demons. Many atheist paranormal investigators or haunting victims will recount their stories of demons, despite the fact that they don't believe in the religious side of demonology.

As for what you'll get from reading this book, at the very least, you will gain an understanding of what present-day ghost hunters believe about demons. It might also help you if you want to identify, understand or put an end to strange goings on in your own home.

You might plan on using the knowledge contained within this book to help others with their demonic issues or eradicate their demonic haunting. If this is your intention, then even more important than knowledge of demons is possessing respect, understanding, and the patience to listen to the victim's issues. You'll need some analytical and critical thinking skills in order to validate, verify, and diagnose your clients' claims in an ethical way.

There's also another, more controversial way that knowledge of demonology can be used: summoning or provoking demons. Using demonology to summon demons requires ongoing research and practice, as it often involves reciting passages and incantations. These are much more effective if you can say them with confidence and an understanding of their meaning, without stumbling or pauses as you read from the book. If you can commit these phrases to memory, you will be able to deliver them much more naturally. It is confidence and belief that are said to give these passages their power.

Warnings

You might expect a book about demonology to come with a disclaimer about irresponsible use of the techniques used by demonologists or a warning not to try any of the methods described yourself, but that's not really the case with modern demonology.

The very nature of demonology has changed a lot over the centuries. Traditionally, the only way to become an accredited demonologist was to be sanctioned by a church. Today, modern demonology is very different, as outdated superstitions have fallen aside through the generations.

Demons were once considered to be exceedingly life-threatening entities, but the truth is, there have been no recorded deaths that have been attributed to demonic possessions or hauntings ever. Of course, there are many reports of people being pushed, scratched, or hit by a malevolent spirit, but claims of demons becoming physically violent are very rare.

Those living in houses which are said to be haunted by a demonic entity often describe a negative atmosphere, an increase in accidents and illness, this can lead to violent behaviour, depression and even suicide, but these stories tend to be anecdotal. It's unlikely a coroner would list "death by demon" as the cause of death of a suicide victim; "paranoid delusions" is more likely.

Hundreds, if not thousands, of locations are believed to be haunted by demons and are open to the public without any reported injury or loss of life. In fact, many of these locations are places where paranormal event companies run ghost hunting events for members of the public, who actively encourage supernatural activity at these locations. Yet, despite their demonic presence, these places and activities are deemed safe enough for the general public to participate in.

Having said that, many people report bad experiences as a result of dabbling with demons because they believe they will. If you are weak in mind and heart, then you may feel as if you have been possessed or feel discomfort after dealing with a demon. This may be all in your mind, but the fact that it's all in your mind doesn't make it any less scary.

Even if not life-threatening, demons can be troublesome and are responsible for very negative haunting phenomena, so don't summon demons where they are not wanted. If you summon demons into this realm, then be sure to return them afterwards so as not to cause discomfort or suffering to yourself or others.

If you have any serious doubts about demonology, then this topic isn't for you. Similarly, if it is against your religious beliefs, then stay clear as it may cause feelings of guilt or conflict. If you are nervous or unsure about demonology, there are a few things you can do to protect yourself, and we'll look into those methods later.

However, if you're feeling strong, willing, and able, then let's delve into the world of demonology.

What are Demons?

It's difficult to define what a demon is without relying on religious texts because we really have no way of knowing if we've encountered one or not. However, if someone feels they are a victim of a demon, then this is essentially a demonic haunting. You should approach it respectfully, because even if you don't believe a demon is responsible for the haunting, the witness does.

Many different traditions and cultures have different beliefs on what a demon fundamentally is, but as a multi-faith paranormal investigator, the best way to describe a demon is simply as a non-human malevolent entity.

Demons are often characterised as being evil, controlling, and menacing, but just as there are good and bad people in the world, there should also be good and bad spirits of the dead. This makes it very hard, if not impossible, to tell whether you are dealing with a demon or the ghost of an evil person.

Ghost hunters who believe in demons often agree upon the claim that an evil human spirit is much less powerful than a demon. Over the years, they have come up with a few methods that signal differences between demonic hauntings and those caused by a malevolent spirit.
Belief in demons has risen throughout the 20th century, even though demonic hauntings are rare. These terrifying intelligent hauntings, sometimes called interactive hauntings, involve the presence of a supernatural being that is able to manifest or communicate in some way, which can include leaving signs, clues, or moving objects. It's also believed that intelligent hauntings are the cause of cold spots in rooms.

Unlike normal hauntings, demonic hauntings aren't the result of deceased human spirits; demons were never humans. They have never been alive and have only ever existed purely as malevolent energy, which is intent on causing suffering to those that it haunts.

Some traditions go as far as to say that demons may not even be from our plane of existence, instead believing them to be entities that have survived from a former universe or have found a way to cross over from a parallel universe. Wherever it is they come from, demonologists tend to call it the "infernal realm."

Those who have reported seeing demons have usually described them as being hideous, grotesque, or evil-looking. They almost always appear wearing black or as a dark animal, and they are said to be unclean and foul-smelling.

It's said that when they manifest, demons can take any form, although usually it is a human form. They also less frequently take animal-like forms, most often a black dog. When in human form, it's said that there is almost always something not quite right about their appearance that gives away the fact that they are demons. They may have facial disfigurement, black eyes, missing body parts, malformed limbs, or cloven feet. On rare occasions, demons have been said to manifest as a hybrid - half man and half animal.

Demons are believed by some to be the hidden cause of all of humankind's problems, including physical and mental illness, bad luck, pain, and suffering. They are much more powerful than human spirits and have abilities that humans don't possess, whether alive or in spirit form. These abilities include telepathy and telekinesis.

It's claimed that demons use these supernatural abilities to weaken and torment their victims. Telepathy allows them to uncover a victim's fear or worry and use this knowledge against them. Telekinesis combined with demons' evil and violent tendencies allow them to move larger objects and even scratch, push, or hit victims.

In whatever form a demon takes, its intentions are always the same. They aim to break down their victim's free will and weaken them so that they can possess and control them. As well as possessing humans, demons can also attach themselves to objects, most commonly dolls and children's toys.

Demonic hauntings which can spontaneously begin anywhere at any time and often begin slowly and non-menacing, with activity similar to any non-demonic haunting, including unexplained knocks and bangs, the disturbance of electrical equipment and disembodied voices and whispers.

A demon grows stronger by feeding on the fear, depression, and sadness of their victim, as paranormal activity intensifies. It can escalate to recurrent nightmares on a weekly or nightly basis, loud noises, growls, unpleasant smells, and physical attacks on humans. Demons don't usually manifest early in the haunting as they don't want to reveal their true nature, but as their hold on the victim grows, full apparitions are witnessed.

One set of phenomena that is exclusive to demonic hauntings is materialisation. This is when a demon can make substances appear out of thin air; often, it's a substance of an unknown nature. This may be in the form of liquids oozing from walls, flowing from taps, or appearing in puddles on the floor. Reports of these mysterious liquids range from nothing more than water to dark, tar-like substances and even blood.

The opposite of materialisation is dematerialisation, which is when something vanishes, and demons are often blamed for this too. It's said that they can dematerialise objects only to have them re-materialise somewhere else or at some time in the future. The levitation of objects is also frequently associated with demons, as are objects being broken in precise and calculated ways to make it clear that there is an intelligence behind the damage and that it's not just accidental damage.

Demons are deceitful; they frequently lie and mix lies with truths to confuse their victims. They often try to trick their victims into thinking that they have left them while quietly waiting for an opportunity to take advantage of them when they are weak and at their most vulnerable.

They also attempt to deceive their victims and paranormal researchers by taking on an angelic form or the appearance and characteristics of a child. For this reason, you should always be wary of a location that is said to be haunted by the ghost of a child. Demons may also pretend to be children or loved ones when communicating via Ouija boards and other methods of spirit communication.

Possession and Attachment

The most common type of possession experienced by a paranormal investigator is emotional possession, sometimes referred to as a temporary spirit "walk-in" or "step-in." This normally happens when the investigator gives any spirits present permission to use their energy and enter their body.

This is not a demonic possession; it is a non-aggressive spiritual exchange involving a human spirit, not a demon. The spirit will normally use this opportunity to share their emotions or feelings with the investigator so that they can experience what the spirit went through in their final moments.

While in this state, investigators have reported feeling totally different, sometimes not recognising the people around them who should be familiar to them. After the incident, they may have missing memories and feel very weak and drained, as walk-ins can be quite a shock to the body.

This type of possession is harmless, temporary, and, most importantly, non-demonic. It is not generally what people are referring to when they talk about a possession. Demonic possession is when a demon takes over a human body for its own evil gain. Only humans and animals can be possessed, but demons can attach themselves to a home or an object. Attachment is sometimes called infestation, but this isn't possession either. Attachment is much more common than possessions, which are very rare occurrences.

One expert in demonic possession, Dr. Richard Gallagher, has dealt with more than 25,000 cases of alleged possession over his 25-year career, but says he's only witnessed about 100 true cases of demonic possession in all that time.

Some proponents of demons believe that most cases of possession start with a Ouija board, and while spirit boards aren't evil or dangerous themselves, what you make contact with and call forward might be. Using a Ouija board is no more dangerous than picking up a phone; it's just a method of communication with spirits and, in almost 100% of cases, is completely safe.

Every day, hundreds, if not thousands, of people use Ouija boards at allegedly haunted locations, on ghost hunts, or just at home for the thrill of seeing the planchette move around the board. If a demon does make contact through a Ouija board, it's often hard to tell as they only communicate by spelling out words. You can't see or hear them, so you have no way of knowing who is really communicating with you.

Even if you do encounter a demon during a séance, it is still very unlikely that it will possess you. In almost all possession cases, demons only prey on the weak and susceptible. They are naturally attracted to negative and unhappy atmospheres, such as homes where there is a lot of resentment or arguments, or dirty or unhygienic living conditions. Their victims are almost always the weak or the emotionally unstable.

Before a possession takes place, victims go through a stage called "oppression." This is more like a traditional haunting, where the demon doesn't have full control over their victim but uses its influence to weaken them further until it can fully take hold and enter the body.

It is said that demons enter the body through the solar plexus, the back of the neck, the left side of the body, or by having sexual intercourse with a person.

The belief is that their reason for possessing the living is that, in order to walk the Earth, they are trying to get their victim's soul, which will allow them to take a physical form and perform its evil deeds as a human. When a demon possesses someone, they slowly break them psychologically and physically. Eventually they will hurt their victim, and in extreme cases, they will drive them to suicide. After death, the demon is said to be able to claim the victim's soul.

When someone is possessed, it's said that they are unlikely to notice at first. It is normally the people around them who first notice that something is wrong. This might be strange or paranormal activity happening around the possessed. One commonly stated early indication is that the victim experiences periods of missing time or black outs.

As the demon takes hold, the symptoms of possession are said to become more obvious. The usual signs are severe changes to someone's personality, inexplicable strength, and supernatural abilities, like those of a psychic. The possessed might demonstrate knowledge of future events or be able to divulge information about someone that they shouldn't be aware of, like secrets, thoughts, or experiences the person has never shared with them.

They may also display an ability to speak languages they've never previously learned or spoken, including ancient dialects like Latin. Demonic possession sometimes also involves the demon speaking through the possessed in a voice other than that of the victim. They often speak in a raspy or deep guttural masculine voice, or otherwise unnatural voice.

Sometimes the voice is said to come from the vocal cords, although it won't be recognised as the voice of the person who is possessed, or the voice comes from outside or around the body. Demonic voices occur in one of two situations, either when the soul of the possessed is dislodged by the demonic presence leaving just the demon's voice. Or when the presence cohabits the body with the soul, in this case the demon and human can speak at the same time.

It's been reported that in rare cases, demons can also cause the body to transform and contort in ways not normally possible. This can involve the manifestations of bodily wounds and scars, which may take the form of words or symbols, like an inverted cross, three scratches, or the number six.

The demon hopes that all this torment and suffering will scare the victim, wear them down, and break their will, eventually driving them mad, driving them to suicide, or making them more prone to accidental death due to tiredness or lapses in cognitive functions. However, cases that have gone this far are very rare, and in many cases, they are anecdotal or unproven to be the result of demonic influence.

There are instances where people have voluntarily let demons possess them. This type of willing possession is known as "perfect possession" and often comes about as the result of a summoning ritual or a pact with a demon. In these situations, it is very hard, if not impossible, to exorcise the person involved.

Attachment

Demons cannot possess objects or places, but they can "attach" themselves to them. This is sometimes also known as "infestation." Demons can attach themselves to homes, which of course results in demonic haunting cases. They can also attach themselves to vehicles, occult paraphernalia, and any other object, but they most often choose objects with faces, which is why cursed dolls are so common.

Attachment is also the early stage of possession when a demon first shows an interest in its victim; at this point, it has no hold on the victim and is merely stalking or haunting the victim with the express aim of introducing itself to the intended target through surreptitious means.

A demon is said to be able to attach itself to an item more easily if it has been used in an occult ritual or if it's had a curse placed on it, but demons can attach themselves to just about any object, although conveniently, it's believed that they can't attach themselves to items used for spiritual protection.

Although it's not demonic activity, you should be aware that human spirits are also said to be able to attach themselves to objects, once again blurring the line between ghosts and non-human spirits. The items that human spirits are most often said to create an attachment to are items that were used as a murder weapon or items that someone was very emotionally attached to in life, meaning that in death they find it hard to let go and their spirit becomes attached to the item.

Demonically infested items aren't always visibly active; sometimes they can lay dormant for years or even generations, but may become active when they are unsettled, perhaps by being moved to a new room in the house or a new home all together, or by being sold or given to a new owner.

As with the early stages of possession, infestation of an item can result in typical haunting occurrences, poltergeist-like activity, and a general feeling of unease or negativity when near or handling the object.

Confirming a Demonic Presence

It can be hard to determine if a haunting or possession is truly the result of a demonic entity. As previously stated, not all attachments are demonic, and even possessions may be the result of a human spirit "walk-in." The same applies for hauntings; it's difficult to know if you are dealing with an evil human spirit or a demon. Even a friendly but mischievous human spirit could be so terrifying from the perspective of a living witness that it could appear to be demonic too.

To make it even harder to work out, demons will often lie about who or what they are to avoid detection, and some paranormal investigators claim that human spirits will sometimes pretend to be demons to make themselves appear more powerful and more terrifying. Humans can be good or bad, so obviously so can ghosts. You can get malevolent human spirits, but they are not as powerful as demons.

Demonic hauntings are very similar to poltergeist hauntings; they are both characterised by physical movement as well as manipulation of the environment around the entity. Poltergeist, which means "noisy ghost" from the German "poltern geist", are often dealt with in the same way as demons too, exorcists are brought in to try to help move them on. However, poltergeists aren't believed to be demonic in origin. They are an escalated form of intelligent hauntings where the spirit is often violent, threatening, and malevolent.

Like poltergeists, demons can show themselves in many different ways, including by throwing or moving objects, producing foul smells, turning lights or appliances on or off, and by producing growls, screams, and other loud noises. On rare occasions, it's been reported that poltergeists have intentionally attacked people by pushing, hitting, biting, or scratching them. All of these traits are regularly reported in demonic hauntings too, making it all the more difficult to separate the two.

In both demonic and poltergeist cases, the activity usually starts out slowly and in a playful manner but increases in intensity, slowly becoming more and more malicious. However, with poltergeist, just as suddenly as the activity starts, it can abruptly end, often never to be repeated, whereas demonic hauntings rarely stop of their own accord.

So, during an investigation, it's always wise to evaluate every encounter to determine whether it's a spirit or a demon, especially if the entity claims to be the ghost of a child; this tends to be a common cover story for demons.

Communication

Identifying demonic contact during a séance or instrumental transcommunication session.

During a Ouija board session, demons can often be detected by mischievous behaviour, through inconsistent answers, or clear lies. Usually, when starting a Ouija board session, you call out to any spirits that might be present, "Is there anybody there?" After a while, you should see the planchette move across the board, hopefully towards "yes," but sometimes it moves to "no." This is said to be a strong indication that you've encountered a demon. Another sign is when you ask a spirit its age and the planchette moves to the number zero on the board. There may also be cases where a demon simply introduces itself as such on the board.

It's not just Ouija boards through which demons make their presence known, but through all forms of spirit communications, especially forms of instrumental transcommunication (ITC), a common set of techniques used to contact spirits using electronic means to record or hear their voices.

Two common devices used for ITC are digital audio recorders and spirit boxes. Audio recorders are used to try to capture Electronic Voice Phenomena (EVP). The spirit voices are not heard at the time, but when reviewing the audio, any EVPs will be present.

A spirit box rapidly scans through the AM, MW, and FM radio spectrums, emitting fleeting bursts of white noise and static that can be heard. Spirit boxes usually have various settings that allow you to tweak which bands the device scans through and how much of each frequency step you hear; this usually ranges from a hundredth of a second up to a second. Just like with audio recorders, you should be able to hear EVPs amongst this white noise, but the answer will be audible in real time.

Whichever method you are using, you should call out to any spirits that might be present and encourage them to come forward, talk to you, and answer your questions. If using a recorder, leave a gap for the spirit to answer, or when using a spirit box listen for their answers within the noise of the spirit box, ideally a response which spans across several steps of the frequency scan.

When reviewing the audio from a recorder or listening to responses through a spirit box, it's not uncommon to hear voices in the audio answering questions, but if the voice sounds gruff, deep, or animalistic, then you may have encountered a demon. Demons are also sometimes captured in EVPs as growling.

It is better to use headphones, rather than the small and inadequate speakers in the recording device itself to monitor the audio. However, the best way to review the audio is to transfer it to a computer, which allows you to review the audio in greater detail. You can use free audio editing software like Audacity to boost the audio level and hear responses more clearly.

Attachment

Identifying demonic influence over a building or object, or the precursor to possession.

If a demon attaches itself to a house, an object within a house, or a person in the household, then the result will be the same: the household will experience haunting phenomena that closely resemble the activity you'd expect in a poltergeist case. Those living in the house may feel a general sense of discomfort or dread, witness objects moving, or even see apparitions.

It can be very difficult to determine if this activity is the result of a demon or just a malevolent spirit, but here are a few ways to help you decide.

In demonic hauntings, the entity often starts by ensuring the environment is safe for them; unfortunately, this might result in the sudden and unexpected death of pets. It's believed that this is because pets are thought to have some perception of the spirit world and could therefore potentially warn their owner of a demonic presence.

You may also find that protective or spiritual items are destroyed or inexplicably lost; traditionally, this would have just been religious objects such as a crucifix, bible, or rosary, but in the modern day, it could be anything that is charged with positive energy in order to offer protection, such as sentimental jewellery or good luck charms.

In demonic hauntings, activity usually happens in threes or sixes; for example, you might hear six knocks or find three scratch marks on a wall. They also result in negativity between family members or friends, which increases and leads to arguments, fights, and general discord.

As with poltergeist hauntings, demonic attachments often centre around one person, and the entity often poses as a child, especially when the victim is a child themselves. This may be explained away as an imaginary friend to start with, but eventually the demon may begin to show itself to others in the household. One thing to look out for if a demon does manifest is its movement. According to some paranormal investigators, even if it is visible as nothing more than a shadowy mass, demons often move from left to right across a field of view.

Other signs to look out for include entire homes or rooms being ransacked even though nothing has been taken, and writing on walls or other places in the building. In extreme cases, victims may awaken at night to a feeling of being held down in bed and, upon waking, discover unexplained bruises or scratches on their body.

Possession

Identifying a demonic hold over a living human's body.

There are a few possibilities when it comes to confirming a demonic possession. Firstly, there may be no possession at all; the alleged possession could be a result of mental illness, delusion, or nothing more than a faked incident. These possibilities should obviously all be considered when diagnosing a case. Secondly, the case might not be demonic in nature and could just be a spirit walk-in or another type of spirit attachment. Third and finally, it could be a genuine case of demonic possession.

It's said that the easiest way to confirm whether a possession is demonic is to use a protective item without the victim's knowledge. We'll explore protective items more in the next chapter, but this can be any object that is charged with positive energy or has religious significance, or holy water if that has meaning to you.

You should hold the protective item behind the head of the possessed without them knowing to see if they react. If they are truly a demonic entity, then they should react to its proximity. You can also try using regular items; if the possession is real, they will not react to an item that isn't blessed or empowered in some way. If using holy water, try sprinkling both regular tap water and blessed water over the victim to see if they react differently to each.

Signs that someone is possessed are that the person does not blink; they may become withdrawn and start to pull away from their family and friends; and they may lose interest in their usual hobbies, interests, and commitments. They may also become emotionally intense, specifically in the form of anger directed at those around them.

Also look out for unexplained marks on the body such as scratches, bites, and bruises, especially if they are in places where the victim shouldn't be able to inflict those injuries on themselves.

They may also show inexplicable signs of illness and weakness of either the body or mind. Signs of this might include weight loss, hair loss, change in skin tone, loss of appetite, vomiting, and loss of energy. Contrary to this, those who are possessed are sometimes said to have extreme strength beyond their normal abilities.

One other indication is that a demon might start to communicate through the possessed and identify itself as a demon.

Protection Against Demons

The risks of negative side effects from investigating or interacting with demons are very low, but it's still a good idea to ensure that you feel spiritually and mentally protected. Therefore, when entering into an investigation or performing a séance, you should ensure that you are not ladened by negative emotions, are not tired, and that you are guilt and stress-free.

If you have a spirit guide or guardian angel who you can call upon, then ensure they are aware of what you are attempting to do and call upon them for their help and support. If you are religious, you could pray for protection or bless your surroundings.

Many people advise that you shouldn't allow yourself to be alone in the presence of someone who is possessed for any length of time. Their negative energy may be infectious and drag you down, making you susceptible to possession too.

Unless you are intentionally trying to summon one, it's advised that you never say a demon's name aloud. If a demon has previously identified itself to you, then using its name acts as an invitation and helps it grow in strength. Demons are said to always be watching and waiting.

You should also avoid provoking or angering demons, be polite when asking them questions, and thank them for their efforts. If you are using a Ouija board as part of a séance, then one important measure that should be taken is to close the board after a session. To do this, you should physically slide the planchette across the board to "goodbye." This will ensure that any demons that have been called forward will return to where they came from after the session.

As we've learned, demons can attach themselves to any object, and it might not be obvious that the object is infested until it is moved or changes owners; therefore, you should never bring second-hand items into your home without cleansing them first.

Cleansing

It is often advised to use burning sage to drive away demons and evil spirits. This is known as "smudging," and the technique can be used to cleanse an object, a building, yourself, or another person. Smudging is most often performed with white sage as part of many belief systems, including Neopagan spirituality such as modern Wicca and paranormal investigations.

Sage has been burned by many Native American traditions for centuries to aid spiritual healing; perhaps due to its natural anti-bacterial properties, its smoke is said to clear bacteria out of the air. Some research has suggested certain extracts of sage may have positive effects on human brain functions. Sage smoke is also said to be an odour remover and a bug repellent.

Smudging involves burning dried sage; it is believed that the smoke can purify a space and drive away negative energy. It is said to be a form of ritual alchemy; the smoke filling the air element is said to help humans better connect with the spiritual world around them. It is rooted in the similar tradition of burning incense, which can be traced throughout the East in parts of Asia and dating as far back to Ancient Greece.

Sage can be bought in a pre-wrapped bundle of dried herb, known as smudge sticks; this is a better option than buying loose-leaf sage as it is easier to burn. You can also grow and make your own smudge sticks. You'll find smudging sticks for sale online or anywhere that incense is sold.

Smudging is an ancient ceremonial ritual that differs by culture. Many of these traditions have been forgotten and may not be in line with your beliefs, so it's best to come up with your own ritual that you are comfortable with and that means something to you.

To ensure smudging is your own meaningful ritual, perform your ritual slowly, with full awareness, and in a mindful manner. You should allow at least 10 to 15 minutes to complete the ritual. White sage is most commonly used, but you can also use different varieties of sage like desert sage, Russian sage, or mugwort (black sage). You can also use cedar, sweetgrass, and lavender.

If you are smudging yourself or another person, then it is best to have the person being smudged remove metal jewellery, belts, and shoes in order to prepare themselves mentally and spiritually. Next, start the ritual by mentally focussing your energy before lighting the tip of the sage with a match, lighter, or candle, then gently waving the smudge stick in the air until the tip begins to smoulder. Throughout the ritual, be aware of glowing embers falling onto the floor.

Simply take your smouldering smudge stick and pass it around the body so that the smoke surrounds them. Start with the area above the head and continue down to the feet; be sure to take your time.

This same procedure can also be used to cleanse any object; simply move the burning sage all around it, engulfing it in the sage smoke.

If you are smudging a building or room, you'll need to move around with the burning sage. It's a good idea to carry a plate with you as a means to catch any smouldering ash. Keep a means of lighting the sage with you too, as you may find you need to re-light the herb during the session.

Ensure that there is at least one door or window open throughout. The sage smoke will drive the demon away, and an open exit route gives the demon a clear indication of where it should go.

When smudging a building, most people start at the front door or main entrance, while others begin at the east or west wall. Then, if possible, consistently move in one direction around the building in either a clockwise or anti-clockwise movement; again, this is up to you, but don't forget about smaller rooms like utility rooms, ensuite bathrooms, and the garage.

In each room, fill the whole space with the sage smoke, being sure to let the smoke drift into all corners and dark or shadowy spaces in every room, as it's said that corners can accumulate stagnant energy.

Nowadays, people tend to direct the smoke around the room by simply waving their hand through the air to waft it in the direction they want it to go, but traditionally an eagle or hawk's feather was used. These feathers are now difficult to get hold of, so in modern times, a turkey feather is more commonly used.

If you pass an open door or window, waft the smoke outside to carry the negative energies from your home with it. To ensure the practice is meaningful, you should focus on the cleansing process during the ritual or recite an incantation that means something to you, either aloud or in your head. One popular incantation is "air, fire, water, earth. Cleanse, dismiss, dispel."

Once you have smudged all areas of the room or building and returned to the starting point, gently extinguish your sage bundle by stubbing it out on a non-flammable, heat-resistant surface. Let the ashes cool down and then pack them away; they can be used in your next session. You can also return the leftover sage to the earth if you wish.

Protective Items

Traditionally, demonologists would carry protection in the form of a cross, holy water, the Bible, or rosaries. Although these items are still perfectly acceptable if they fit your religious stance, nowadays many paranormal investigators carry a form of spiritual protection or a defensive item that has specific meaning to them and their beliefs.

It doesn't really matter what the object is; if you feel strongly about it, then the belief is that it is charged with your positive energy. Most commonly, it's a form of jewellery like a bracelet, necklace, or medallion. It can also be a tattoo, some kind of sacred item, or anything else that makes them feel safe and secure.

Protective jewellery often includes symbols like the Celtic triple knot, known as a triquetra. Also a pentacle, specific runic symbols or a blue eye symbol usually made out of glass called a nazar, but often referred to incorrectly as the evil eye. It's actually a Middle Eastern talisman to ward off the evil eye, which is a curse believed to be cast by a malevolent glare and usually given to a person when they are unaware.

If you're thinking of getting some protective jewellery of your own, then silver is said to be a good choice as it purifies its surroundings and interferes with spirit communication.

You may also consider an amulet of protection or a charm, which is usually made out of natural substances, crystals, or semi-precious stones. There is a long-standing belief that crystals and certain stones can protect people from demons, demonic hauntings, and possession. There isn't really a right or wrong when it comes to choosing the best stone to protect you; you should simply pick something that appeals to you and that you can focus your positive energy on.

Traditionally, stones like amber, black onyx, ruby, amethyst, jade, and tourmaline are used. Peridot is said to ward off demons, and chrysoberyl is believed to specifically protect against possession. Iron is also thought to repel demons; in fact, iron chains are said to be the only type of restraint that works on a demonic entity.

Salt is also a frequently used protective item that is believed to repel demons as well as other negative spirits. It is sometimes worn in the form of rock crystals in a pouch around the neck, giving you constant protection during a paranormal investigation or séance.

Paranormal investigators also use salt, specifically sea salt or black salt, to draw a circle on the floor to make a safe area that demons cannot enter. It can also be used to protect a house by sprinkling it around the perimeter of the building or across doors and windows.

Another way to protect a house is to use a small terracotta bowl known as a "demon bowl." The bowl is inscribed with incantations or religious texts, depending on your beliefs, and is said to either repel or trap demons. Traditionally the bowls were buried in foundations in each of the corners of the house. This may be difficult to achieve in a modern home, but they may be just as effective if placed in windows or entrance halls.

Summoning Demons

We've looked at how to protect yourself from demons, but what if you actually want to provoke or summon them so you can attempt to communicate with them or observe demonic phenomena during a paranormal investigation? This is something many demonologists attempt, often as part of a ghost hunt.

Traditionally, demons were summoned in order to form pacts for personal gain or wealth, get a question answered, or curse someone with pain or suffering. Black magic practitioners and witches would use a grimoire, a textbook specifically for magic. These books usually included instructions on how to do things like create talismans and amulets, how to perform magical spells, charms, and divination, and of course how to invoke supernatural entities, including demons.

Although there are some more modern grimoires, most date back to at least the 16th century, some as early as the 5th century BC. Outside of ancient myth, there's no evidence that any such practises worked. However, modern ghost hunters have often reported successful attempts to summon demons as part of paranormal investigations.

You don't need any specific skills, psychic powers, or experience in order to summon a demon, but the act should be performed responsibly due to a demon's tendency to attach itself to or follow those who summon it. If you are worried by the potential lingering presence of a demon, then you should always do your best to ensure that the demon returns to its own realm after the session for your own peace of mind.

To increase your chances of summoning a demon, it is important to set the mood. It's best to hold your ritual in low light or by candlelight, not in complete darkness. You could also try burning some incense, but avoid burning sage, as this is believed to drive evil energy away. Make sure you're comfortable. Making contact with a demon can take time and patience.

You'll need to make sure you're not distracted during the ritual, so put your phone on silent and shut pets and other distractions out of the room. As with any type of paranormal interaction, like a séance, vigil, or attempt to communicate, you should make sure you are in the right headspace first. You should be alert, feeling positive and confident, and not under the influence of drugs or alcohol.

It is best to attempt to summon demons between 3 and 4am; this is the witching hour, also known as "high noon" of the demonic day. Dusk till dawn, around 9pm to 5am is said to be the most paranormally active time of day, but 3am precisely is the single most active time of day.

Of course, there are countless sightings of ghosts and demonic activity, not only in the dead of night but also in broad daylight and lit houses, but paranormal investigators and demonologists tend to prefer to work in the dark.

Many paranormal investigators believe that ghosts and demons are a form of psychic or electrical energy. It's claimed that in order for a demon to manifest, it needs to draw on all of its energy to take on a physical, or at least visible, form. The belief is that in a light environment, a demon doesn't always have enough energy to manifest and become visible; it's being drowned out by surrounding energy fields. Occasionally, a demon will be strong enough to overcome this barrier and manifest during the day, but generally, it is thought to be more difficult.

The effect is similar to the principle that a radio has better reception at night; you'll find you're able to pick up radio stations from further away. This is because during the day, solar radiation from the sun ionises our atmosphere. This heavy ionisation in the atmosphere is known to drown out certain forms of electrical activity, such as radio and television broadcasts, and it is this same energy that is reducing demonic manifestation.

Invocation

Invoking a demon might sound daunting, but it can be as complicated, ritualistic, or simple as you want it to be. It could be as easy as eliminating distractions by sitting alone in a darkened room and asking the demon to come forward.

It's important to remember that demons are unpredictable by nature, so you should avoid angering or antagonising them at all costs, not because they might hurt you but in order to ensure they cooperate with you. Be sure to treat the demon with honesty and respect; always be polite; and most importantly, don't make demands or command the demon; you should only make requests.

Invocation involves asking demons to come forward by calling out to them. This is when a paranormal investigator or medium speaks aloud in an attempt to encourage any spirits or demons that might be present to communicate with them or show themselves. The classic ghost hunter's trope is, "Hello, is anybody there?"

When trying to contact demonic entities, you need to be a little more specific. You should call out encouragement to any demons that can hear you to come forward. If a demon has previously identified itself to you, then the best way to do this is to call it by name, as a demon's name holds power.

Under normal circumstances, you should never say a demon's name aloud; it can be taken as an invitation by the demon. Of course, in this situation, it is intended as an invitation, so repeat the name over and over. When you feel the time is right, you should start to recite words or incantations that are meaningful to you. The power isn't so much in the specific words you are saying as in the belief behind them. If you know the demon's name, you should use it in these incantations.

You could try phrases like:

• I invite the forces of darkness to bestow their infernal power upon me and show me you're here.

• Come forward, forces of darkness, and greet me.

• I invoke thee [demon's name].

• Come forth and answer to your name

• Come forward, [demon's name], where I can see you.

• I summon you into visible form before me.

Once you feel a demon has made its presence known, you should tell it exactly why you have summoned it. You need to get the demon on your side, and chances are you're not the first paranormal investigator on their patch. They might already feel like a performing monkey. Demons are unlikely to be happy existing for no other purpose than to amuse you, so tell them you're not here to mock them and that you come with respect and want to communicate. Ask the demon if they need help or have a message. Ask them to show you a sign that they are here so that you can talk to them, perhaps even to help them move on.

Demonic entities are said to only be able to give very subtle clues to the fact that they are present. They might use our energy to communicate through a Ouija board, knock over an object, tap on a hard surface, or make a sound in someone's ear. It's unusual to hear a loud noise, a clear voice, or see an object deliberately being moved for any sustained period of time.

So, we can assume that demons have to muster up a lot of energy in order to give us these signs. Therefore, you should thank the demon for their efforts if they do something that you've asked them to do. Give them encouragement. Let them know that what they've shown you is great, but ask them to do a little more if they can.

Be sure not to shut the session down prematurely. One common mistake is to say things like, "Give us a sign that you're here, and then we'll leave you alone." To be true to your word, if the demon does give you a sign, then you're going to have to pack up and end your investigation. Otherwise, you'll have lied, and the demon is unlikely to trust you again or do as you ask.

At this point, you might want to switch to another method of communication, such as a Ouija board, a spirit box, a digital audio recorder in order to capture EVPs, or any other method you are comfortable using. This might enable you to have a more meaningful conversation with the demon. Below is a list of example questions and phrases that you can use to try to encourage the demon to communicate with you. You shouldn't copy these exactly; it is better to be yourself and talk in a natural and open way as you normally would.

• If you can hear me, tap on the floor.

• Can you make a noise to let us know you are here with us?

• If you're here, can you show yourself to me?

• Can you throw something?

• Can you copy me? [then tap on a surface or whistle]

• My name is XXX, can you tell me your name?

• Tell us who you are, introduce yourself, please.
• If there's somebody here with us now, can you walk towards us?

• Are you happy for us to be here? Two taps for yes, one for no.

• Can you come and talk to us?

Of course, if you establish a dialogue with a demon, then you can ask more in-depth questions. Try to ask questions that no one in the room would know the answers to so you can rule out fakery or people subconsciously affecting the outcome.

After the Ritual

Once your session with the demon comes to an end, you should do all you can to ensure that the demon is not still present in that location. Even if you think you were unsuccessful, you should still take the precaution, as there is always the chance that you successfully called something forward but it refused to interact with you.

If you are using a Ouija board, it is advised to close the board by moving the planchette to the word "goodbye." This will ensure that any demons that have been called forward won't follow you after the session.
It is also a good idea to tell the demon that it must not remain. When ending the session, simply call out to the demon and say something like, "Thank you for making yourself known to me this evening. You must now return to the realm you came from; you cannot stay here."

You can also use the cleansing and protective techniques from the previous chapter to drive the demon away, and in the next chapter, we'll look into techniques that you can use to exorcise a location, which can also be used after you have summoned a demon.

Exorcisms

Exorcisms are usually elaborate rituals of some kind, designed to remove demons and negative energies. It is a traditional and ancient practise that is part of the belief systems of many cultures and religions, most notably the Catholic faith. In fact, the Catholic Church still takes exorcisms very seriously to this day and recently announced that the demand for exorcisms is on the rise.

Until recently, only a limited number of priests could perform the ritual, as the texts are written in Latin. To meet this new wave of demand, the church has been distributing its guidelines on exorcism in English, meaning that the ritual will be accessible to more priests.

The church would argue that even if you had a copy of their exorcism guidelines, you still wouldn't be able to conduct an exorcism yourself without being an ordained priest. As with many other aspects of demonology, this is a dated concept, and there's no reason to assume that all demons only respond to a Catholic ritual.

Exorcism is not and has never been limited to just one religion. We know that exorcisms are said to be effective, whichever religion or belief system they are based upon. Beliefs and rituals that could appropriately be labelled "exorcisms" are found in the traditions of almost all cultures and faiths. Clearly, the religious aspects of these ceremonies help those performing the ritual to focus their energy using a strong, powerful force that they believe in; in the case of religious exorcisms, this higher power is God.

The church might try to monopolise exorcisms, but the truth is, anyone can perform an exorcism, even a layperson. The exorcist can do this by building on their own belief system and drawing on their own spiritual beliefs, whether this is God, a spirit guide, a guardian angel, the power of a charm or crystals, or their own positive energy.

The aim of any exorcism is to free a place, object, or person from some form of negative or demonic influence, and ultimately, it is your own strength and faith that will command the demons out. It is important that you have strength of mind during the ritual; if you are fearful or half-hearted, you will not see any results.

In order to conduct any kind of exorcism, you'll need to develop your own meaningful ritual, which will allow you to exorcise objects, places, and people in a positive, compassionate, and confident way. These rituals are a world away from the dramatic, inaccurate rituals portrayed in movies and the media.

Once you have completed the ritual, do not stir things up again. Don't acknowledge the demon, don't talk to it, and don't attempt to contact it in order to see if it is still present. This can be taken as an invitation and permission to remain or return. Don't in any way attempt to re-investigate the disturbance after the exorcism; just let things naturally settle down.

Ridding a Location of a Demon

As we've already discussed, people can open themselves up to demonic hauntings in many ways, but in the case of an attachment to a house, the demon may already be there, laying dormant. When you move in, this change may be enough to unsettle or provoke the demon, or renovations could trigger a demonic haunting.

If you have a demonic presence in your house or someone else has asked for help with an entity that haunts their house, then the guide presented below will help you move the demon on. These steps should be effective against demons as well as both benign and malevolent spirits.

Before beginning the rite, ensure that you are in a fit state to do so. You should be free of stress, guilt, and anger. You should be alert, unladen by negative emotion, and not under the influence of drugs or alcohol. Although traditionally the power behind exorcisms came from a higher power, namely God, today paranormal investigators, demonologists, and spiritualists know that the power comes from within. A ritual like this is less likely to succeed if you are fearful, as we know demons feed on negative energy. If you are not emotionally fit and confident enough, then it may be better to ask someone else to lead this rite.

It is a good idea to start by cleansing the house. Start by decluttering and cleaning the house from top to bottom; this creates a positive atmosphere. Open the curtains or blinds and let the light into the house. Then you should smudge the location as described in the previous module about protection from demons. As this is more than a pre-emptive protective measure, you may want to be a little more thorough and ensure that you smudge inside of wardrobes, cupboards, crawl spaces, the attic and basement. Ensure you smudge the environment before and after the ritual.

The next step is to walk around the house or base yourself in an active area of the building and call out to the demon. Be firm and confident, and command it to leave and never return. Avoid using an angry, aggressive, or confrontational tone. Let the demon know that you mean it no harm, but make it clear that the physical world is not their place anymore and that they should return to their own realm.

You should invest a good amount of time into this step; of course, it depends on the size of the property, but about an hour is a good guide. During this time, don't let fear creep in. If you hear strange noises or experience anything odd, don't let it bother you. Ignore it; speak over it; drown it out.

What you call out is really up to you. If you are religious, then you might want to command the demon to leave in the name of God, or you might want to call upon your spirit guide or guardian angel to help push the demon out. If you have none of these, then you could focus on your own inner strength or the power of an item that holds meaning to you, such as a piece of jewellery, a crystal, or a protective object.

Remember that names hold power. If you know the name of the demon you are trying to banish, then using their name will give you greater power and control over them. Use their name frequently in your incantations.

You might want to try some of the example incantations below, but don't worry about copying them exactly. It's better to be yourself and talk in a natural and open way as you normally would.

- I consecrate and clear this space. Let nothing but joy linger here.

- I call upon you, [demon's name]. Obey my commands and leave here.

- I command you to return to the infernal realm, you are no longer welcome in this place.

- This house is protected from all evil. No negative entity will enter this house.

Once you feel a change in the atmosphere and the environment settles, you should end the ritual by once again smudging the entire building. You may also want to draw protective symbols around the house. The symbol can be anything you want; people often choose a cross, the Celtic triple knot, a pentacle, or runic symbols. Draw the symbol anywhere something could enter the house, like doors, windows, chimney breasts, and ventilation. You may also want to encircle the house with salt. Simply shake the salt out in a complete line around the outside of the building.

Freeing a Person From a Demon

Exorcising a person is a lot more serious than ridding a house of demons; if you don't practise the ritual with compassion, respect, and sensitivity, you could end up making things worse. There are three very important things you need to establish first.
The first and most important thing you need to know is whether the victim truly does need to be exorcised. We covered confirming a demonic presence in a previous module, but you really need to be sure of this before going any further.

Secondly, you categorically need their explicit and direct consent in order to perform the ritual on them. This is because an unneeded or unwanted ritual can make things worse for them, plus the ritual you have planned may not be in line with their personal beliefs.

The third thing you need to establish is whether the person is mentally stable enough to go through this process. Even if you think that the person is genuinely possessed and they have given you their explicit permission, you still need to know that they are emotionally strong enough to deal with an exorcism and that the ritual won't make things worse.

Consult the person in a calm and honest conversation in order to clarify these three points. Ensure to remove all doubt and do not pressure or rush the victim. A key part of an exorcism is evaluating the victim's claims and ensuring they are free of mental health and emotional issues and that they are not having an epileptic fit or a psychotic episode. If you are able to rule out anything supernatural, you should then support the victim in finding appropriate help.

Traditionally, people have refused to undergo an exorcism, and the exorcist has taken this to be the demon talking and gone ahead with the ritual anyway. Exorcisms performed without consent often end up being violent, aggressive, and terrifying for the victim. This is never acceptable. If it is clear that the person needs help but is refusing your assistance, then you should encourage them to speak to a professional or trusted friend or family member who can find them alternative help.

Once you've established that the victim is mentally and emotionally stable enough to continue, you need to make sure you are too. You need to be sure that you are feeling strong, confident, stress-free, rested, and not under the influence of drugs or alcohol. This ritual relies on your positive energy; if you are fearful or not emotionally fit and confident enough, then it may be better to ask someone else to lead this rite.

An exorcism should NEVER be violent or aggressive in any way. There does not even need to be any physical contact with the possessed.

In some ways, exorcising a person is very similar to exorcising a house. However, ridding a person of demonic attachment is much harder than a house. Demonic possession is a vicious cycle. The demon preys on the weak, drawn to them by their negative energy, but as the demon takes hold, its victim will become more withdrawn, depressed, and negative. This negative feedback loop will help the demon gain strength and get a tighter hold. Therefore, it might take several attempts at an exorcism to break that cycle, so don't expect instant results.

It is a good idea to start by cleansing the person. You might want to suggest that they take a herbal salt bath and use a white sage body scrub. Both salt and sage are said to be powerful substances that spiritually cleanse and drive away negative energy.

The next step is to cleanse the person using the smudging technique we covered in the previous module on protection from demons. First, ask the victim to remove all metal jewellery, belts, and their shoes. Then mentally focus your energy before lighting the tip of the sage with a match, lighter, or candle, and gently waving the smudge stick in the air until the tip begins to smoulder.

Take your smouldering smudge stick and pass it around the body so that the smoke surrounds them. Start with the area above the head and continue down to the feet; you should allow at least 10 to 15 minutes to complete this part of the ritual.

The next step is to ask the demon to leave. You should invest a good amount of time in this step. During this part of the exorcism, be sure to listen to the victim to ensure they are comfortable throughout. If at any point they want to stop or need a break, then you should allow them to take as long as they need.

In a calm and non-confrontational tone, command the demon to leave its victim's body at once. Be strong and confident in your request. Do not show any anger or frustration, and reassure the demon that you mean it no harm. Make it clear that the demon is not welcome in this world and that it should return to its own realm.

The exact phrasing that you use during this step of the rite is up to you. You should draw on your own inner strength, positivity, and beliefs. Remember that knowing a demon's name gives you power over them, so use it frequently in your incantations.

You might want to try some of the example incantations below, but don't worry about copying them exactly. It's better to be yourself and talk in a natural and open way as you normally would.

- I call upon you, [demon's name]. Obey my commands and leave this person.

- I command you to return to the infernal realm, leave this person alone.

- This person is protected from all evil. No negative entity may remain here.
- I consecrate and clear this person. Let nothing but joy linger in them.

Once you notice a change in the victim, or they indicate that they have noticed a change themselves, you should once again smudge them before smudging the whole house to ensure the negative energy is driven away for good.

Cleansing an Object of a Demon

As in the above guidelines for exorcising a person or place, when working with items with an attachment, you first need to confirm that the object is in fact hosting a demonic presence. If this is definitely the case, then ending a demonic attachment with an object is much easier than with a person, and you have a few more options to choose from.

One thing you definitely should not do is either give the item away to someone or throw it away. This doesn't solve the problem; it just transfers the negative energy to someone or somewhere else.

If you don't mind destroying the object, then the best way to deal with it is to burn the object, as fire always has been and still is used in purification rituals. Obviously, this method only works for objects that are flammable. Avoid burning plastics and other materials that release potentially toxic fumes when burned.

The best way to burn an object is to first light a fire, either outdoors or in a fireplace. Once the fire is burning well, carefully throw the object in and let it burn. Do not extinguish the fire yourself; wait for it to naturally burn out.

After the flames have died down, allow the ashes to cool down and pour salt into them. This spiritually purifying substance will ensure that the evil energy has completely left the remains of the object. Mix the salt and ashes together, place them in a container, and bury them as deep as you can in the ground.

The best place to bury the ashes is at a crossroads. Crossroads are sites where paths cross, and over time, many people's energies cross here. They are said to be very supernaturally active and a point where two realms can meet. In the UK, there is a tradition of burying criminals at crossroads, those who cannot be buried in consecrated ground.

If the object isn't flammable or can't be burned, then another option is to simply bury it and abandon it at a crossroads. Some also say you can remove the object from your home and place it on a stone, allowing this natural substance to absorb the negative energy. You can then dig a hole, place the stone in it, pour salt over it, and then bury the stone, leaving the object untouched and free of evil.

Before you bring the object back into your home, be sure to smudge it with sage as an extra precaution. Simply light your sage and, once smouldering, pass it over the object, surrounding it in the smoke.

Another method for items that can't be burned is to throw them into a living body of water, like a river or an ocean. Ideally, it should be salt water, and the faster it's moving, the better.

Whether you burn the object, throw it into water, or bury it, as a precaution, you should smudge your whole house with burning sage when you return to your home.

Scientific Theory

Energy, Fields and Frequencies

Defining Energy

The word "energy" gets used a lot during paranormal investigations. Often, people will talk about investigators having positive energy that spirits can use to manifest or produce signs they are present. You may have also heard that people with negative energy can put a damper on paranormal activity.

This use of the term energy really just refers to positive and negative "vibes." In the case of paranormal investigations, it's about someone's willingness to be enthusiastic, to get involved, and to call out to the spirits and encourage them to engage with you.

It's said that certain people radiate positive energy and others negative energy, but this sort of energy is merely a metaphor and bears no resemblance to "energy" in the scientific sense of the word. It's just people appropriating technical terms for emotional states.

While we are able to detect certain energy from the human brain in the form of electrical impulses, there's no scientific instrument that can detect either positive or negative energy emanating from the human body.

However, there is one thing that can detect and interpret this energy, and that's our bodies. A lot of what people interpret as positive and negative energy is really just sensory input that we process unconsciously. When we get a "vibe" from someone, we're simply reading their body language, attitude, posture, and many other intangibles. You may not be aware of these factors, but this is what forms your emotional reaction to a person.

For most people, the human subconscious is really good at reading the body language of other humans. We've all experienced that situation when we walk into a room where an argument has just taken place and, although the disagreement is over, we're able to pick up on a negative vibe and just know that those in the room have been arguing.

The tension that you can cut with the proverbial knife is very real, but it's an emotional experience inside our own heads based on how we observe people's behaviour, not an active field of energy. When this is done on a subconscious level, our conscious minds aren't thinking about the tensed muscles of the other people, the jaw clenching, or the other subtle movements the others are making that show their distress. Our subconscious mind takes these clues in and gives us an uncertain feeling, a vibe.

An easy thought experiment you can try is to imagine walking into that same room if you were deaf and blind. Do you think you'd still be able to pick up on that negative vibe? It should be clear that you're being affected by the things you're sensing through your five senses. Unless, of course, you are clairsentient or have psychic abilities, there is no provable scientific understanding of how this works, and it wouldn't rely on conventional energy.

As for what gives people either an outwardly positive or negative vibe, it depends on their past, their mindset, their dominant thoughts, and their perception of the world. Sometimes that energy is easily felt, and other times it manifests subtly and subconsciously.

Positive people are loving, happy, compassionate, kind, and supportive. You intuitively feel safe, happy, and relaxed around them. Their vibe is welcoming.

Negative people are judgmental and unhappy, and they like to put others down. You instinctively feel insecure, unhappy, and tense around them. Their vibe is off-putting and standoffish.

That's why, on a ghost hunt, it is important that you are radiating positive energy. After all, the spirits around you are likely to make you just as able to pick up on a negative, standoffish vibe and be drawn towards communicating with those who are positive and welcoming.

We all have our off days, but simply put, positive energy is a group of positive attitudes, emotions, and thinking patterns. So, if you're feeling restless, agitated, tired, or nervous before an investigation, you may need to take some time out to focus your thoughts and change your outlook.

It is also said that a location or haunting case can have a lot of energy. Again, this isn't energy in the scientific sense but instead refers to activity. If a location has a lot of energy, then it is very active. The term energy is used in the same way you might call a lively child "energetic." This is not an actual scientific measure of energy.

Energy in the Realm of the Paranormal

In physics, energy is a measure of work or potential that, in accordance with the law of conservation of energy, cannot be destroyed or created, only transferred or converted. By work, we mean when a force causes any form of movement or state change, such as heating, melting, evaporating, or changing its shape. For example, when we boil a kettle, electrical energy causes the kettle's element to heat up, converting electrical energy to thermal energy. This energy is then transferred into the water, making it hot and causing it to boil.

The human body requires energy in order to function. We get our energy from food in the form of chemical energy in the food we eat, which is primarily stored in carbohydrates, fats, proteins, and ethanol. The energy content of food is measured in kilojoules (kJ) or, more commonly, calories. The more calories there are in a meal, the more energy you will have to move, think, and exist.

When we eat, we normally consume more than we need to keep us going for the day. The body stores that energy as carbohydrates and sugars, like glucose. If we have an excess of energy in our system, the body stores it for longer-term use in fats and oils called lipids.

Where this becomes relevant to the world of the paranormal is when trying to determine how paranormal activity can occur. If a spirit knocks on a surface, then this is a transfer of energy. In the case of a human knocking on a surface, the potential energy stored in our cells is converted to kinetic energy in order to perform a mechanical movement. The action of our knuckles tapping the surface causes it to vibrate, which in turn vibrates the air around it, creating a sound wave that we can hear.

When it comes to ghosts and hauntings, especially poltergeist hauntings, we need to question how something without a solid, physical form can transfer its energy into sound and movement, bearing in mind that it doesn't have potential energy stored in cells like we do. Even if a ghost did have a means of storing and using energy, what would the source of that energy be? Do ghosts eat? We will attempt to answer these questions in a later chapter.

Does Negative Energy Exist?

Due to the psychology and emotional connotations of the term, it's often assumed that negative energy is bad because that's what we associate with the word "negative." However, in science, positive and negative energy are more about balance and the differences between amounts of energy.

In the previous section, we clarified what energy is and isn't, and what is meant by positive and negative energy. But can negative energy exist in the universe in a scientific sense?

Hypothetically, the answer is yes, but we've never encountered it, and how likely it is that negative energy actually exists in our universe is still unknown. The term negative energy is a concept used in physics to explain the nature of certain fields. The term negative is most frequently used when talking about attraction, which is of course most relevant when describing the effects of gravity.

The universe is very good at balancing itself out. For example, magnets have two poles, and electricity flows between the negative and positive poles. Negative energy is simply the exact opposite of ordinary energy and would move in the opposite direction from its momentum and accelerate in the opposite direction of an applied force.

All this confirms that negative energy, in the scientific sense, is no different from positive energy. We just happen to live in a universe made up of positive energy, and our positive energy is attracted to negative energy. There could be other dimensions or realities where this is flipped and the negative is dominant.

Although not strictly negative energy, this can be observed in our daily lives. Electricity is negative energy in the literal sense. It is a flow of negative particles called electrons, which are drawn towards the positively charged terminal. Despite being negative in nature, electricity is the lifeblood of our modern-day lifestyles.

In more speculative theories, negative energy is involved in wormholes, where it is needed to keep the wormhole open. If there was an equal amount of positive and negative energy, then there would be zero total energy. Negative energy, if it exists, could potentially be used to stabilise wormholes.

As a wormhole directly connects two locations that may be arbitrarily far apart in both space and time, stabilising wormholes could offer near-instantaneous travel between them.

Negative energy would also warp spacetime in the opposite way from ordinary matter, meaning that it may enable a theoretical principle for a faster-than-light (FTL) warp drive for spaceships.

The Electromagnetic Spectrum

For most paranormal investigators, electromagnetism is just something that is associated with EMF meters, a popular ghost hunting gadget that picks up electromagnetic fields. However, the frequency range that these devices are sensitive to is actually tiny, and they are only measuring a small fraction of the electromagnetic spectrum.

EMF meters are only sensitive to the electromagnetic fields generated by electrical devices, but the whole spectrum is made up of various types of radiation, including visible light, x-rays, radio waves, and even the heat generated by things like your oven.

The types of radiation that occur in different parts of the spectrum have different uses and dangers, depending on their wavelength and frequency. Radio waves have the lowest frequencies and longest wavelengths, while gamma waves have the highest frequencies and shortest wavelengths.

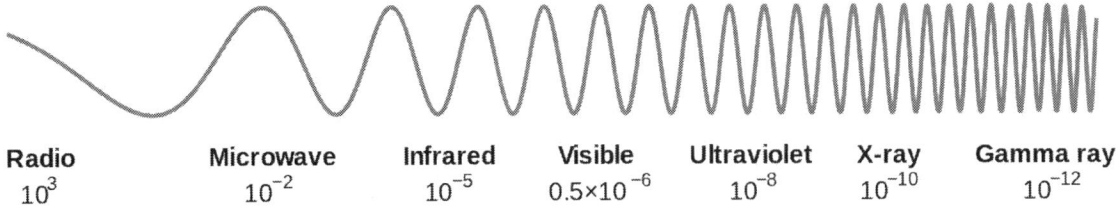

Radio	Microwave	Infrared	Visible	Ultraviolet	X-ray	Gamma ray
10^3	10^{-2}	10^{-5}	0.5×10^{-6}	10^{-8}	10^{-10}	10^{-12}

Only a very small portion of the EM spectrum is visible to the human eye in the form of white and coloured light. White light can be split up to form a spectrum using a prism, which ranges from red to blue. On either side of visible light are infrared and ultraviolet.

Infrared radiation has a longer wavelength than visible light and is therefore invisible to the human eye, although IR is used by cameras to facilitate night vision. Ultraviolet radiation, which is found naturally in sunlight, has a shorter wavelength than visible light. It is also invisible to the human eye. However, insects, birds, and some mammals can see near-UV light.

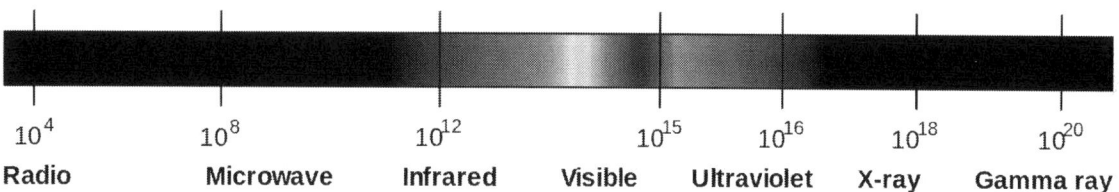

10^4	10^8	10^{12}	10^{15}	10^{16}	10^{18}	10^{20}
Radio	**Microwave**	**Infrared**	**Visible**	**Ultraviolet**	**X-ray**	**Gamma ray**

Over-exposure to certain types of electromagnetic radiation can be harmful. The higher the frequency of the radiation, the more damage it is likely to do to the body. This can range from the internal heating of body tissues and skin burns through to damage to cells causing cell death or mutations, which may lead to cancer.

Electromagnetic Field Meters

An electromagnetic field meter, or EMF meter, is one of the most popular pieces of ghost hunting equipment. They are simple to use, often consisting of nothing more than an on/off switch. They alert you when they detect an electromagnetic field from 50 to 20,000 Hz. This means it picks up the part of the EM spectrum with a wavelength ranging from about 14 to 6,000 km. The device gives instant feedback via a digital display or LED indicators, usually five.

An EMF meter can be used to communicate with spirits during a séance. When using an EMF meter you should call out to any spirits that might be present and encourage them to come forward and try to trigger the lights on the meter in order to show that they are present or to indicate an answer to a question.

There is no scientific understanding of how spirits can communicate using an EMF meter, but there are two major schools of thought within the paranormal community.

The first is that ghosts can disrupt the ambient EM field. For the EMF meter to trigger, a spirit would need to cause a spike or fluctuation in this ambient field in order to bring it up to a level that the device can detect. Quite how a spirit has the ability to manipulate an EM field is unknown and highly questionable.

The ambient EM field is a field that is created by wiring and electrical devices nearby. For this reason, an ambient field would only exist in a home or building, near power lines, or near broadcast equipment. If spirits rely on an ambient field to manipulate, then an EMF meter would be ineffective in remote outdoor locations or in isolated locations like underground.

For most homes, the average ambient EM field strength is about 0.1 milligauss (mG), which would be too weak to trigger an EMF meter. The first green light on an EMF meter lights up at around 1.5 mG, and a field of 20 mG or more would light all five LEDs.

It is often mistakenly claimed that the ambient EM field is generated by the Earth's geomagnetic field. However, this is not the case as EMF meters detect electric and magnetic fields, which oscillate at a frequency of at least 50 Hz. The magnetic field of the Earth is fundamentally different and does not oscillate in any regular pattern, so it cannot be detected by an EMF meter.

The second school of thought is that ghosts create and emit their own EM field. This is based on the fact that the human brain uses tiny electronic impulses to think and control our bodies. It's believed that this synaptic energy can live on as a disembodied consciousness after death, and it is this that EMF meters can detect.

This explanation would mean that EMF meters would work in locations where there is no ambient EM field. If electromagnetic radiation is something that naturally lives outside the body, then it avoids the issue of how a ghost could manipulate an EM field.

However, there is a flaw in this belief too, and it's one you can easily test yourself. If you hold an EMF meter near your or anyone else's head, there is no change in the EM field strength. This is because EMF meters can't detect "brainwaves." In fact, even if our brains did kick out a strong enough current, it still wouldn't be detected, as EMF meters aren't designed to detect it. Brainwaves cycle at 12.5 to 30 Hz, lower than the minimum 50 Hz threshold of an EMF meter.
If both of these two beliefs are flawed, then why are EMF meters so widely used on ghost hunts? Well, the original reason for taking an electromagnetic detecting device along on a paranormal investigation has been lost.

EMF meters were originally used to try to rule out the possibility that artificial EM fields could actually be causing people to experience certain haunting phenomena. This is because strong electromagnetic fields can induce strange experiences in people exposed to them. When field strength is high or aggressively fluctuating, it can affect the temporal lobes of the brain.

The symptoms can range from seeing light anomalies, feeling a perception of a presence, or experiencing sensations of being touched. The effect can be replicated in a lab when a subject's head is placed between the poles of an alternating current magnet in a darkened room. As the field strength is increased, the person will begin to see a faint glow and strange lights. These odd sensory anomalies could be mistaken for ghostly goings-on.

Michael Persinger, a Canadian neuroscientist, has been recreating the phenomenon in his laboratory for years. He uses a specially designed helmet that uses a weak pulsed magnetic field to induce the feeling in volunteers. According to his findings, someone exposed to these kinds of fields for just 15 minutes can start to feel like there's an invisible presence in the room.

This could explain some reports of hauntings in locations where there is an erratic or strong electromagnetic field, which is why investigators began using EMF meters to ensure that there are no constant or erratic fields in or around the property in order to validate the haunting. If you find that the location has a high or changeable field strength, you should bear in mind that people in the building may be susceptible to these fields and use methods other than human senses to validate the claims.

For example, you may want to discredit light anomalies seen with the naked eye and instead rely on evidence captured on camera, which shouldn't be affected by high-level EM fields.

Light Frequencies

The visible light spectrum is the portion of the electromagnetic spectrum that we know best. It is the range of electromagnetic radiation that a typical human eye can detect, with wavelengths ranging from about 380 to 740 nanometers. In terms of frequency, this corresponds to a band in the vicinity of 430–770 THz.

Light travels in straight lines at approximately 300,000,000 metres per second. It travels in waves that can pass through a vacuum (empty space). They do not need a substance to travel through, like sound waves do through air or a solid medium. Light can travel through transparent substances like air, glass, and water. These substances transmit light with very little absorption.

Translucent or opaque materials, like lamp shades and sunglasses, transmit some light but are not completely clear. Some wavelengths or colours of light are absorbed and do not pass through to our eyes. The material acts as a filter. All colours are absorbed except for the colour of the filter. For example, a red filter transmits red light but absorbs all the other colours. If white light is shone through a red filter, only the red wavelengths will be observed by the human eye.

The visible light range of the electromagnetic spectrum is made up of a spectrum of colours. This is a continuous range of colours. In order of increasing frequency (and decreasing wavelength), they are: red, orange, yellow, green, blue, indigo, and violet.

Visible light is made up of three primary colours: red, green, and blue, each with a different frequency. Light in these colours can be added together to make the secondary colours magenta, cyan, and yellow. All three primary colours added together make white light.

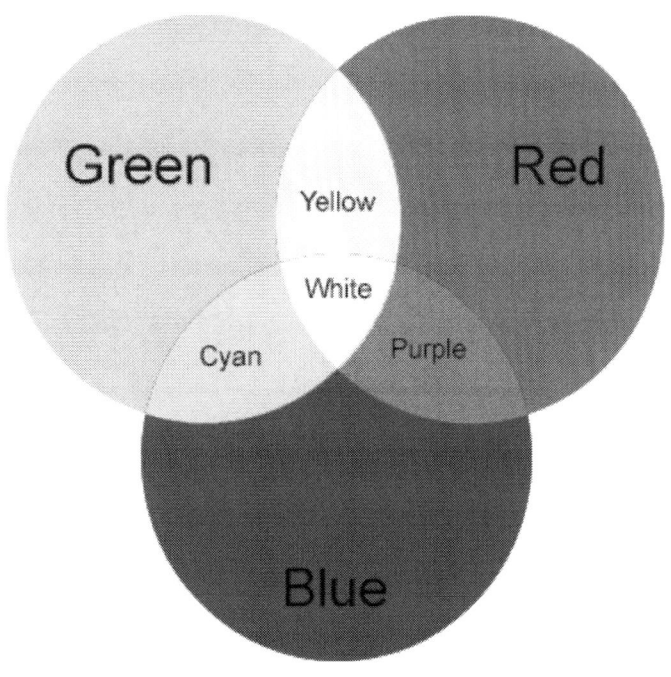

When light hits a surface, some of it is absorbed and some of it is reflected. The light that is reflected is the colour of the object. For example, grass absorbs the red, orange, yellow, blue, indigo, and violet lights. It reflects only green light and appears to be green to the eye.

In white light, black objects appear black because they absorb all colours of light and reflect none. Objects also appear black in any single colour of light if their colour is not the same as the light. For example, a blue object appears black in any other light than blue (or white, which contains blue) because there is no blue light shining on it to reflect into your eyes.

When it comes to the paranormal, there are plenty of gadgets that are used to detect electromagnetic waves in order to prove the existence of ghosts. The most commonly used of these is a camera.

Cameras are devices that focus light from an object onto a photo-sensitive material using a lens. In a traditional film camera, the photo-sensitive material was camera film. When the film absorbed light, a chemical change produced an image in the film, called the negative. This was used to produce a photograph on photosensitive paper.

In a modern camera, like a digital compact, an SLR, or the camera in a mobile phone, the photo-sensitive material is the camera's charge-coupled device (CCD). When light hits the CCD, it produces electrical impulses, which are used to produce an image file.

Camera CCDs are capable of capturing wavelengths of light from about 350nm to over 1,000nm. This is a wider range than visible light (380–740 nm), and it can capture both near infrared and ultraviolet light, which are invisible to the human eye. Camera manufacturers put a filter over the CCD to prevent this unwanted light from being captured. This filter can be removed to turn the device into a "full-spectrum camera."

Infrared

Infrared is possibly the most important range in the electromagnetic spectrum for paranormal investigators. Not only does it give investigators the power of night vision, but it also allows for heat sensing technologies like infrared thermometers and thermal imaging cameras.

Night Vision

Any night vision video camera uses an active source of illumination, which is in or near the infrared band. This is usually in the form of an external top light mounted on the camera or a small in-built illuminator on consumer camcorders. This frequency of light is just outside the visible spectrum of the human eye, but it can be picked up by the camera's sensor. So, although the scene looks dark to you, your camera will see a brightly lit space.

Video captured using this method appears in monochrome, either with a greenish tint or in black and white. This is because the camera cannot see visible light when in night vision mode. It is only sensitive to IR light, which has no colour.

The IR light source on your camera is similar to the light-emitting diode in a television remote control and in some home and commercial security systems, where a PIR (Passive InfraRed sensor) can detect movement even in a darkened room. As there are so many potential sources of this invisible light in a building, you should remember that although a room appears to be dark, there may actually be several sources of light, which could result in your camera seeing shadows that you didn't expect to see or lens flares.

As well as infrared night vision, full-spectrum cameras have also grown in popularity among ghost hunters in recent years. A full-spectrum camera is just like an ordinary camera, but as the name suggests, it can see the full light spectrum, including light in the infrared and ultraviolet frequencies that the human eye can't see.

When a full-spectrum camera is paired with an infrared light source, it too can act as a night-vision camera. However, a full-spectrum camera will still be able to see visible light and colours alongside the IR-illuminated images. Rather than being green or grey, the night vision image produced by a full spectrum camera has a pink-purple hue, which gives it a unique look when used to film investigations.

Full-spectrum cameras aren't easy to get hold of and aren't generally commercially available. This is because paranormal investigators modify their cameras to turn them into full-spectrum cameras. This can be done to pretty much any camera, whether it be a compact stills camera, a digital SLR, a camcorder, or a professional video camera. However, the modification isn't easy. It involves taking the camera apart and stripping it down to its sensor in order to remove the tiny glass filter that stops IR and UV light from hitting the sensor. There are companies in the UK, US, Australia, and other parts of the world who will modify a camera for you. A lot of these companies also sell pre-modified new and used cameras.

One of the downsides of this modification is that once the filter has been removed, the camera can't be used as a regular camera. Although some more expensive cameras do allow users to fit an external filter over the lens, which effectively temporarily converts the camera back to being a regular camera.

It's possible that some ghosts or even light anomalies are only visible in IR or UV light, a full-spectrum camera therefore increases the odds of capturing this evidence. After all, when investigating, recording the most amount of information possible is clearly beneficial, and that's exactly what a full-spectrum camera does.

Thermometers and Thermal Imaging

Infrared can be used as a way to measure the heat radiated by an object. In the case of heat loss, this is the emission of energy as electromagnetic waves. If an object is very hot, like molten metal or the filament in a lightbulb, you will see it emitting visible light, but cooler objects emit most of their energy in the infrared range. For example, hot charcoal may not give off light, but it does emit infrared, which we feel as heat.

Any object with a temperature above absolute zero (-459.67°F or -273.15°C) radiates in the infrared range. Even objects that we think of as being very cold, such as an ice cube, emit infrared. The warmer the object, the more infrared it emits.

A thermal imaging camera, or thermographic camera, to use its correct name, is a detector that gives a visual representation of the otherwise invisible infrared energy emitted by objects. Thermal infrared images let you see heat and how it is distributed.

Thermal imaging cameras have lenses, just like cameras that use visible light, but in this case the lens focuses waves from infrared energy onto an infrared sensor array. Thousands of sensors on the array convert the infrared energy into electrical signals, which are then converted into an image. The temperature of objects is indicated with colours. Hot areas show as shades of yellow, orange, and red, depending on how hot it is. Very hot areas will appear white. Cold areas will show as shades of blue, with very cold areas being black.

Thermal imaging cameras are relatively expensive but are a popular piece of ghost hunting equipment, especially since the advent of cheaper devices that work as an add-on to Apple or Android phones.

Sudden drops in temperature and cold spots are a commonly reported phenomenon in haunting cases. Some believe that cold spots are a sign that a spirit is present or even close to manifesting in a physical form. Others think these reports are caused by explainable drops in temperature caused by things like draughts or open windows. It's also possible that a perceived drop in temperature is merely a psychological response to long periods of inactivity while sitting in the dark during ghost hunts.

Whatever the reason for cold spots and sudden temperature changes, as a paranormal investigator, you're probably going to want to validate these claims and try to establish what has caused them, whether they are a result of the paranormal or not.

However, it is very important to understand that thermal imaging cameras don't measure air temperature. They only measure the temperature of the object they are pointing at.

While air does emit IR, thermal cameras are tuned to ignore the frequency range at which air emits IR waves. This is done intentionally to make the air appear transparent so that the user can effectively gauge the temperature of objects without having to worry about air temperature skewing the image.

This means that if someone reports feeling cold, a thermal camera won't give you an accurate reading of the temperature around the person.

They are also susceptible to reflection. This means that if you point the camera at a shiny or reflective surface in front of you, you may see your own heat being reflected back at the camera, which can show either a hot spot or even a full human figure, which of course can result in some undue excitement during paranormal investigations.

If a thermal camera is a bit out of your price range, then a cheaper alternative for detecting temperature fluctuations associated with hauntings is a point-and-click infrared thermometer. Like a thermal camera, they don't require any contact with the object. They simply measure the temperature of the object you're pointing it at based on the infrared radiation it is emitting. You point the device at the object and press the trigger to take a reading.

Although they are very useful for easily reading the temperature of solid objects, there is one drawback. Like thermal imaging cameras, contactless infrared thermometers can't measure air temperature, only the heat radiating from a solid surface, and like the camera version, they are also susceptible to reflection.

If you want to accurately record the air temperature, then the best tool to use is a digital thermometer, which gives you a real-time reading of the current air temperature. This type of thermometer is often built into other ghost hunting devices, such as multi-meters.

Radio Noise & White Noise

Radio noise is something that crops up often in the field of paranormal research, most often referred to as "white noise." It is beneficial to understand exactly what produces radio noise, its practical applications, and how it can affect an investigation.

If you're listening to the radio at home or in the car, the last thing you want to hear is radio noise. These unwanted noises and the hiss you hear in between radio stations are the result of random electrical signals always present in a radio receiver in addition to the desired radio signal.

Radio noise is made up of a combination of three main sources:

Radio Frequency Interference (RFI)
Manmade radio frequency interference from other sources, such as electrical switches, motors, vehicle ignition systems, computers, and other electrical devices, is picked up by the receiver's antenna. These noises are often referred to as "static".

Thermal Noise

Thermal noise is present in the receiver input circuits, caused by the random thermal motion of molecules, and thirdly, natural electromagnetic atmospheric noise.

Atmospheric Noise

Atmospheric noise, or "spherics," as it is referred to when relating to radio broadcast and reception, is created by electrical processes in the atmosphere. Primarily, this is caused by lightning discharges in thunderstorms. On a worldwide scale, 3.5 million lightning flashes occur daily (about 40 lightning flashes per second). The sum of all these lightning flashes results in atmospheric noise.

Radio noise is most commonly encountered during paranormal investigations when using a Spirit Box. These devices work by rapidly scanning through the AM, MW, and FM radio spectrums. As it does, fleeting bursts of white noise can be heard. Spirit boxes usually have various settings that allow you to tweak which bands the device scans through and how much of each frequency step you hear. This usually ranges from a hundredth of a second up to a second.

The belief is that spirits can use the snatches of radio broadcasts as well as the noise between the frequencies to communicate with the device's user. A spirit is said to be able to do this by reorganising sounds in the noise into coherent words for us to hear.

Like a lot of paranormal research, there is no scientific understanding of how an entity can cause a change to this noise, but the researcher's belief stems from countless paranormal investigations where they obtained what they believed to be valid and relevant audible responses to their questions through the device.

When using this sort of device, it is very important to ensure that any words you hear are a direct and meaningful response to your questions. These are called "intelligent responses." This is because, unless you are in a cave or well-shielded building, you will almost certainly hear fragments of speech and music from radio stations.

Some investigators actively use radio noise during their investigations. They use white noise to try to capture examples of Electronic Voice Phenomena (EVP). EVPs are disembodied voices believed to be those of spirits, which are captured using anything from an old cassette deck, reel-to-reel machine, pocket digital audio recorder, a laptop, or a mobile phone.

White noise is a specific type of noise that has equal intensity at different frequencies, giving it a constant power spectral density. It is referred to as "white" noises because the random electrical interference that creates it is spread across the whole audio spectrum of frequencies. In the same way that white light is made up of colours of all frequencies, white noise is made up of sounds of all frequencies. These random bursts of varying frequencies have an overall intensity that is constant.

Based on the theory that spirits can reorganise radio noise to form words, some investigators use a white noise source to give spirits a base of raw sound to use to form words. This is done by playing back a pre-recorded sample of white noise, by recording near a source of static noise like a television or radio, or by using a white noise signal generator to artificially produce random and constant white noise.

The drawback to using this technique is that the white noise contaminates the recording, making it hard to analyse the audio. However, some EVP experts use audio editing software like Adobe Audition and Audacity or bespoke audio filtering software to remove the white noise, leaving only the more sustained sound in the recording, which could include spirit voices.
White Noise is used to help with sleep, improve concentration, aid relaxation, and calm infants. In healthcare, it is used to treat hyperacusis, an increased sensitivity to normal environmental sounds, or to camouflage the annoyance caused by tinnitus, a ringing in the ears that occurs without any stimulus. White noise is

also used to mask background noises that might occur naturally in an environment. For example, if you live in a city, white noise could help block out noises associated with traffic.

Although all the frequencies that make up white noise are produced at equal intensity, it sounds bright and high-pitched. This hiss-like noise is due to the nature of our hearing, which doesn't sense all frequencies equally. To balance this out, there are two further common variants of white noise: pink noise and brown (or brownian) noise. These, too, could be useful during an investigation. In these two cases, the distribution of the frequencies used to make up the sound has been skewed or weighted. Pink noise is given a boost in the lower frequency range to compensate for the hiss-like property of white noise. Brown noise puts even more emphasis on the lower frequencies.

Energy in the Body

A lot of ghost-hunting gadgets claim to use electromagnetic detection methods to detect ghosts. This is a bold claim when you consider that there aren't even any devices that are capable of detecting a living human based upon their electromagnetic signature alone. However, humans do create a magnetic field and emit EM radiation, but they are very weak. For comparison, the magnetic field of the Earth is just strong enough to move the needle of a compass. Signals from the brain are a billionth of that strength.

This magnetic field can be measured using an instrument called a Superconducting Quantum Interference device. The experiment is normally conducted in a magnetically shielded room to filter out external interference. Various parts of the body can be measured. The heart generates the largest electromagnetic field in the body. The magnetic field from the brain is called the magnetoencephalggram, or MEG.

The body's internal magnetic field is generated by the extraordinary amount of internal electrical activity, which is produced in several different types of cells, including neurons (also known as nerve cells) and muscle cells. Animal electricity was discovered by Luigi Galvani around 1780 by applying electric discharges to the leg of a dead frog. The leg moved every time a discharge was given, establishing a direct connection between animal tissue and electricity.

Nerve impulses are electrical energy signals, and like all electricity, they create energy fields around the body and electromagnetic energy waves that can travel away from the body.

These "bio-photons" are emitted in the visible and ultraviolet spectrums but are too weak to be seen with the naked eye. There are creatures in the animal kingdom that are capable of seeing this energy using cells called chryptochromes, and humans have those receptors too, but the current consensus is that humans cannot sense magnetic fields or non-visible light, even on a subconscious level.

There is another frequency range of EM that the body emits, something we covered previously: infrared. Like all objects, human bodies emit thermal radiation that is dependent on their temperature. Most of the radiation emitted by the human body is in the infrared region, mainly at a wavelength of 12 microns.

The warmest parts of the body emit more thermal radiation than cooler ones, which is why you will see different coloured areas on the body when using a thermal imaging camera. Handheld infrared ear or forehead thermometers are used to probe body temperatures by detecting the infrared radiation emitted by human bodies.

Static Electricity

In a circuit, an electrical current flows between the negative and positive poles. Where there is no circuit or flowing current, we have static electricity. This is the result of an imbalance of electric charges within or on the surface of a material. The charge remains until it is able to move away by means of an electric current or electrical discharge.

The effects of static electricity are familiar to most people because they can feel, hear, and even see the spark as the excess charge is neutralised when brought close to a large electrical conductor. The familiar phenomenon of a static shock (an electrostatic discharge) is an example of this.

In the paranormal world, static electricity is used as an alternative to EMF meters in devices that radiate their own static field. They're called REM-Pods, or radiating electromagnetism pods. A REM-Pod is essentially a capacitive circuit paired with an oscillator to generate an EM field.

Traditional electromagnetic field meters used in the paranormal field are tuned to detect the fields produced by flowing currents. Because the REM-Pod radiates its own static EM field, it can detect much more, which in theory makes it easier for spirits to use the device to communicate.

The REM-Pod can detect a difference in field strength when a conductive material enters its EM field. This means it can detect things moving in and out of its fields, which, from a ghost hunter's point of view, are hopefully spirits approaching the device's telescopic antenna, which allows for 360-degree coverage.

When the devices are triggered, one of five coloured LED lights illuminates. Each of the five lights (red, green, blue, yellow, and purple) is accompanied by a distinct audible tone to indicate the strength of the field disturbance.

The technology is nothing new. The device is basically a modified theremin, a musical instrument invented by the Russian scientist Lev Sergeevich Termen in the 1920s. Unlike other musical instruments, the theremin is played without making physical contact with it. Just like the REM-Pod, the closer the musician moves their hand to the instrument's control antenna, the higher the note that is emitted.

Instrumental Transcommunication

ITC is an umbrella term that refers to all forms of spirit communication using any kind of electrical instrument. The best-known method of ITC is electronic voice phenomenon, or EVP, which is a small sub-set of the wider topic of ITC.

The term instrumental transcommunication was coined in the 1970s by Prof. Ernst Senkowski, a scientist with a background in experimental physics who went on to conduct experiments to try to find out the source of unexplained voices on audio tapes. This is of course known as EVP.

The term ITC isn't limited to audio devices. It encompasses any communication between the living and spirits or other discarnate entities through any electronic device. This can be anything from tape recorders through to computers, and in more recent years, ghost hunting gadgets such as smartphone apps.

ITC also covers visual forms of communication, normally conducted with the use of a television and video camera feedback loop, which creates the Droste effect, where a picture recursively appears within itself, or simply by observing patterns in static. One famous example of this occurred on the day of the funeral of EVP researcher Friedrich Jürgenson. His colleague had tuned his television set to an empty channel so that it just showed static. He claims that Jürgenson's face appeared on the screen.

Jürgenson himself had gained notoriety in the EVP world after he captured audio recordings of two voices while recording bird songs in the wild: one was a male, and the other was the voice of his mother. He conducted his research two decades before the term ITC was coined in the 1970s, but the field of research dates back even further.

The first known experimentation with spirit communication using electronic devices was conducted by a priest named Roberto Landell de Moura in 1910. He used a small box-like device that he could speak into, and voices would answer back. The inner workings of his box were kept secret, which is a little suspicious as Landell was a pioneer in developing voice transmission technologies.

One of the best known names involved in early ITC experimentation was the American inventor and businessman, Thomas Edison, who has been described as America's greatest inventor of all time. In the 1920s, it's believed that he was working on what has been called "Edison's telephone to the dead", but his work was never completed before his death in 1931. The device was based on the inventor's firm belief that consciousness lives on after death. He is quoted as saying, "If our personality survives, then it is strictly logical or scientific to assume that it retains memory, intellect, and other faculties and knowledge that we acquire on this earth. Therefore, if we can evolve an instrument so delicate as to be affected by our personality as it survives in the next life, such an instrument, when made available, ought to record something."

One of the most fascinating cases of early ITC was demonstrated by Marcello Bacci. Starting in 1974, over a period of about 20 years, Bacci gave public performances of his spirit communication technology to an audience in Grosseto, Italy. Audience members were given the chance to hear the voices of their deceased loved ones.

Exactly how Bacci's spirit radio worked was a closely guarded secret. All that is known is that the radio relied on white noise in the short-wave radio band. During his demonstrations, the white noise would die down, and the voice of a spirit would clearly come through.

Many sceptics tried to debunk Bacci's work, and the experiments were carried out in controlled conditions, but the results were the same, even when the radio was isolated inside a Faraday cage, which blocks all external radio and electrical signals.

Today, ITC is more actively investigated by parapsychologists and spiritualists than ever before. The array of devices available to carry out experiments is endless. Long gone are the days of secretive devices. Modern paranormal investigators can get their hands on plenty of commercially available gadgets.

The first of these modern devices was the Frank's Box, named after its creator, Frank Sumption, which he developed in 2002. There are many similar devices available on the market today. They're now generally referred to as ghost boxes or spirit boxes. The most common are the P-SB7 and P-SB11 spirit boxes.

Another popular modern form of ITC is electronic speech synthesis, like the Ovilus and Echovox. These types of devices can be quite expensive. However, there are cheaper versions available as apps for smartphones. They work as either random word generators or by generating random sounds, the phonics that make up words. It's said that spirits can affect the random nature of these devices to form intelligent responses to the user's questions.

Most devices of this type use atmospheric sensors to generate their random output. They monitor conditions such as temperature, pressure, humidity, and electromagnetic flux. It uses these signals as a random number generator, and this number is used to reference a database of words or sounds. The atmospheric sensors give the spirits a way to influence the random nature of the device.

An EMF meter can also be used as a form of ITC, but only when used for communication as opposed to taking baseline electromagnetic field measurements or looking for EM spikes. In order to use an EMF meter to communicate with spirits, the user should encourage the spirits to come forward and try to trigger the lights on the EMF meter to show that they are present or to indicate an answer to a question.

These are just a few of the most commonly used electronic devices in the ITC field, but the list doesn't end here. Over the years, there have been reports of just about every type of electrical device being used to communicate with spirits, from telephones and fax machines to battery-powered children's toys and flashlights.

Understanding Frequencies and Audio Waveforms

As a paranormal investigator practicing ITC, you'll often be required to analyse audio recorded during investigations in order to determine if any spirit voices or audible phenomena have been captured in the recording. Proper analysis of the audio requires you to understand terms like frequency, amplitude, wavelength, and pitch.

The best way to analyse a waveform is with software such as Adobe Audition or Audacity. These applications allow you to view the waveform, zoom into it, pick out sounds in the recordings, and amplify them. When looking at a waveform as a whole recording, it's hard to pick out anything useful, as the image above shows. However, it is clear to see areas of loud noise and silence.

Sound waves in a recording will normally be fluctuating vibrations consisting of many different frequencies and amplitudes, but to simplify things, we're going to introduce you to the parts of a uniform oscillating wave.

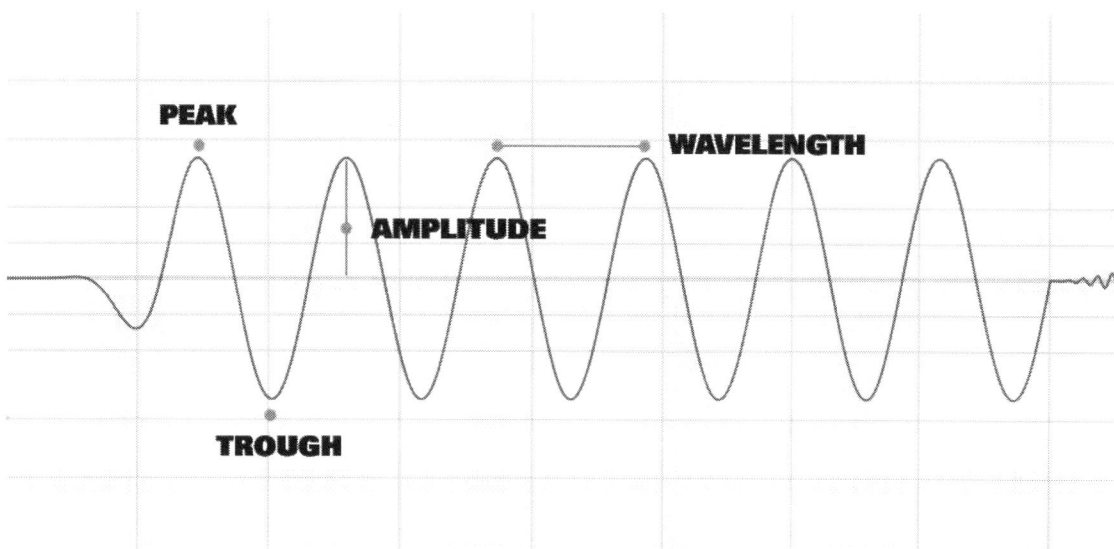

In the diagram above, you can see the important parts of a waveform, which you should understand in order to properly analyse an EVP session that you've recorded. These parts are:

Peak - the highest point above the rest position (the red line through the centre of the wave)
Trough - the lowest point below the rest position
Amplitude - the maximum displacement of a wave from its rest position
Wavelength - distance covered by a full cycle of the wave, usually measured from peak to peak or trough to trough
Another important property of a wave is its frequency, something which is commonly misunderstood in the paranormal field. It can't

be measured directly by looking at a waveform, but it can be calculated. The frequency of a waveform is what determines the pitch. We either hear the sound as low-pitched or high-pitched. It is measured in Hertz (Hz) as the number of waves passing a point each second.

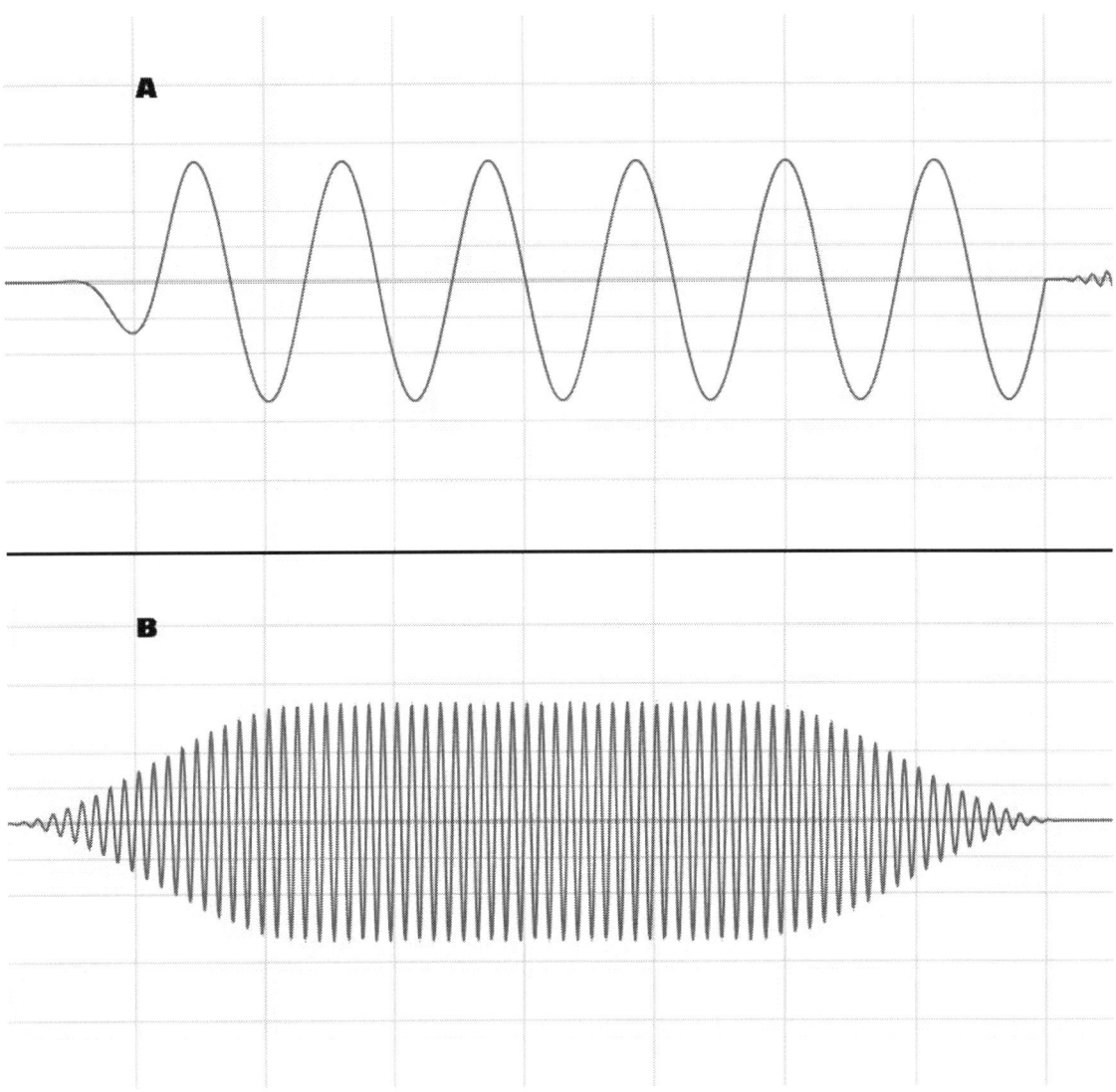

In the example above, the top waveform (A) has a lower frequency and, therefore, a lower pitch than the bottom waveform (B), which will sound higher pitched.

It seems to be a common misconception within the paranormal community that the height of a wave is an indication of its frequency. As the diagram above shows, this is not the case, as waves A and B are the same height, but the higher number of full cycles of the wave over the same time period in wave B shows that it has a higher frequency than wave A.

Below we can see two sounds, A and B. Both are made up of varying frequencies. Each of the two sounds starts at a low pitch but becomes higher. Wave B is much taller than wave A. This indicates that it has a higher amplitude, measured in decibels (dB).

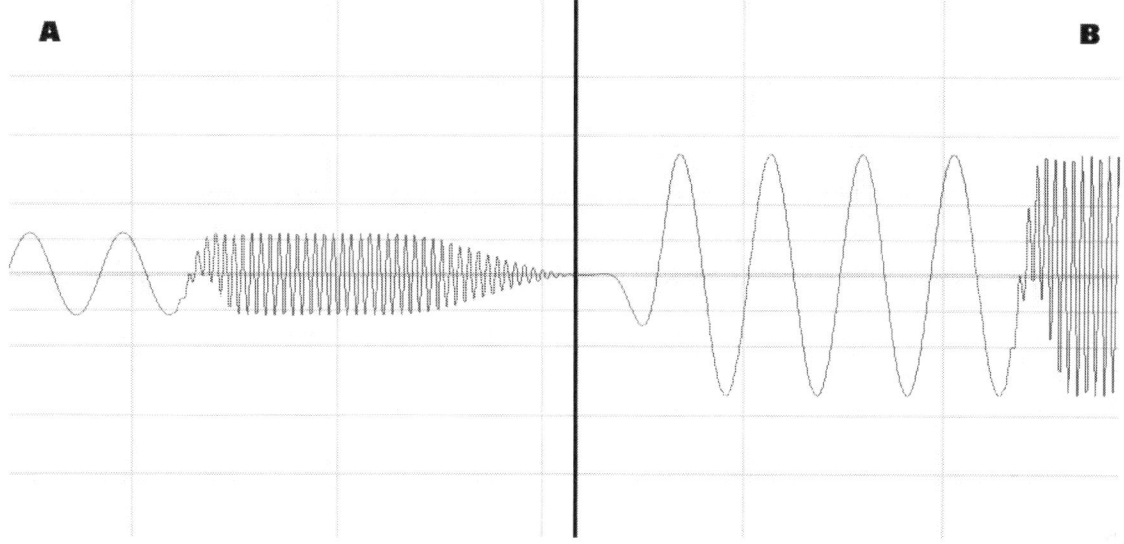

The amplitude of a sound wave determines its volume. We can tell by looking at the diagram above that wave A is quiet while wave B is loud.

When analysing the audio in order to pick out EVPs, you will most likely amplify the recording to see its features more clearly. Amplifying the audio increases its amplitude, making the wave appear taller, but it doesn't affect the waveform's frequency or wavelength. These two properties are independent of amplitude.

In reality, your waveforms won't be as clear as these examples, especially when dealing with speech, as every voice has a different pitch and words are made up of various different sounds and tones that merge into one erratic waveform that may also include background noise.

The human ear detects sound. Sound waves enter the ear canal and cause the eardrum to vibrate. Three small bones transmit these vibrations to the cochlea. This produces electrical signals, which pass through the auditory nerve to the brain, where they are interpreted as sound.

Ultrasound & Infrasound

Ultrasound

Ultrasound waves have a frequency higher than 20,000 Hz, which is outside the upper limit of human hearing. The cochlea in the human ear is only stimulated by a limited range of frequencies. This means that humans can only hear certain frequencies. The range of normal human hearing is 20 to 20,000 Hz, but some animals like dogs can hear the ultrasound.

Ultrasound has several applications in healthcare. It is used to break kidney stones. The vibrations caused by the ultrasound shake apart kidney stones, breaking them up. The principle is the same as the opera singer's trick, where a glass may shatter if the singer makes a high-pitched sound near the glass. It is also used to scan the inside of the body, creating a picture of something that cannot be seen directly, such as an unborn baby in the womb.

Ultrasound occurs in almost every situation. There is noise around us all the time, but we may not be hearing all of it. Any sort of movement can create a vibration, which in turn creates sound waves. These can be in the ultrasound range as well as being audible. A lot of the electrical equipment we use on a daily basis emits ultrasound.

Microphones, including those in smartphones and digital audio recorders, are designed specifically to pick up the frequency range that roughly matches the range that the human ear can hear. Humans can hear sounds between 20 and 20,000 Hz, but most microphones aren't quite as sensitive and fall within this range at about 50 to 18 kHz. Some very expensive specialist microphones are able to pick up audio outside of this range, but you wouldn't find this sort of microphone in any consumer device.

This means that if you are using a digital audio recorder to try to capture EVPs, you know that the device isn't going to pick up any sounds that you can't hear with your own ears. Of course, this is pretty logical anyway, as if a device did catch something outside of your ear's frequency range, you wouldn't be able to hear it when you played it back.

So, if there is an EVP in your audio recording, then you know it must have been created in one of two ways:

1. The sound was audible at the time of recording and was extremely quiet. It must have been either very close to the microphone or nearer to the microphone than you were, so it picked up the sound but you didn't. Or the device is more sensitive to low-level noise than your ear.

2. The sound was not audible at the time but has made its way into the recording via a form of electrical interference, which affects either the device's circuitry or storage medium.

It's not commonly practiced, but some paranormal investigation teams use ultrasound detectors as part of their investigations. These types of detectors are mainly used to pick up ultrasound signals emitted by bats, insects, or other animals. These devices are capable of translating high frequencies into audible sounds we can hear in real time, as well as recording them on a memory card.

This device could be used during paranormal investigations to obtain a baseline reading of ultrasound at the location, but also as a means of capturing EVPs at a higher frequency than we can normally hear or capture using a recording device.

Infrasound

Infrasound is a very low-frequency sound vibrating from 0.1 to 20 Hz. It's below the human range of hearing, and it is a cause of mistaken reports of paranormal activity. These low-frequency vibrations have been known to cause people to report discomfort in the form of disorientation, feeling panicked, and an increased heart rate and blood pressure.

In extreme cases, infrasound has been attributed to feelings of depression, a general feeling of unease, as well as visions of apparitions.

Scientists researching the low-frequency noise created by wind turbines and traffic noise discovered the effects of infrasound on humans. They found a link between infrasound and the sensations often described as getting chills down the spine.

As specialist audio equipment is required to detect infrasound, it can be hard to eliminate this from your investigation. However, keeping doors and windows closed will help to keep these frequencies out of the building. It should also be noted that some machinery and even fans can produce the low frequencies associated with infrasound. This is another reason why care should be taken to turn off any electrical equipment that could interfere with your investigation.

The link between infrasound and paranormal activity was first researched by some of the early paranormal investigators, including Harry Price, who would make a basic tilt switch using mercury in order to detect tremors that could produce infrasound waves.

In 1980 by Vic Tandy, an experimental officer and part-time lecturer in the school of international studies and law at Coventry University in the UK. He was working alone late one night in a lab, which has a reputation for being haunted. He reported feeling anxious and claimed he could see dark objects out of the corner of his eye, but when he turned to face the greyish blob, there was nothing there.

The next day, the researcher noticed what some might describe as poltergeist activity. He was working on his fencing sword, which is made of a lightweight, flexible metal. He had the handle of the foil held in a vice on his desk when he noticed that the blade started vibrating, even though nothing was touching it.

In 2003, an experiment using infrasound was carried out in London. Infrasound was played during a concert in the Purcell Room. Afterwards, the audience was interviewed, and their responses were analysed by psychologists. On average, infrasound boosted the number of strange experiences by around 22% and caused the concertgoers to report feelings of sorrow, coldness, and anxiety.

SLS Cameras

Kinect SLS Cameras are becoming more and more popular with paranormal investigators. The camera works by projecting its own invisible infrared laser grid over a wide field of view. The grid is made up of over one million tiny dots. This structured grid of laser dots is what gives the device its name, SLS, or Structured Light Sensor. The camera's sensor is able to calculate the distance between these infrared dots in order to build a three-dimensional model of its view.

This three-dimensional model doesn't rely on visible light or colours. Instead, it "sees" a physical representation of the space and objects around it. This means that if something moves within its field of view, there will be a change in the distance between the dots, which the camera recognises as movement.

The reason this technology is used by paranormal investigators is that the camera's software has the ability to recognise and highlight human figures in the images it captures. The software "sees" people by detecting limbs and movement.

Everything the camera sees is displayed in real time on a screen, usually a connected tablet, and any figures it detects are highlighted by overlaying a bright green stick figure, which is why the device is sometimes called an SLS Stickman Camera.

Some think that this "skeletal movement tracking" is not only able to recognise human forms but also detect human-shaped paranormal entities that are invisible to the naked eye. The technology is appealing to paranormal investigators, as the video evidence captured can be recorded directly to the camera or a memory card.

Another plus for paranormal investigators is that SLS cameras work in total darkness as well as in full daylight. Like a lot of ghost hunting gadgets, SLS Kinect Cameras are based on technology that was primarily built for another purpose. Their main component is a Microsoft Kinect, a piece of hardware that adds motion control to the Xbox 360 and later the Xbox One.

The Kinect sensor is modified, which enables it to run off of a battery pack to make the device portable, and is adapted to connect to a tablet, usually one running Windows 10 with the Kinect SLS software installed.

It is normally the now-out-of-production first generation Kinect sensors that are used to make SLS cameras, those that were compatible with Xbox 360. Some more advanced devices use second-generation sensors that have the added ability to detect body heat, changes in facial expression, and heart rates. Of course, none of these upgrades are particularly useful in the spirit world.

The Kinect was originally designed to spot a human body and track it in great detail, but ever since the release of the Kinect motion sensor controllers in 2010, gamers have found that the device sometimes marked out stick figures at random, behind them or in their house, when there was no one there with them.

The problem with SLS cameras for ghost hunting is that they are designed to do something else. Its original task is very specific, and the device itself isn't foolproof. Many gamers experience motion control failing while playing games from time to time. Sometimes it fails to detect players in the room. Other times, it misidentifies something else as a player.

The software is looking for a human form. It expects to see one or more players in its field of view. This is why gamers found that the camera would spot bodies that weren't there. The software's algorithm has been trained by developers to detect people standing in front of the camera. The device doesn't have the ability to detect ghosts included in its algorithm. Nobody has ever been able to train an algorithm in this way.

Paranormal investigators use this technology in the hopes that they will see a stickman, but that is literally all the device is designed to do - draw a stickman over anything even remotely human-shaped and track its movement. However, the movement of the stick figures of ghosts that the camera draws is often very erratic. They twitch and dance around. They're often not in scale with their surroundings, making them look too small, too big, or as if they're floating in the air. They even spontaneously change positions.

As paranormal investigators normally use handheld SLS cameras, you'll notice that when the camera moves considerably, the figure it has detected vanishes. This is because with a change of angle, whatever the software is mistaking for a human no longer looks like a human. That's the reason why the stick figures are always erratic, contorted, or in strange positions.
Walking around with the camera will almost certainly give you false positives because the grid of invisible dots the camera uses to "see" will be constantly moving and distorting, plus the camera only has an intended range of about three metres, so anything beyond that is probably a false positive.

Oscilloscopes

An oscilloscope is a type of electronic test instrument that displays a real-time visual representation (the waveform) of an electrical signal. The graphical representation shows the electrical signal in a similar way to that of an audio waveform that we've looked at previously, with the X-axes representing time and the Y-axes showing the signal's voltage. This allows you to see the amplitude, frequency, and wavelength of the wave.

Oscilloscopes are mainly used for analysing and debugging circuits, but they also have a use in the paranormal field. Using an oscilloscope for ITC is similar to using an EMF meter. The hope is that any spirits present can somehow manipulate the electrical signal being displayed or generate their own in order to communicate. A modern oscilloscope will show you the waveform on an FFT digital screen. The scope usually has a ground clip that clips to the negative terminal of a circuit and a probe that clips to or is pushed onto the positive terminal.

In the paranormal field, investigators often connect allegedly haunted items to an oscilloscope. This can be done in one of two ways:

1. The ground clip is connected to a grounded contact, like a radiator, water pipe, or similar. The probe is clipped onto the item itself. This is then measuring the voltage potential between the object and ground. You should make sure the item is not on a grounded surface.

2. Both clips are placed on opposite sides of the item in the hopes that an electrical current might flow across the object. When using this method, if the object is conductive, you should see a resistance reading on the device. If it is non-conductive, there will still be some waveform activity, but it will be minimal.

You can also use an oscilloscope with an artificial signal generator. This is the equivalent of using white noise in an EVP experiment. It gives the spirits the raw waves that they can then hopefully manipulate in some way. You can even ground the oscilloscope and connect the probe to any object in the vicinity of your investigation.

Whichever method you choose, you should then call out to any spirits that might be present and encourage them to communicate with you. You may find that they are able to change the amplitude or frequency of the waveform or change the object's resistivity.

If a spirit does become responsive, you may be able to ask it to change the shape of the waveform, increase or decrease its frequency, or completely drop the amplitude and "flat line" the scope.

Consciousness and the Soul

Can science shed any light on the age-old debate about life after death and the paranormal? Well, interestingly, it seems that scientists are using the exact same branch of science to support their conflicting arguments.

Cosmologist Sean Carroll thinks that quantum field theory proves that human consciousness cannot live outside the body after death, while British physicist Sir Roger Penrose says that this same branch of science proves that consciousness is a property of the universe and can live outside the body.

Sean Carroll is just one in a long line of scientists to make the outright claim that there is no such thing as an afterlife or ghosts. It's agreed upon that in order for there to be an afterlife, consciousness would need to be entirely separate from our physical body. The physicist from the California Institute of Technology argues that this is not the case.

He says, "Claims that some form of consciousness persists after our bodies die and decay into their constituent atoms face one huge, insuperable obstacle: the laws of physics underlying everyday life are completely understood, and there's no way within those laws to allow for the information stored in our brains to persist after we die."

However, Sir Roger Penrose, an advocate for the quantum consciousness theory, argues that consciousness, like all forms of energy, can't be destroyed and therefore lives on outside of the body when someone dies. Penrose first proposed that a quantum consciousness might exist in his 1989 book 'The Emperor's New Mind'.

Sir Penrose thinks that when a person temporarily dies, their conscious energy is released into the universe, only to return to the body's cells if the person is revived and brought back to life. This, he says, explains how people have near-death experiences.

Researchers at the Institute for Physics in Munich also subscribe to Roger Penrose's theory and say that our awareness of a physical universe is just a perception. When we die, there is an infinite existence beyond the physical universe in the form of energy.

Dr. Hans-Peter Dürr, former head of the institute, said, "What we consider the here and now, this world, it is actually just the material level that is comprehensible. The beyond is an infinite reality that is much bigger."

So, if scientists like Dürr and Penrose are correct, when the body dies, the spiritual energy continues, and Dr. Dürr adds, "In this way, I am immortal."

Whichever side of the argument you support, the evidence that supports it is rooted in quantum field theory, and this is where the debate gets interesting. While one group of scientists argues that quantum field theory proves that there is a shared consciousness and life after death, the opposing group uses the same branch of physics to prove their argument that consciousness cannot live outside the body after death.

We all understand the concept of consciousness. We know when we're conscious because we hear our conscious thoughts and understand the difference between being asleep and awake. Consciousness is often defined as the ability to observe yourself.

The American medical doctor and scientist, Robert Lanza, wrote in an article that "we are all the ephemeral forms of a consciousness greater than ourselves." He claims that the mind of every human being is instantly connected to each other, "a part of every mind existing in space and time."

The principles of this belief are based on our current quantum mechanical view of reality, and for this reason it has been called quantum consciousness or the quantum mind.

If the existence of a quantum consciousness can be proven, then it will answer some long-debated questions about the afterlife and even the existence of ghosts. If our souls can live outside the body as some form of mental energy, then there's the potential for the living to pick up on the energy of the dead in the form of ghosts or spirits.

Penrose says that the energy leaves the body after a person dies. He said, "If the patient dies, it's possible that this quantum information can exist outside the body, perhaps indefinitely, as a soul." So, in order for our consciousness to survive after death, it would need to exist as a quantum field of its own.

Of course, this isn't the only theory about how consciousness works. The more generally accepted theory is that consciousness is a mechanistic byproduct of our incredible brains. Neuroscientist Giulio Tononi of the University of Wisconsin-Madison has proposed the integrated information theory, which states that consciousness is the result of the vast amount of information that comes into our brain. Our brain interweaves a sophisticated information web from sensory and cognitive inputs.

Shared Quantum Consciousness

In theoretical physics, quantum field theory is a framework that encompasses our understanding of subatomic particles and gives us a mathematical model that describes the types of fields that make up these subatomic, or quantum, particles. The scientists also look at the bigger field of quantum mechanics, which includes some very strange phenomena such as quantum entanglement and superposition.

Quantum field theory states that there is one field for each type of particle. This means all of the photons, which make up light, in the universe are part of one field. All electrons make up another field. The same is true for gravitons and every other type of subatomic particle.

British physicist Sir Roger Penrose believes that this theory, combined with the first law of thermodynamics, which states that energy cannot be created nor destroyed, means that, like other quantum fields of energies, there is one uniform field of consciousness that exists throughout the universe and that cannot be destroyed.

If you believe in a shared consciousness, this would mean that all consciousness that has ever existed and will ever exist is present in the universe right now. Sir Penrose says that he believes consciousness to be packets of information stored at a subatomic level. The scientist believes that this mental energy is stored in microtubules within the cells of our brains.

He believes that these protein strands reside inside the neurons in our brains and can store and process information and memory. Apparently, these microtubules are quantum devices where information comes together into an instantaneous calculation, called "quantum coherence."

Many other scientists have suggested that quantum effects are indeed involved in the process of consciousness, but even those who advocate this belief admit that the hypothesis remains unproven. Until they make a prediction that is tested by experiments, the hypotheses aren't based on empirical evidence. Some experts go as far as saying that the hypothesis is possibly unprovable.

Penrose's theory has been criticised by some, who say the brain is too warm and wet to sustain the quantum processes. The effects would be destroyed due to a process called decoherence, which is expected to be extremely rapid in living cells. Physicist and cosmologist Max Tegmark calculated that the brain can't process information as fast as it would have to to make this theory possible.

Others who oppose the theory do so on the basis that if "spirit particles" or mental energy exist, then we should be able to detect it, which we haven't. Adrian Kent of the University of Cambridge estimates that there is just a 3% likelihood that we will be able to experimentally detect a link between consciousness and quantum theory in the next 50 years.

Professor Brian Cox stated that if some kind of spiritual energy existed, the experiments at CERN (the European Centre for Nuclear Research) should have detected it using the Large Hadron Collider (LHC), the world's biggest and most complex science experiment, a particle accelerator 17 miles in circumference built underground on the border of France and Switzerland.

Professor Cox said, "If we want some sort of pattern that carries information about our living cells to persist, then we must specify precisely what medium carries that pattern and how it interacts with the matter particles out of which our bodies are made."

Talking about this proposed conscious energy, Brian said, "It must interact with the particles out of which our bodies are made. And seeing as we've made high-precision measurements of the ways that particles interact, then my assertion is there can be no such thing as an energy source that's driving our bodies."

If Professor Cox is right, then all this means that there is no "life force" within us with its own distinct energy that can leave the body to live on as a ghost or spirit after the body has died.

You may be thinking that perhaps these "spirit particles" simply can't be detected. Well, that's possible, but if they can't be detected, then this raises questions about how these particles interact with other particles so as to exert their influence on the human brain in order to give rise to consciousness.

From a paranormal standpoint, if ghosts are manifestations of this spirit energy, but this energy cannot be detected, then a ghost wouldn't be able to interact with its surroundings. Not only does this mean poltergeist activity wouldn't be possible, but it would also mean that ghosts wouldn't reflect light and would therefore not be visible to the naked eye. They would also be unable to manipulate the air in order to produce the sound waves required for speech.

But many, including Roger Penrose, believe that we're not able to detect this energy due to the weird properties of quantum mechanics. There's one odd principle in quantum mechanics known as the observer effect that nobody really understands. As nobody understands the nature of consciousness either, many think the two could be linked.

The Observer Effect

One of the strangest phenomena in quantum physics is the observer effect, which can be demonstrated using the double-slit experiment, the outcome of which is often described as mysterious, a term not often used in the scientific world.

The reason for this label is because the outcome of the experiment depends on whether we observe or measure the results.

The experiment involves shining a beam of light at a panel with two parallel slits in it. Some of this light passes through the slits, forming two paths. The emerging light from the slits acts like waves. They interfere with each other. The interference can be seen when the light hits a second panel as a series of alternating brighter and darker spots. The pattern appears brighter where the waves converge and reinforce each other.

This experiment shows us that photons, which are particles of light, can behave like waves as well as particles. The same test can be carried out on quantum particles, like electrons, and can be used to prove that these tiny subatomic particles also behave like waves and particles at the same time. It's called wave-particle duality.

Where this starts getting weird is when you fire a single electron towards the slits. Although there is only one particle at a time, over time, the same interference pattern builds up on the panel. This implies that the particle passes simultaneously through both slits and interferes with itself. This phenomenon of being in two places at once is known as a superposition state.

When scientists put a detector behind the slits to try to establish which slit the electron had passed through, they encountered something very odd. Observing the experiment in this way seemed to force the particle to pass through one specific slit, not both. However, when this happens, the interference vanishes.

So, just by observing the electron's path in a way that doesn't disturb the particle's motion, we change the outcome. Physicist Pascual Jordan said in the 1920s that "observations not only disturb what has to be measured, they produce it. The electron is forced to a decision. We compel it to assume a definite position."

If the way the world behaves at this fundamental quantum level can change depending on whether we observe it or not, then what does this mean for reality as a whole?

Sir Roger Penrose thinks that the microtubules in our brain are capable of changing their state in response to these peculiar quantum events. He proposes that they could even enter a superposition state themselves, like the particles in the double-slit experiment. Could this be how our brains hold two mutually exclusive ideas at the same time?

Phosphorus atoms are common in living cells in the form of phosphate ions, which means they've bonded with an oxygen atom. These cells are able to place the ions into groups. Matthew Fisher from the University of California thinks that pairs of these phosphate ions might enter an entangled state. This is another weird phenomenon associated with quantum mechanics.

The nucleus of phosphorus atoms has a property called spin. When two particles are in an entangled state, the spin of each atom cannot be described independently of the state of the other, even when the particles are separated by a large distance. This, of course, supports the theory of quantum consciousness and massively increases the processing power of the brain.

Penrose thinks that our ability to perceive the world around us and process as much information as we do instantaneously far exceeds the capabilities of any computer currently in existence, but an emerging technology known as quantum computers is predicted to one day be capable of accomplishing much more than regular binary computers. Perhaps this type of computer could match our own cognitive ability and may even form its own consciousness.
Sir Penrose speculates that even if you connected every traditional computer in the world, it's unlikely that it would create consciousness, but he thinks a quantum computer probably could become conscious.

There is currently no evidence to support Penrose's theory that our consciousness depends upon superpositioned particles within our neurons, but oddly, the use of lithium-based drugs to treat bipolar disorder could be a clue that there is some truth in the theory.

Although lithium is widely used to treat these sorts of mental disorders, no one is really sure how they work, but a scientific paper noted that lithium had different effects on the behaviour of rats depending on what variant, or isotope, of lithium was being used. The differences were noted even though different isotopes behave almost identically in a biochemical system.

If lithium worked like a conventional drug, the isotopes should all have had the same effect. However, atoms of different isotopes can have different spins, and Matthew Fisher thinks that this quantum property might affect the way lithium drugs work.

Although Fisher isn't a supporter of quantum consciousness, the fact that the differing quantum properties of a drug can affect the brain in different ways leans towards the belief that our brains work on a quantum level.

All this brings us back to our mythical spirit particles, which we now know must exist as a unified field like other types of particles. If this fundamental field of unified mental energy exists and can interact with our brain chemistry but can't be measured because of superpositioning and the observer effect, then this could explain why we can't detect, photograph, or otherwise measure ghosts or paranormal activity.

The Weight of the Soul

We've talked about immeasurable and intangible energy resulting in human consciousness, but some researchers think that the soul is measurable. In fact, they think it weighs exactly 21g and that it can be detected escaping the body after death.

This figure was calculated back in 1907 by Duncan MacDougall, a doctor working in Haverhill, Massachusetts. He spent much of his career trying to find evidence of the human soul, with the ultimate aim of capturing an image of it within the body using x-ray.

His most notable work is based around his belief that if humans have a soul, then it must exist in the body as some kind of material, and that material must weigh something. In order to test this, MacDougall converted a hospital bed into weighing scales so that he could measure the change in weight of a patient at the moment of their death.

MacDougall had opted to pick patients who were dying of tuberculosis. This was because the bed balance was sensitive, and any muscular movement or flailing around at the time of death could affect his results. Writing about his experiment in the American Medical Journal, he said, "It seemed to me best to select a patient dying with a disease that produces great exhaustion, the death occurring with little or no muscular movement, because in such a case, the beam could be kept more perfectly at balance and any loss occurring readily noted."

Because the patient was lying on a bed, any bowel movements or urination at death did not skew the results, as that all stayed on the bed, but should anything leave the bed, like the soul, MacDougall's experiment would detect it. After completing several tests, MacDougall found that the human body lost up to three-fourths of an ounce upon death, which is equal to 21g. He believed this was the weight of the soul departing.

To back up his findings further, he conducted the same experiment on 15 dying dogs. This was because he didn't believe that dogs have souls, and his experiments showed that dogs didn't lose any weight after death. He wrote in his paper, "Here we have experimental demonstration that a substance capable of being weighed does leave the body at death."

However, MacDougall's experiment has since been heavily criticised and even described as an embarrassment. MacDougall's sample size was small. He only managed to obtain permission to test his theory on six dying people. His scales were inaccurate, and his data varied dramatically. He failed to consistently pinpoint the exact time of death, and the time taken for the weight loss to occur ranged from an immediate drop in weight to a drop over several minutes.

He responded to this criticism by saying, "The soul's weight is removed from the body virtually at the instant of the last breath, though in persons of sluggish temperament, it may remain in the body for a full minute."

The more likely explanation for the loss of weight in dead bodies that MacDougall was recording was down to tiny, intercellular structures called lysosomes that release enzymes to break the body down into gases and liquids. These gases would escape the bed into the air, and the liquids would evaporate.

The Anatomy of a Ghost

We all know that in the land of the living, humans are mostly made up of water, but what happens when someone comes back from beyond the grave? How do they manifest into a ghost, and what are spirits physically made of?

The defining property of a ghost is its lack of flesh. It's not made up of organic matter, blood, and organs like a living human. But if people are able to sense the presence of a ghost, detect them with ghost hunting gadgets, or even see an apparition, then there must be something measurable and tangible that creates them.

To answer this question, we first need to break ghosts down into a couple of types of hauntings. There's a belief within the paranormal world that some ghosts are intelligent and capable of interacting with their surroundings, and then there are residual hauntings, which are said to merely be past events being replayed.

Residual hauntings are thought to be an imprint of energy that has been left behind by someone who suffered a tragic, traumatic, or premature death, usually a murder, suicide, or execution. The energy used by the body and the brain in resisting death can be so immense that those events can be replayed either on the anniversary of the event, when atmospheric conditions are similar, or when someone is susceptible to or in tune with that energy. The energy of strong positive or negative emotions may also cling to its surroundings.

The phenomenon is known as "stone tape theory" due to the belief that energy is captured and stored like video recordings in the surrounding bricks, woodwork, stone, and possibly even the soil. When the conditions are right, these materials release this energy, and you sense or see the event occur in exactly the same position as it did years ago.

As residual hauntings represent nothing more than a reflection of the past, you can't communicate with them. The visions seen are not aware of their surroundings. They cannot interact with you and are not aware of your presence.

Whatever form of energy is responsible for residual hauntings, it's clear that they don't have a physical presence as they don't interact with their surroundings, and apparitions are often seen to pass through walls, often in locations where a door has been bricked up. The ghosts relive the actions they performed when they were alive.

But some parapsychologists think that if we were to define ghosts as non-physical spirits that can't interact with their surroundings or the physical world around them, then it would be impossible to see one or interact with one in any way. This suggests that if ghosts can't interact with their surroundings, that would include not just objects, buildings, and people, but would also mean they can't interact with the air, light, and other forms of electromagnetic energy around them. Light would not be able to hit a non-physical spirit and bounce off, which would mean they would not be visible to the human eye. They would not be able to interact with the air around them, making speech and sound impossible.

When it comes to intelligent hauntings, it's a little different. These types of hauntings are the classic "ghost." They can reportedly move objects, push or touch people, slam doors, and even throw objects across a room. So clearly, when they manifest, there is some kind of physical force behind them.

Many paranormal researchers believe that when someone dies, they continue to live on outside of their body as a form of electromagnetic energy, similar to the electrical impulses in the human brain. Some think that it is this EM energy that is responsible for ghosts. This is why ghost hunters often use electromagnetic field meters to detect the presence of ghosts.

However, as we learned in the previous chapter, there are those who dispute the idea of energy living outside the body, notably Professor Brian Cox, who thinks that the Large Hadron Collider has proved that there is no unknown or undiscovered psychic energy that is driving the body.

If there were some kind of force or energy within our bodies that controlled our limbs and gave us our "life force," then we should be able to detect that energy interacting with the atoms within our bodies, but we can't, which would suggest this force doesn't exist.

Paranormal investigators would argue that the paranormal falls outside of the realms of normal science and that it is by its very nature unmeasurable, but a sceptic would challenge this with the statement that "the unmeasurable is essentially the non-existent."

The Physics of Haunting

A lot of the areas of study in the field of physics relate to cause and effect. As we learned previously, for any form of movement or state change, such as heating, melting, evaporating, or changing shape, a transfer or conversion of energy must occur.

The law of conservation of energy states that energy cannot be destroyed or created, which means that if you knock on a hard surface or push something over, some of the chemical energy from your body is used up. When it comes to hauntings, it is harder to establish where the required energy comes from.

In the case of poltergeist activity, if something is pushed, thrown, or broken and the energy to perform this work isn't coming from somewhere else, then the energy has been created, which is a violation of the law of conservation of energy.

Another form of energy transfer we've discussed is when light reflects off of an object and is focused by your eye onto your retina. This part of the eye contains cells that are sensitive to light. The energy of the light is converted by these cells into electrical impulses when they absorb light. These impulses are passed along the optic nerve to your brain, which interprets them as a vision of the object.

This whole process is pinned on the fact that an object can reflect light. If it couldn't, then the light would pass straight through it and it would be invisible. There are countless reports of ghosts walking through walls and solid objects, which means they don't have a physical form and are incapable of reflecting light, and the mechanics of how they are seen are unknown.

Sound also requires a physical form. When we speak, small bands of tissue on our voice box expand and contract as the air from our lungs rushes through them, causing the bands to vibrate. The vibration makes the air around us vibrate, and the air vibrations enter the ears of those around us and vibrate the eardrum, which passes the signals to the brain through the auditory nerve, and our brain interprets these signals as sound.

For a ghost to be able to speak or make a sound, it needs a physical form so that it can create the vibrations in the air required to transmit sound.

These factors are a sticking point. If an apparition is fundamentally unable to be seen due to its inability to reflect light, cannot be heard, and is unable to move anything, then how and why do so many people report experiencing these things?

There are a lot of inconsistencies when it comes to which materials spirits can manipulate, and ghost stories typically get this all wrong. In almost all ghost reports, the spirit switches states. Sometimes ghosts can interact with their surroundings. They're able to move objects, be seen by the human eye, or communicate using sound. Other times, spirits can pass through solid objects seemingly at will. Think of Casper the Friendly Ghost. He can typically pass through walls but interacts with solid objects.

The only possible plausible explanation is that ghosts change states. Whether this change occurs at will or is the result of environmental or atmospheric conditions is unknown. This is an area of research that you may wish to investigate further.

Perhaps the truth is that it doesn't really matter. While some ghost sightings can be written off as hoaxes, the majority of ghost sightings come from people who genuinely believe they have seen something supernatural. So, whether ghosts are electromagnetic energy, a reflection of the past, or a trick of the mind, you can't take the experience away from someone who has witnessed a ghost.

Alternative Causes for Physical Movement

You must have experienced that phenomenon when you're sitting at home and suddenly something on a shelf falls off for no reason. There's no one near it, and it's been sitting on that shelf for months. Why should it randomly fall now? Is it paranormal, is there a spiritual meaning, or is there a rational explanation for these items' unexpected movements?

There are plenty of reasons why this might happen. The object could have been perched precariously in the first place, meaning the slightest nudge or draught could cause it to fall over.

Items can also fall off of a piece of furniture over time due to tiny forces generated from within the home, things like the vibration from a desktop fan, air conditioner, plumbing, or a nearby washing machine. Even a sudden change in air pressure due to opening a door or window could cause an object to topple over.

There are also plenty of external sources that can cause vibrations, like road works outside the house, heavy traffic passing by, an earthquake, low-flying aircraft, or a gust of wind through an open window. In fact, even with the windows closed, a strong gust of wind can affect the pressure inside due to the elasticity of the glass.

A gust of wind or an earthquake is enough to break an object from a position of stable mechanical equilibrium in just one blow, but what about when there is no apparent reason and no obvious vibration?

You may not think that vibrations can cause an object to fall, but this can be a slow process. This is why these objects fall after being left on a shelf or tabletop for days, weeks, or even months. The object doesn't appear to move, but it is, just very slowly, and then at some point the object's centre of gravity changes and it falls over.

Every time you switch on your washing machine, the vibrations could be slowly edging an object in the house slightly closer to the tipping point, until one day it falls. The most common way an object can be affected by these kinds of vibrations is by your own movement through the house, especially if you have wooden floors. Each time you walk through a room, you create vibrations. Opening or closing doors could also be a cause, as could banging on a wall.

A good example of this is if you have a small toy or piece of stationery on your desk, and also on the desk is a speaker that is playing loud music. The vibrations from the speaker can cause the object to inch closer to the edge of the desk by a fraction of a millimetre at a time, and eventually it will fall off the desk.

A change in air pressure can also cause something to fall off a desk. Let's say you've put a book down on a desk in a hurry, and half the book is on the desk and the other half is hanging over the edge, but it's balanced and stable. It could stay like this for days, but if you've happened to balance it in just the right way and suddenly there's a change in air pressure, then that book's balancing point might change and it will fall.

Another factor that can make something fall is gravity and how it affects an object as it changes state. A towel, for example, is placed on a towel rail in the bathroom. It can be hanging over the rail quite happily, then all of a sudden it slips and lands in a heap on the floor.

In this case, the towel is slightly uneven. There is more of the towel over one side of the rail than the other. It's being pulled down by gravity, but very slowly, as the friction of the towel on the rail stops it sliding off quickly... but it is moving, and the heavier side is getting longer and heavier compared to the shorter side. Eventually there's not enough resistance and gravity is able to overcome friction, and all of a sudden the towel simply slides off of the rail.

The towel drying over time could also change how gravity affects it. If one side of the towel is wet, it will be heavier. As it dries, it will get lighter and change the balance of the towel.

It's a little harder to find a rational cause when an object appears to have been thrown across the room, but there are non-paranormal ways to explain this too. When something falls, usually it hits the floor and stays roughly where it landed, but there's a chance it might hit something on the way down and get deflected, land on something, roll, bounce, or a combination of all of these actions. In this case, the landing position and orientation can be very hard to predict.

It's a little like when you drop a coin into a penny drop at an amusement park: it's almost impossible to get a coin to drop in exactly the same way two times in a row.

Practical Investigation

Proving Ghosts Exist

Stories of ghosts have existed in every culture going back thousands of years. A recent survey conducted in the US revealed that 60% of Americans believe they have seen a ghost, and thousands of paranormal investigators are actively researching the topic around the world. Yet, the existence of ghosts is still not recognised by mainstream science, especially as hauntings aren't something you can recreate in a laboratory.

Firm believers in the paranormal tend to take a dim view of sceptics. They often deem them to be close-minded and pedantic, but a sceptic would view a believer in the same way. It's not that either group is close-minded. It's just that they've both already formed an opinion on the paranormal and will therefore, in most cases, only consider evidence that supports their stance.

For example, if a sceptic doesn't believe that it's possible to capture the voice of a spirit in audio form by using the technique known as EVPs, then they will never accept an EVP as evidence. No matter how many examples you play them, they will simply put the voices down to being audio pareidolia, the human brain's tendency to hear recognisably familiar sounds in abstract noise.

It's as hard to convince a believer that ghosts don't exist as it is to convince a sceptic that they do. However, it's easy to see it from both points of view.

Believers often say that sceptics make irrational and endless demands for more and more evidence and that they feel like the sceptic is judging them, but if you are trying to convince that sceptic that ghosts exist, then you have opened yourself up to judgement and scrutiny, and you need to provide evidence in order to convince that person. If you turn the tables, a believer would require an equal amount of evidence to convince them that ghosts don't exist.

Another argument that believers use to attack sceptics is that a sceptic can't possibly make a judgement on the existence of ghosts when they don't know anything about the topic, but this is unfair. There's no reason to assume that a sceptic isn't well-read in the paranormal. They may have embarked on more paranormal investigations than a believer in order to come to their opinion.

So, what exactly would it take to prove that ghosts exist once and for all? What proof would take the paranormal from a fringe or pseudoscientific field of study to a mainstream scientific field of study?

Since most people will never witness a ghost themselves, it will take more than a few anecdotal stories to convince them. In order to prove the existence of the paranormal, the scientific community would be looking for empirical evidence that withstands peer review and, most importantly, is reproducible.

If you were capturing EVP recordings and you called out to any spirits that might be present and said, "If there's someone here with us, can you tell us your name?" and a voice said "Victor," then that could just be audio pareidolia. If you could then say, "Can you confirm your name, please? Say it again?" and it once again replied with "Victor," then that becomes good evidence. But what would make this evidence strong enough to convince the general populous would be if that spirit could give its name via EVP every time it was asked by every investigator who visited the location.

If every investigator was able to carry out this experiment, get the same result, and rule out anything that may be interfering with the experiment, then this would be irrefutable evidence that couldn't be debunked. The fact that different, independent investigators could repeat the same results would satisfy the peer review requirement.

This is simply the scientific method. A scientist always ensures the results can be repeated and withstand peer review. For example, if a scientist was conducting an experiment to determine if salt exists in sea water and the results of their experiment appeared to confirm this, they wouldn't pack up and go home. The next step would be to repeat the experiment multiple times using different samples and invite other scientists to do the same.

To prove that the paranormal really exists, one would actually only require one irrefutable example like this, but unfortunately, this kind of repeatable, measurable evidence is a world apart from a muffled voice in an audio recording that sounds like it could be saying "Victor."

Ghost sightings generally aren't repeatable. There are many spooky stories of the ghosts of soldiers walking through a castle at night or of a lady in grey who appears in a church on the anniversary of her death. If these stories were true, then any sceptic could be taken to that castle at night or to the church on the correct date, and they should be able to see the ghost, but they don't and can't.

Another thing that goes against the evidence generated by paranormal investigators is that the explanations that scientists give for some paranormal phenomena are empirical and reproducible. For example, psychologists have documented the common phenomenon of sleep paralysis, where a person awakes to find they are incapable of moving their body due to a chemical process in our bodies that prevents us from living out our dreams as we sleep. This uncomfortable and scary experience is often accompanied by visions of a dark or shadowy figure, but there is nothing paranormal about this.

Sleep paralysis is supported by empirical evidence because we can measure the effects of the neurotransmitter glycine on the muscles in the human body and they are reproducible. Some people experience it so regularly that it can be observed and requires treatment.

Strange mists are often caught on camera. These mists could be ghosts, or they could be the photographer's breath lit by the camera's flash or a lens flare. One photo proves nothing unless it can be repeated and the possibility of things like lens flares are removed. Why, in 200 years of photography, has no one ever found a haunted location where the spirit of someone can always be caught on camera sitting in the chair they died in?

Similarly, no psychic medium has ever been able to prove that they are able to contact the dead, despite the One Million Dollar Paranormal Challenge, set up by James Randi to pay out a cash prize to anyone who can demonstrate supernatural abilities.

Most evidence presented by mediums is no more convincing than guesswork and chance. The problem is, even if a psychic correctly predicted this week's lottery numbers, that could still be deemed to be chance. A chance of one in 45 million, but still someone guesses it right most weeks. If a psychic could predict the lottery numbers every week, now you're talking.

One interesting experiment that has been discussed by members of the paranormal and skeptical communities is testing a psychic's abilities and proving the presence of a spirit. The results of this experiment would be measurable, reproducible, and impossible to debunk. The experiment would work as follows:

Given that psychics claim to be able to interact with the ghosts that roam around a haunted location, a good test would be to place a device at one end of a room out of view of the psychic. The device would generate a random six-digit number and display it on its screen. The medium would then ask the spirit to move to that part of the room, read the number, and come back and tell them what number was being displayed. The psychic could then relay the number, which could be verified against the number on the screen.

As there are countless haunted locations around the world and thousands of practising mediums, it shouldn't be too much of a stretch to find the right person and the right spirit to successfully prove the existence of the paranormal in this way.

This may sound like an over-the-top and unnecessary experiment that's a world away from evidence like the sensation of being tapped on the shoulder or the sound of unexplained knocks, but if you pose the question, "What would it take to prove ghosts exist?" Then, like it or not, this is what it would take.

You might argue that perhaps ghosts can't perform on demand in this way because, by their very nature, they are not measurable or repeatable. That's alright, and if that's the case, then you simply have to accept that there is no way you are ever going to convince anybody.

Conflict and Misinformation

Although public ghost hunting events are becoming more popular and new paranormal investigation teams are forming all the time, there is a consensus in the paranormal community that no one is actually conducting proper paranormal investigations any more.

Although humans have been fascinated by the supernatural and life after death since ancient times, we actually know very little about ghosts and spirits. What we do know is that people report seeing, hearing, being touched by, or otherwise sensing a ghostly presence in just about any location at any time of day or night.

Yet modern ghost hunters ignore their own senses and embark on investigations in darkened buildings while arming themselves with an array of elaborate ghost hunting gadgets. Most commonly, devices like EMF meters are used.

Some believe that EM spikes can indicate the early stages of a ghostly manifestation or act as evidence of a haunting, but this isn't likely to be the case. EMF meters were first introduced into the paranormal field as a way to debunk hauntings. A paranormal investigator should always be looking for ways to eliminate rational explanations of happenings from their investigation. If all rational explanations are removed, then what is left must be proof of the paranormal.

Today, EMF meters are incorrectly used by most paranormal investigators as a form of spirit communication rather than to determine whether spikes in EM levels could be causing people to think that they are experiencing paranormal activity.

Of course, there's nothing wrong with testing a theory that electromagnetism might be linked to the paranormal, but EMF meters should be used in the right way in order to help debunk claims. It shouldn't be the primary method of experimentation in all paranormal investigations.

Electronic speech synthesis devices are another commonly used tool by ghost hunters. They can be found in the form of physical devices as well as mobile phone applications and are pre-loaded with a library of phonetics and word elements. These words are randomly spewed out by the tool. The idea is that any spirits present are able to interfere with the software and affect its random nature in order to form sentences and communicate. Spirits can do this by manipulating various sensors built into the device, including the phone's microphone and motion detector.

Again, there is nothing wrong with testing this theory, but both of these types of devices have never been categorically proven to be an effective way to contact spirits. There is no evidence to suggest that after death, humans naturally acquire the necessary skills that allow them to interfere with the random word generation algorithm of an electronic speech synthesis tool or manipulate an EMF meter to cause it to trigger. These are clearly not skills we naturally possess in life.

Traditionally, ghost hunters were armed with nothing more than a notebook to jot down their findings, and their senses were their first and most important method of spiritual detection. Today, a digital audio recorder is more commonly used and just as acceptable. It gives you the ability to play back the audio from the investigation and listen out for anything you might have missed at the time.

However, many investigators don't use audio recorders in the same way they used to use notebooks. They've gotten lazy. Upon entering a vigil or being part of an investigation, the investigator should always speak into the recorder and say something along the lines of, "Investigation of the Great Hall, 4pm. Three people are present." This is your only record of the proceedings. You might have forgotten who was present when you play the audio back, which means you might not be able to identify the source of a sound made by another member of the team during the investigation.

One of the oldest paranormal groups in the world, the Society for Psychical Research, was formed in 1882, and amongst its members were famed paranormal investigators like Harry Price, Maurice Grosse, and Guy Lyon Playfair, who investigated the famous Enfield Haunting. Combined, their members have far more experience in the field of paranormal investigation than any amateur or small paranormal team and have clocked up significantly more hours at haunted locations than even the teams on the longest-running ghost hunting reality shows.

The organisation's guidelines clearly state electronic ghost hunting devices are not an effective way of investigating a haunting. Their guidelines are publicly available and published in a short book entitled 'Guidance Notes for Investigators of Spontaneous Cases', a new version of which was published in 2018 and is a must-read for anyone calling themselves a paranormal investigator.

The SPR defines a "spontaneous case" as one that can occur unpredictably at any time and cannot be recreated in a lab.

The SPR advises using nothing more than a few simple tools when investigating the paranormal, all of which were available in Harry

Price's time. Firstly, a notebook. We've already mentioned that today, this is often substituted for an audio recorder. The SPR agree with this substitution but offer guidance on how to record your findings in audio form.

SPR's suggested kit list:
- Notebook
- Wristwatch
- A camera
- An audio recorder
- A torch
- Sensible clothing
- Food and other refreshment

Other than the last few items on the list, you can see that the tools suggested by the SPR mimic the human senses. A wristwatch provides a measure of our perception of time and also lets a team of investigators synchronise their findings. A camera captures apparitions and other visual phenomena that people have reported seeing with the naked eye for generations. And, an audio device like a tape recorder, digital audio recorder, or dictaphone allows you to capture any auditory phenomenon, the type of evidence that the victim of a haunting would naturally be able to pick up using their own ears.

A digital thermometer might also fit into this way of thinking. It allows us to obtain an accurate measure of the ambient air temperature at a location, confirming the existence of "cold spots", which are often felt by witnesses of hauntings. But, just like the EMF phenomenon, although cold spots are said to be the first indication of a manifestation or a spirit's presence, there is no evidence to back this up. It's simply a belief. So, if using a thermometer, it should be used to confirm whether someone present at the investigation is really experiencing a temperature change or whether it's psychosomatic. A temperature change should not be taken as definitive proof of the paranormal.

The explosion in paranormal devices and their usage as part of ghost hunts is most likely a result of the media and television shows. Want-to-be paranormal investigators look up to these shows, which not only go way overboard in their use of ghost hunting gadgets, but also fail to use any scientific professionalism when dealing with claims of the paranormal.

So, if you want to really investigate the paranormal, then put down the gimmicky gadgets with their flashing lights and experience the paranormal the way humankind has for thousands of years, with your own senses. To learn more about how a genuine and effective study of the paranormal should be conducted, we highly recommend Steven Parsons' book 'Guidance Notes for Investigators of Spontaneous Cases', which is available to buy through the SPR website.

Capturing and Analysing EVPs

Defining Electronic Voice Phenomenon

The quality of EVPs varies from sounds like groans, whispers, and growls to clear, human-like voices in the form of an intelligible sentence or phrase. Sometimes amplification, noise filtering, or enhancement is used in order to hear the voices.

At their best, an EVP can be a recognisable voice. You'll be able to clearly identify words, and the tone of the voice will indicate whether the voice is likely to be that of a man, woman, or child. If clear enough, the pace, intention, or vocabulary may even allow you to identify the voice as a specific person. You may also be able to determine the state of mind of the speaker through the tone of their voice; the speech might sound angry, sad, or happy, for example.

Unfortunately, you're not likely to encounter this best-case scenario on every investigation. It's more likely the voices you capture will be gruff or made up of breathy groans, grunts, or even growling. The EVP is most likely to be one word, perhaps two or three, but whole sentences are rare and dialogues are almost unheard of.

Ideally, you are listening for intelligent or direct responses. These are words and phrases that directly respond to your questions, the current conversation in the room, or a statement that is timely or in context with what's going on in the environment.

The source of these voices is still not fully understood by paranormal investigators, and it is written off as pseudoscience by skeptics. Of course, many parapsychologists and paranormal investigators believe that EVPs are produced by the spirits of the dead communicating with us. It's said that these spirit voices can be unintentionally recorded or intentionally recorded on demand. There are also several other commonly shared theories relating to the source of EVPs, including subconscious psychic projection and sounds from another dimension or time.

Electronic Voice Phenomenon is a form of Instrumental Transcommunication (ITC). ITC is an umbrella term that refers to a wider field of spirit communication using any kind of electrical instrument that isn't just limited to voices.

The term "Instrumental Transcommunication" was coined in the 1970s by Prof. Ernst Senkowski, a scientist with a background in experimental physics who went on to conduct experiments to try to find out the source of unexplained voices on audio tapes.

The term "ITC" isn't limited to audio devices; it encompasses any communication between the living and spirits or any other supernatural entity through any electronic device. This can be anything from tape recorders through to computers, and in more recent years ghost hunting gadgets and smartphone apps.

ITC also covers visual forms of communication, normally conducted with the use of a television and video camera feedback loop, which creates the Droste effect, where a picture recursively appears within itself, or simply by observing patterns in static.

Today, ITC is more actively investigated by parapsychologists and spiritualists than ever before. The array of devices available to carry out experiments is endless. Modern paranormal investigators can get their hands on plenty of commercially available gadgets.

The first of these modern devices was the Frank's Box, named after its creator, Frank Sumption, which he developed in 2002. There are many similar devices available on the market today; they're now generally referred to as "ghost boxes" or "spirit boxes." The most common being the P-SB7 and P-SB11 spirit boxes.

Another popular modern form of ITC is electronic speech synthesis, like the Ovilus and Echovox. These types of devices can be quite expensive; however, there are cheaper versions available as apps for smartphones. They work as either random word generators or by generating random sounds, the phonics that make up words. It's said that spirits can affect the random nature of these devices to form intelligent responses to the user's questions.

Most devices of this type use atmospheric sensors to generate their random output. They monitor conditions such as temperature, pressure, humidity, and electromagnetic field strength. It uses these signals as a random number generator, and this number is used to reference a database of words or sounds. The atmospheric sensors give the spirits a way to influence the random nature of the output.

An EMF metre can also be used as a form of ITC, but only when used for communication as opposed to taking baseline electromagnetic field measurements or looking for EM spikes.
An EMF meter, or electromagnetic field meter, is one of the most popular pieces of ghost hunting equipment. They are simple to use, often consisting of nothing more than an on/off switch. They detect and alert you to fluctuations and spikes in EM flux, and the device gives instant feedback via a digital display or LED indicator.

In order to use an EMF metre to communicate with spirits, the user should encourage the spirits to come forward and try to trigger the lights on the EMF metre to show that they are present or to indicate an answer to a question.

These are just a few of the most commonly used electronic devices in the ITC field, but the list doesn't end here. Over the years, there have been reports of just about every type of electrical device being used to communicate with spirits, from telephones and fax machines through to battery-powered children's toys and flashlights.

Direct Voice Phenomenon

Electronic Voice Phenomenon shouldn't be confused with Direct Voice Phenomenon (DVP). DVP is sometimes also referred to as an AVP or Audible Voice Phenomena, but the terms are interchangeable.

DVPs are similar to EVPs in that they are disembodied voices that are heard during paranormal investigations, séances, or at a haunted location. The difference is that they are audible at the time and are spoken directly to the investigator or witness. No audio or electrical equipment is needed to hear a DVP; they are heard in real time with nothing more than the human ear.

Direct voice phenomena are much more rare than EVPs, almost as rare as full-bodied apparitions, but it's not uncommon for people to report hearing laughter, cries, or even menacing voices shouting "get out" while at an allegedly haunted property.

Although DVP relates to audible voices, the phenomenon shouldn't be confused with voices produced in cases like the famous Enfield Poltergeist haunting, when a gruff male voice seemed to be coming from Janet Hodgson. This is not a DVP, as in this case Janet was the instrument of communication, meaning it was not direct. That is why the phenomenon is called "direct voice" or "independent voice" - no equipment is involved, and the voice isn't spoken through a third party.

Although rare, DVPs are a concept that most investigators are familiar with and disembodied voices is something they are actively listening for during ghost hunts, but traditionally direct voice phenomenon was more closely associated with a unique branch of mediumship. In séances, it wasn't uncommon for a direct-voice medium to facilitate voice communication.

It was believed that the medium was able to encourage and give the spirit the energy to come forward and communicate, but sitters claimed that the voice didn't come from the medium themselves. Instead, it was heard coming from mid-air in front of the medium or elsewhere in the room, and the words were spoken in the spirit's own voice.

There are plenty of examples of spirits who are able to manifest audible voices. One of the best known cases is the tale of the ghost of Sarah Siddon, who is said to haunt the Bristol Old Vic theatre in England. The building is one of the oldest continually operating theatres in the world, built between 1764 and 1766.

Sarah's boyfriend hanged himself at this theatre, and her ghost is thought to continue to mourn the loss. Staff working at the theatre have reported hearing a female voice telling them to "get out," a classic example of a DVP.

The key to hearing a DVP during an investigation is to be patient and quiet and to offer lots of encouragement to the spirits. Call out and ask any spirits present at an allegedly haunted location to use their voice to talk to you. Ask them to use your energy to communicate and remember to encourage them and don't make demands of them. After calling out, stay still and quiet and give the spirits time to answer.

Of course, if you have recording equipment with you during an investigation and a DVP is heard, then there's a good chance that you could capture the audio in your recording. Recording a DVP doesn't make it an EVP, as by its definition, an EVP is a voice heard through electronic means only.

Origins of the Voices

How an EVP is actually captured in a recording is still not understood by parapsychologists. Of course, what we do know is that ghosts and spirits don't have physical bodies; therefore, they have no vocal cords, so it could be argued that they can't produce a voice in the same way that living humans do.

However, this isn't strictly true. It's widely agreed upon by paranormal investigators that ghosts are sometimes able to move objects, slam doors, and break items. Therefore, they must at times be able to take a physical or partially physical form, or at the very least be able to manipulate the physical world around them. If this is the case then they may also have the ability to vibrate the air around them in order to make sounds, which are at a basic level vibrations in the air.

The idea that they can do this, either at will or under certain conditions, is backed up by the common belief that ghosts are also able to produce direct and audible voices; we hear the sound of their clothes rustling and even their footsteps.

In the early séances of the late 1800s, mediums believed that spirits were able to spontaneously form physical vocal cords to speak through using a substance called ectoplasm. This is one theory that could explain direct voice phenomena, but when it comes to EVPs, the voice isn't actually heard out loud, so it could be that the voice is imprinted in the recording using a kind of psychic energy or manufactured electrical interference.

No matter what method is used to make the recording, the leading theory about the origins of EVPs is that they are the voices of the dead - whether that be in the form of residual or intelligent spirits - this isn't the only theory. It's entirely possible that the voices heard in EVPs aren't voices of the dead but are, in fact, voices from another point in space, time, or a different dimension.

Many within the paranormal field believe that a portal or vortex can allow an entity to cross over into the physical world we live in from the plane of existence that ghosts inhabit - the spirit world. There's also a growing number of claims that they could be inter-dimensional gateways or even doorways to a different point in time, either the past or the future. This is based on claims that objects and artefacts have fallen through portals. Items like feathers, arrowheads, and ancient coins have been found in places where they have no business being.

The idea of other planes of existence isn't too far-fetched. There's growing support from leading scientists for the many-worlds interpretation, which suggests that there are one or more, perhaps an infinite number, of complete universes co-existing with us on a plane we are not aware of.

It's for this reason that some paranormal researchers believe that hauntings could be caused by beings from another dimension and that ghosts could be explained as beings living in one or more parallel dimensions. When conducting experiments with EVPs, it's just as likely that we are inadvertently communicating with living humans in a parallel universe as it is that we're communicating with the spirits of the dead.

It might not just be the barriers between realities that ghost hunters are breaking down but also those between space and time. Ghost hunts are usually conducted in haunted houses, castles, or other locations believed to be haunted. This means that over several years, many different groups of paranormal researchers focus their attention on the exact same location in an attempt to make contact with spirits. Some believe that it's possible that psychic energies from different time periods could be converging and could be what is causing spiritual contact and even the voices in EVP recordings.

If it isn't the spirit of the deceased that we're communicating with and it is, in fact, the focussed energy of ghost hunters from the past, then these people from the past have made contact with us here in their future. This means it could also be possible for today's ghost hunters to make contact with people in the future.

Communication between the dead and the living, or in this case, the two points in time, doesn't normally consist of a linear conversation; instead, it's a voice imprinted in an EVP recording, the movement of the planchette over a Ouija board, or tapping to indicate "yes" or "no." Perhaps this is because subconscious psychic energies are being drawn to each other. Those taking part in an investigation may not even realise what messages they're throwing out into the past or future.

Space and time is so intrinsically linked as the spacetime continuum, that if it's possible to communicate through time, then it should also be possible to communicate with different physical locations throughout the universe.

There's no real way to know where the voice in an EVP recording is coming from. Even if the voice identifies itself by giving you its name in the recording, this could mean you're communicating with the spirit of that person, but you could also be in communication with their living counterpart in an alternative reality.

Of course, as well as the many possible supernatural explanations, there are also plenty of natural explanations for EVPs. Skeptics maintain that EVPs are merely the result of poorly conducted recording sessions where unwanted noise is introduced through over-amplification, noise reduction, or enhancement, which can cause recordings to take on qualities significantly different from those that were present in the original recording.

Other natural causes include interference from broadcast sources, including radio broadcasts, CB radio transmissions, transmissions from wireless baby monitors, sounds caused by the recording device being moved or handled, or the sounds of the inner workings of the recorder itself.

Subconscious Imprinting

A final theory on the origins of EVPs is that they're not coming from a spirit or another being at all; instead, they are audible imprints of the EVP practitioner's mental thoughts that are subconsciously recorded through psychokinesis, especially given that our thoughts are an electrochemical process in the brain.

Spirits are believed to be our souls or the energy that gives rise to our consciousness, which lives on outside the body. If we are willing to accept that this disincarnate energy is capable of affecting an audio recorder, then it could also be the case that the energy or soul within a living human can have the same effect.

The living are consciously aware of the intent of what they are about to say, as well as the words, before we form the sentence aloud. If a spirit's conscious energy works in the same way, then it's possible that it is this mental intent that causes an imprint in an audio recording. This means that a paranormal investigator who is focussing on the question they've just asked to the spirit could unwittingly mentally project the answer they hope for or expect onto the recording. It might be that the investigator is subconsciously willing the spirit to answer with a specific word or phrase.

Famous EVP researcher Konstantīns Raudive's work might have helped confirm that EVPs are the result of some form of psychic projection rather than an audible sound. He often used a germanium diode in a radio circuit to capture EVPs. Modern-day researchers now plug a similar diode into an audio recorder instead of a microphone. A germanium diode is a low-resistance electrical component and isn't capable of capturing audio in the same way that a microphone does. This means that any voices captured using this method were never audible.

If EVPs are a result of our own subconscious thoughts being imprinted in the recording, then it becomes harder to tell if the voices heard come from the depths of our psyche or from a spirit. In order to validate that a voice isn't the result of our own thoughts, the EVP would have to impart information that none of the investigators present are aware of and that can be validated later. This would help to prove that the voice hasn't come from the investigators themselves as they didn't have this information before-hand.

However, where information is known to an investigator or generic phrases are spoken in the EVP, it's impossible to rule out the fact that the EVP could be unwittingly caused by the investigator themselves. For this reason, when attempting to capture EVPs, you should aim to collect information that you are not aware of but that can be corroborated later. Information such as dates of birth, next of kin, or anything else that you could verify in records after the investigation.

If you want to explore this theory further, then you could try a psychic projection experiment. This involves using an audio recorder and intentionally focussing on one specific word that has been decided on in advance. You could either try this alone or with a group of people all concentrating on the same word. Leave the audio device recording for 30 to 60 seconds; this should be enough time for the imprint to occur without the need for you to review long audio recordings afterwards.

The person reviewing the audio shouldn't have been part of the original experiment and shouldn't be aware of the word in advance. It is their job to listen to the audio objectively and write down any words they hear. If the theory is correct, then the word they write down should match the one you decided upon before the experiment.

If the experiment is unsuccessful, continue to repeat it and retry it with a different word each time. EVPs aren't captured on every attempt and there's no scientific understanding of what allows them to be captured, so it may be that you have more luck in subsequent attempts.

Scalar Waves

Scalar waves are a proposed type of exotic energy that some paranormal investigators think could be linked to the transmission and capturing of EVPs.

Some believe that different frequencies of scalar waves are responsible for supernatural phenomena like telepathy and clairvoyance. So, it might be possible for mediums or those who are sensitive to be able to consciously or subconsciously pick up on scalar energy.

It's also been suggested that scalar waves could be the mechanism that imprints spirit voices in audio recordings, essentially powering EVPs.

The belief is that scalar waves can pass through ordinary matter, even right through the core of the Earth and out the other side. EVPs have been captured when the recording devices have been electromagnetically shielded in a Faraday pouch; this could be possible if the wave carrying an EVP could pass through an object such as a Faraday cage.

However, there's no agreed-upon scientific understanding of how this could work, but if scalar does represent an undiscovered branch of science, then this might mean that the principles and processes of scalar waves are still to be discovered and they could work in the way described.

Creating a device that can detect scalar waves is an interesting challenge, especially if the waves behave as they are said to. If scalar waves are able to pass through solid objects, including metals, then there is no way to detect them with an aerial made of metal. The waves shouldn't interact with any type of machine.

The current understanding in the scalar theory research community is that you'd have to detect a scalar wave's influence by measuring more conventional fields. In fact, most designs for scalar wave detectors take the approach of recording the unseen waves' effects on electromagnetic fields. If scalar can influence traditional electromagnetic waves, then it could influence electrical devices in such a way that voices could be transposed into recordings.

Scalar-wave research is still very new and generally not accepted by mainstream science. Scalar within the paranormal world is even more specialised, with just a handful of investigators experimenting with it.

The History of EVP Research

The spiritualist movement began in the 1840s, when holding a séance was the most common way to attempt to contact spirits, usually through a medium. This was about 100 years before audio recording technology was invented. As technology evolved, so did the methods used to attempt to contact spirits.

The first radio transmission had been made by the Italian inventor, Guglielmo Marconi, in 1895, and by the early 1900s, the possibility that radio-based equipment could be used to contact the dead was being explored.

Father Roberto Landell de Mour, a Brazilian Catholic priest and inventor who was an early pioneer in long-range radio broadcasting and voice transmission technologies, was the first to experiment with electronic spirit communication. In 1910, it's said that he laid the groundwork for future generations of ITC researchers when he demonstrated a device that produced EVPs through radio technology.

Landell's work is little more than a legend, and very little is known about his session in which he spoke to spirits. Even at the time, the inventor refused to talk about the inner workings of his device, as communicating with spirits through any other method than prayer is frowned upon in the Christian church.

However, it could also be seen as a little suspicious that the man, who some claim sent a voice transmission before even Marconi, had a box that was able to hear his questions when he spoke into it and answer back by producing a voice.

In the 1920s, the American inventor Thomas Edison fuelled the possibility that technology could be used to communicate with spirits. Edison was a prolific inventor who contributed to such technologies as the electric light, the phonograph, and the nickel-iron battery, but in 1920 he shared his belief that it may be possible to build a machine that could communicate with human personalities that live on after death.

In the article entitled 'Edison's Views on Life and Death' in the October 1920 edition of the magazine Scientific American, Edison said, "I have been thinking for some time of a machine or apparatus which could be operated by personalities which have passed on to another existence or sphere. Now follow me carefully; I don't claim that our personalities pass on to another existence or sphere."

He claimed that "it is possible to construct an apparatus so delicate that if there are personalities in another existence or sphere who wish to get in touch with us in this existence or sphere, that this apparatus will at least give them a better opportunity to express themselves."

Edison went on to state that he doubted other methods of spirit communication; he gave unreliable examples such as table tipping, rapping, Ouija boards, and mediumship. He said, "In truth, it is the crudeness of the present methods that makes me doubt the authenticity of purported communications with deceased persons. Why should personalities in another existence or sphere waste their time working a little triangular piece of wood over a board with certain lettering on it? Why should such personalities play pranks with a table? The whole business seems so childish to me that I frankly cannot give it my serious consideration. I believe that if we are to make any real progress in psychic investigation, we must do it with scientific apparatus and in a scientific manner, just as we do in medicine, electricity, chemistry, and other fields."

It seems that what Edison was proposing to do was give investigators a more scientific approach to spiritualism than the other more "crude methods" employed at the time. He said, "What I propose to do is to furnish psychic investigators with an apparatus that will give a scientific aspect to their work."

He described his vision of the apparatus as a valve-like device, probably similar to the type found in old vacuum tube radios. He said that it should be capable of massively amplifying even the slightest effort to effect it. This would make it much easier for a spirit to interact with it than sliding a planchette across a Ouija board or tipping a table.

In another article published on October 15th, 1920 in the Canadian news magazine Maclean's, Edison is quoted as saying, "I am engaged in the construction of one such apparatus now, and I hope to be able to finish it before very many months pass."

In the same publication, Edison is quoted as saying, "If our personality survives, then it is strictly logical and scientific to assume that it retains memory, intellect, and other faculties and knowledge that we acquire on this earth. Therefore, if personality exists, after what we call death, it is reasonable to conclude that those who leave this earth would like to communicate with those they have left here."

Thomas Edison died in 1931, having never completed the device or given any further information on the theory behind it or its operation.

Early EVP Recordings

As technology evolved, recording equipment became accessible, and with this innovation came attempts to capture spirit voices in recordings, the true origins of the modern-day EVP movement. It was an American psychic of Hungarian descent named Attila von Szalay who was at the forefront of this new approach.

At the time, Szalay was working as a photographer in California, where he specialised in spirit photography, the art of photographing ghosts or spirits. In 1941, to expand his work, he decided to attempt to capture the voices of spirits. He did this using one of the first commercially available home recording devices - the Packard Bell Phonocord.

The phonocord recorder cutter used an external microphone to record sounds to a 5-inch blank record spinning at 78 revolutions per minute. The device was also capable of playing back the recordings. From 1950 on, Szalay teamed up with psychologist Raymond Bayless, and together they continued experimenting, and in 1956 technology once again leaped forward and the researchers began using a reel-to-reel tape recorder.

They conduct their EVP experiments in much the same way as mediums did in early séances. A microphone was placed in an insulated spirit cabinet. The medium, in this case psychic Szalay, would sit in the cabinet in order to channel the spirits. The microphone was connected to the tape recorder, which was outside the cabinet.

The researchers found that they had captured many unexplained sounds in their recordings that were not heard during the experiment. Some of these sounds were recorded at times when there was no medium in the cabinet.

Reverend Charles Drayton Thomas, a British Methodist minister and spiritualist, also became one of the first to capture a spirit voice in a recording in the early 1940s. Thomas, a member of the Society for Psychical Research, was investigating the validity of a well-known medium of the time, Gladys Osborne Leonard. During one of their sessions together, Thomas found that he had captured on tape the disembodied voice of his own father.

The next leap forward in the field of EVP research came in 1959 when Friedrich Jürgenson, a painter and film producer from Sweden, captured what he thought sounded like voices on tape. The recording happened by accident while Jürgenson was attempting to record bird song in woodland.

Jürgenson concluded that the voice in the recording was clearly human, but was unable to ascertain how it had been recorded as the tape had been blank before, meaning it couldn't have been sound leaking through from a previous recording. The area of woodland he'd been in was very remote, which eliminated the possibility that someone made the sounds at the time of recording.

This led Jürgenson to investigate the phenomenon further. He was able to rule out the possibility of radio interference and eventually started to capture much longer phrases and sentences. He then found that the voices in his recordings started to address him by name, and he was able to identify one of the voices as that of his dead mother.

Later in his research, Jürgenson became the first to combine the technique of recording EVPs with the earlier method of radio contact in order to improve his results. Jürgenson went on to write two books on the subject of EVP, 'Rösterna Från Rymden' ('Voices from the Universe') published in 1964, and 'Radio och Mikrofonkontakt med de Döda' originally published in 1968, then translated into German as 'Sprechfunk mit Verstorbenen' ('Voice Transmissions With The Deceased') in 1981.

Agostino Gemelli also captured an unexplained voice on tape, and like Jürgenson, he captured the sounds inadvertently, and it was the sound of a deceased parent. Gemelli was an Italian Franciscan friar and former physician. He captured the voice in 1952 while working in Milan with Father Pellegrino Ernetti, an Italian priest and scientist.

The pair were attempting to record the sounds of Gregorian chants using a reel-to-reel tape recorder, but they were experiencing technical issues with the microphone. At one point during the recording session, Gemelli looked to the heavens and asked his dead father for help. When Gemelli and Ernetti later reviewed the tape, they heard a voice that Gemelli recognised as his dead father's, and that voice said, "Of course I shall help you. I'm always with you."

Konstantin Raudive

Inspired by the work of Jürgenson, the next big name in the field of paranormal research was Konstantin Raudive, a Latvian parapsychologist, writer, and student of the famous Swiss psychiatrist, Carl Jung.

Raudive got in contact with Jürgenson after reading his book and initially worked with him to capture EVPs in 1965. In one of these early experiments, Raudive heard multiple voices in a recording, with voices speaking in German, Latvian, and French. One of the voices said "va dormir, Margarete," which translates as "go to sleep, Margaret."
In his 1968 book on EVPs, 'Unhörbares Wird Hörbar' (translated into English as "what is inaudible becomes audible," but published in 1971 as 'Breakthrough: An Amazing Experiment in Electronic Communication with the Dead,') Raudive wrote, "These words made a deep impression on me, as Margarete Petrautzki had died recently, and her illness and death had greatly affected me."

Raudive also recorded the voice of a deceased parent. He heard his mother's voice using his childhood name, Kostulit: "Kostulit, this is your mother."

His early experiments drove Raudive to spend the next nine years of his life, until his death in 1974, exploring EVPs with the help of German parapsychologist Hans Bender. It's said that over his career he recorded more than 100,000 recordings. With a career that only spanned about a decade, this would mean that he'd have to have recorded around 30 EVPs per day.

Raudive used several methods of recording EVPs, each method was carried out in strict laboratory conditions, which included screening from external radio interference.

The most simple method employed by Raudive was to use a normal microphone connected to a tape recorder. He left this running in silence, with no one talking. At times he even used this method but without a microphone even connected to the recorder.

He also used a standard radio that was not tuned to any station so that it just produced white noise, which he would record and later analyse for voices. The voices obtained through this method are sometimes referred to as RVPs, or Radio Voice Phenomenon.

The third method was similar but used a modified radio. The method is known as "diode recording" and involves replacing the most important component in a simple crystal radio, the crystal detector, with a piece of germanium. This has become known as a germanium diode or Raudive diode.

The diode was too short to pick up radio transmissions and could not be tuned to a specific station; instead, it acted as a noise generator fed by a broad band of the radio spectrum. It was believed that this wide, untuned band of radio noise provided the raw energy required for the voice formation process.

In order to avoid his own subjectivity, Raudive invited more than 400 impartial volunteers to listen back to the voices he'd captured and to interpret them without bias - all of whom heard distinguishable voices.

Raudive's germanium diode was later put to use by businessman George Meek and his psychic research partner, William O'Neil. Together, they used a similar diode to develop the Spiricom device. At a 1982 press conference, the researchers demonstrated their radio-based device, which also used a tone generator spanning the frequency range of the human voice, and claimed that it made two-way communication with the dead possible.

They went on to record hundreds of hours of voices using this, but only when the device was used by O'Neil. Meek put this down to O'Neil's psychic abilities being an essential component of the system.

Marcello Bacci

One of the most fascinating cases of early EVP research was demonstrated by the Italian medium, Marcello Bacci. Starting in 1974, over a period of about 20 years, Bacci gave public performances of his spirit communication technology to audiences in Grosseto, Italy. Audience members were given the chance to hear the voices of their deceased loved ones.

Bacci started out by using an old military radio that was used on naval ships but eventually moved on to a larger vacuum tube radio set with three loudspeakers, which he said provided better sound and clearer voices. Both of these radios were unmodified.
During the demonstration, he would then tune the radio to a part of the radio spectrum that was devoid of radio broadcasts. In a 2000 interview, he explained, "There is not a particular frequency. I can go all the way from left to right and if the voices want, they come in." After ten to twenty minutes, the white noise from the speakers would die down and the voices of the spirits would clearly come through.

The voices are much clearer and more sustained than those captured by most other EVP researchers. Some of the voices Bacci's radio produced could deliver coherent dialogues that were several minutes long. They are easy to identify as male or female, and each voice sounded distinct and unique.

The most commonly retold explanation for Bacci's demonstration is that he had unique psychic abilities that the experiment relied upon. It's said to be for this reason that Bacci had to be in constant contact with the radio's dials during the demonstration. If he left the room at any point, the voices would stop. His radio also failed to produce results for anyone else who used it.

Many skeptics tried to debunk Bacci's work, and the experiments were carried out in controlled conditions, but the results were the same, even when the radio was isolated inside a Faraday cage, which blocks all external radio and electrical signals.

Some in the paranormal field claim that in order to try to debunk the Bacci experiment, they have unplugged the radio, taken the back off to ensure there are no batteries present, and found that the voices persist even without power. This is not the case. Bacci's radio does require power at all times to operate. However, skeptics have removed all three vacuum tubes from the radio and found that the voices continue.

The Global Movement

As the EVP research movement grew, the American Association of Electronic Voice Phenomena, founded in 1972 by EVP researcher Sarah Estep. It later became known as the Association Transcommunication (ATransC) and survives to this day.

This was followed by research associations forming all around the world, starting with des Vereins für Transkommunikations-Forschung (German Association for Transcommunication Research), which was founded in Germany in 1975.

Estep began her research into EVP using a a reel-to-reel tape recorder in 1976 after reading about the work of Friedrich Jürgenson and Konstantin Raudive. She went on to become a leading researcher in her field, making hundreds, if not thousands, of recordings of voice messages, some of which she identified as deceased friends and relatives and even intelligences of extraterrestrial origin.

Perhaps Estep's best-known legacy is her popularisation of an EVP classification system. It was similar to a previous system of classification proposed by Raudive. Estep's system used the same A, B, and C classes, with "Class A" being used to categorise the highest-quality EVPs and "Class C" being the poorest examples.

In the 21st century, we've seen an explosion of ITC devices. Unlike their predecessors, the new versions are mass-produced and sold to any interested investigator. With the advent of smart phones, the technology has even become the basis of mobile phone apps.

The first of these devices was called a "Frank's Box," which was invented by Frank Sumption. His idea of a device that sweeps through radio frequencies has become commonplace in the paranormal field, more commonly known as a "spirit box" or "ghost box."

Advances in technology have also made it easier for paranormal investigators to capture EVPs while on ghost hunts. Gone are the days of investigators having to lug around large tape recorders. Now, handheld digital audio recorders make it easy to record and quickly review EVP sessions.

Choosing the Right Equipment

Even if you're not attempting to capture EVPs, an audio recorder is a very useful tool to have on a ghost hunt because it mimics the human sense of hearing. Since so many hauntings include reports of unexplained knocks and bangs, footsteps, disembodied voices, and other sounds, it makes sense to try to capture evidence of this.

A digital audio recorder is capable of recording for hours on end, allowing you to create an audio log of the investigation. Should you hear any strange sounds, knocking, or voices, you can play them back to review them.

If using audio to log the investigation, you should ensure that the recorder is running continuously. Audio files are relatively small compared to a modern memory card's capacity, which means you can easily record several hours of audio.

When you start recording, say the time out loud. This will then give you a timeframe for the whole recording. When moving around the property you're investigating, describe your movement out loud; for example, "we're moving into the living room."

It's also a good idea to note in the recording how many people are present in each situation or vigil. This means if a sound is captured in the recording, you'll know if you were in a room alone or not; this will tell you if the sound could have been caused by someone else present - perhaps a fellow investigator simply cleared their throat.

You should also note verbally any non-paranormal sounds that are heard during the investigation. This includes sounds from outside the property, people moving, objects being dropped, coughs, sneezes, and stomach rumbles. Even the sound of the recorder itself being moved across a surface can be hard to identify during playback without a frame of reference.

You might think you'll remember these sounds when you listen back, but things can often sound quite different when captured by the recorder.

Having a running commentary in the recording will enable you to eliminate these sounds from your investigation, leaving only the unexplained sounds to be investigated.

Digital vs. Analogue Recording

Normally, when debating digital versus analogue audio recording methods, digital is the clear winner. Mainly because old analogue devices increase the chance of noise in the recording, this could be in the form of unwanted hiss, pops and rumbling.

But when it comes to the paranormal, it's not so simple, and investigators get results using both methods. Of course, all the early pioneers in EVP research would have been using analogue devices.

A digital method of audio recording would be a modern handheld audio recorder or dictaphone, the audio recording app built into your mobile phone or tablet, or audio recording software on a laptop.

Analogue refers to devices that use a magnetic storage medium, such as a cassette recorder or reel-to-reel tape machine. Today, these devices are considered antiquated, but since these sorts of recording devices proved so popular in the early days of EVP research, perhaps they shouldn't be ignored now.

Because the mechanics of how a spirit voice can be transposed on to a recording is far from understood, we can't rule out that it could be easier for a spirit to speak via an analogue device. After all analogue devices capture raw audio in real-time on magnetic tape.

Whereas a digital audio recorder samples the audio in tiny slices, which are then encoded in a digital format, and saves them to a digital storage medium like a memory card or hard drive. Due to the fragmented way hard drives work, the audio may not even be written in a linear sequence on the drive.

So, logic dictates that analogue might be a better method to capture EVPs, although it does have some downsides. It comes at a higher cost as you'll have to buy tapes if you want to archive your work. There's no easy way to skip back and replay audio instantly or jump between recordings with a tape recorder; you have to use the old-fashioned rewind button.

Most paranormal investigators like the ability to transfer their audio files to a computer for analysis. This is easy with digital devices, as the audio file can be transferred in seconds. With an analogue device, the only way to transfer the audio is by using a sound capture device connected to your computer or laptop via USB. You'll then need to connect the tape recorder's output to the device. This type of transfer is done in real time, so if you recorded an hour of audio, it will take an hour to be re-recorded onto your computer.

This type of transfer is a destructive process, and if high-quality audio connectors aren't used, then noise and interference may be introduced into the recording.

Analogue cassette and tape recorders can be picked up on auction sites for very reasonable prices; everything from vintage reel-to-reel tape recorders to 90s cassette recorders to retro dictaphones that record to mini-cassettes is available. Before committing to buying one, you should ensure that you're able to easily and cheaply buy the tapes you'll need. Surprisingly, new and unused tapes are also available for most types of recorders.

Recommended Audio Recorders

The important thing to remember when choosing an audio recorder is that there is no such thing as a dedicated "EVP recorder." You don't need to buy a specialist device from a ghost hunting store; you just need a normal, off-the-shelf recorder.

There are countless makes and models of audio recorders available on websites like eBay, Amazon, or electrical stores.

The most popular devices are digital voice recorders, most often either Olympus or Sony, which range from about $75 up to $180. The lower-priced recorders in this range are great entry-level devices which have an outstanding battery life and in-built memory that will allow you to record for hours on end. Those at the higher end of this price range are used by many well-established paranormal investigators.

Most of these devices make it easy for you to skip backward and forward when you review a recording. Many of the Olympus models have a button that lets you jump back a few seconds. Some let you slow down playback at the touch of a button, making it easier to listen to any potential voices in your recordings.

However, there are plenty of much more basic recorders that start for as little as $20, and although cheap, many investigators get as good results from a cheap recorder as others do from much more expensive devices.

At the other end of the scale are Tascam and Zoom digital audio recorders. These are professional-level audio recorders that record extremely clean and clear audio. They're of such high quality that they are used by podcasters, radio professionals, and video producers.

Tascam tends to be a little bit cheaper than Zoom, but both are of similar quality thanks to their built-in dual omnidirectional condenser microphones. Omnidirectional microphones are better at picking up sounds no matter which direction they come from. Where as a directional microphone will only hear what is in front of it. Some dictaphones, especially smaller ones, may only use a directional mic to capture just the user's voice as they hold the device.

If you are using a high-end recorder, you may feel like you are capturing fewer EVPs, but the better sound quality is actually preventing you from misidentifying false positives because you can hear those sound events for what they actually are instead of incorrectly interpreting them as a potential EVP.

If you're not yet ready to fork out cash on an audio recorder, then use the one you already have in your pocket. Most smart phones have an audio recording or voice notes/memo app built in that is good enough for paranormal investigations.

If a suitable app isn't installed on your phone by default, then there are audio and voice recording apps available in the app stores. When selecting an app, you should avoid "EVP recorders" or audio apps aimed at ghost hunters, as these apps are likely to include unnecessary features and could even reduce the quality of your audio by applying needless effects and processing.

There is no right or wrong when it comes to choosing an audio recorder for EVPs; what works for one investigator doesn't work for everyone. If you get the opportunity, try out other people's recorders. Make sure they are comfortable to hold, feel solid, that the playback controls aren't too fiddly, and that the sound quality is good.

It's not even really about the price and quality. Some paranormal investigators believe that cheaper, poorer-quality devices could be better for capturing EVPs, although, as previously mentioned, this could be due to lower-quality audio causing false positives.

Later in the book, we will look at EVP classifications in detail. One classification is "Type 1" or "transformative EVP." These are voices captured in recordings where the speech is a manipulation of other dissimilar sounds.

Cheaper or lower-quality recording devices, such as analogue tape recorders, are much more prone to picking up background noise, hisses, hums, and low rumbles. Low-cost audio recorders often have in-built microphones that might not be sufficiently shielded to filter out the sounds of the inner workings of the recorder.

This might sound like a negative, but some believe these normally unwanted sounds might be crucial to the formation of transformative EVPs, as this classification of EVP is made up of background noise that has been transformed.

However, you can still use a high-quality recorder and research transformative EVPs by using a white noise generator or similar random sound or tone generator to introduce background noise into the recording in the hopes that it can be transformed into an EVP.

In addition to your recorder itself, you may also want to invest in one other piece of equipment: an external omnidirectional microphone. These won't be compatible with all recorders, but some models of handheld audio recorders will also have a standard 3.5 mm microphone jack, so you can plug one in.

The internal microphones in recorders are good, but they're not perfect. They are more likely to pick up noises from inside the recorder itself, especially in quiet environments. The built-in microphones are primarily designed to capture human speech, so their frequency range might be limited to the human frequency range. They also tend to be unidirectional so as to pick up the person speaking without background noise.

However, depending upon how much you spend, an external microphone can have a much better frequency sensitivity and can be omnidirectional, which means it picks up sounds coming at it from all directions.

Panasonic RR-DR60 Series Recorder

We covered recommendations, but there's one audio recorder that shouldn't be avoided despite what you might have heard about it. Some paranormal investigators call Panasonic's early dictaphone, the RR-DR60, "the most effective recorder in the world for capturing EVPs," but there are countless arguments stacked up against its effectiveness.

The Panasonic RR-DR60 IC Recorder was launched in the mid-1990s. It was one of the first digital audio recorders to hit the market, and because it was one of the first of its kind, it lacked a lot of the features that newer digital audio recorders have, most noticeably a USB connector and a removable memory card. This meant that the only way to get the audio off of the device was via its headphone jack, an uncommon 2.5 mm socket.

The thing that made the DR60 unique at the time was that it had a "voice activated system" (VAS) feature. This allowed the device to automatically pause recording when no sound was detected. This avoided blank portions in recordings.

This functionality is useful for those using the dictaphone for the purpose it was originally designed for - making voice memos and notes, but the reason paranormal investigators liked this recorder was because they could leave it in the voice-activated mode and call out to any spirits that might be present. They could then leave a gap and remain silent before moving on to the next question. When reviewing the audio, the silence between the questions would not have been recorded unless someone or something had made a noise. If a voice was heard answering the question, this was deemed to be an example of an EVP.

The VAS feature made the DR60 perfect for quick-fire EVP sessions where the investigator would record for a minute or two and then review the audio before continuing. The lack of drawn-out silent periods in the recording sped this up dramatically, and working in this way reduced the need to go through hours of audio after an investigation. It also meant that if an answer was heard as an EVP, the investigator could question the response further in their next quick-fire burst of questions.

The DR60's instruction manual doesn't list its frequency response; this is very unusual for an audio recording device and is probably due to the fact that its range is so poor. There have been varying results from those who have tested the device, but they generally agree that the upper limit of the DR60's frequency range is about 18 kHz, although most state the figure to be 15 kHz. The human ear can hear sounds up to around 20 kHz, so the RR-DR60 doesn't outperform the human ear for high-frequency sounds as claimed.

At the low end of the scale, we can hear sounds from around 20 Hz, but it's claimed that the DR60 can record sounds as low as 4 Hz, although this seems very unlikely as this was a first-generation digital recorder that used a very basic audio codec that was first used in 1985. Based on this, the frequency response of the device could be much closer to that of a telephone call, which is optimised for voice only at around 300 to 3,400 Hz.

The Panasonic IC Recorder wasn't just troubled by a poor frequency response; it also had a very poor sample rate. The higher the sample rate, the crisper and clearer the audio sounds, but unfortunately for the DR60, it was only able to sample the sound six times per second. To put that into perspective, a compact disc contains music that is sampled 44,100 times per second.

When you take the Panasonic RR-DR60's poor frequency response and its truly awful sampling rate into account, you end up with very muffled and poor-quality recordings at the best of times, as you'd expect from a 20-year-old recorder. Then, when you switch on the voice activation feature, it cuts out the silence in between any sounds, leaving just the noisy parts of the recording bunched up together. This means that what could have started out as tiny but natural sounds spread out across a long recording ends up as a short but constant sound made up of these noises. This is made worse by the device's onboard noise reduction and auto-gain functions.

Essentially, the device creates short bursts of noise through poor audio processing, triggers itself to record, and these noises get distorted due to poor audio compression. The silence between the noises is ignored, so the noises become a more sustained sound.

The other problem with the silent parts of the recording being removed is that you'll have lost the chance to enhance the quieter parts of the audio in order to listen for lower volume EVPs, which might have been under the minimum threshold required to cause the device to start recording.

Computer Recording

In the same way that you can carry out research using a mobile phone, you can also use a computer, or more likely, a laptop. The good thing about recording on a laptop is that the audio is captured directly in the audio software that you will later use to analyse it.

The most commonly used software is a piece of free, open-source audio software called Audacity. Those who are more experienced working with audio might prefer to use Adobe Audition, which offers users many tools for creating, mixing, and editing audio.

Both Audacity and Audition are available for Windows and Apple Mac, and at their core, they both have a very similar waveform editor.

One of the advantages of using a computer to capture EVPs is that you can see the audio waveform appear on screen as you record. If a sound is captured that you didn't hear aloud, it will show up as a peak in the waveform, and you can then stop recording and instantly review it. Having a waveform available in real time makes it much quicker and easier to skim through and check for EVPs. Moments where an investigator is speaking and when the room falls silent can clearly be distinguished from the shape of the waveform.

Laptops are also good because they let you connect external devices via their standard 3.5 mm microphone jack or USB port. This means you can plug in external omnidirectional microphones. The USB connection allows for microphones to be powered, so you can use a condenser mic, which is much more sensitive and can generally pick up a wider frequency range than a normal unpowered dynamic microphone - the type you'd find in cheaper audio recorders, mobile phones, and the laptop itself.

The possibilities are really endless when you factor in external devices paired with a laptop. You can use radio mics to monitor or record audio from another room, or even use multi-track and multiple inputs to record the audio from several areas at once in one master recording file.

One thing to be aware of if using a laptop to capture EVPs is that the microphones in these sorts of devices are designed to primarily be used as part of a video call, so in most cases they will be tuned to pick up audio in the human vocal range that is close to the microphone while trying to exclude any background noise like the distant sound of people talking in another room.

The same is partially true for digital voice recorders; they too are tuned to be more sensitive to the human vocal range, but since one of their primary uses is to record lectures and group conversations, they will pick up more than just a voice immediately in front of the microphone.

Laser Beam EVPs

Many paranormal investigators believe that ghosts and the electromagnetic spectrum are intrinsically linked, and since laser light is part of the EM spectrum, laser beams can be used to capture EVPs.

It's not uncommon to use a device called an EM pump as part of an investigation. The gadget pumps energy out into the environment around it in the hopes that spirits can draw on that energy and use it to manifest or communicate.

The obvious fact that is often overlooked is that you can pump electromagnetic energy into your surroundings using just about anything, from a flashlight to a fan heater; in fact, even the human body gives out electromagnetic energy in the form of heat.
Another source of EM energy, similar to a flashlight, is a laser. Light, including laser light, travels in waves of varying frequencies in much the same way as radio waves, which are also part of the same spectrum. Of course, radio waves are capable of transmitting data - everything from wifi and mobile phone data to FM radio broadcasts in the form of music and speech.

The radio wave portion of the electromagnetic spectrum is the ideal frequency range for sending audio because the energy kicked out by a radio transmitter travels so far, but just about any form of EM energy can transmit data, including laser light. In fact, before Bluetooth took over the world, wireless headphones that used an invisible infrared light source to transmit the music were common. They worked in much the same way as your television remote control, which sends invisible light signals that your TV can decode.

A visible laser, like the common red and green laser pens that can be bought commercially, can be modified to send an audio signal to a light-sensitive receiver. This means that audio can be wirelessly sent across a room, meanwhile pumping EM energy into the environment. This is where it gets really interesting for paranormal investigators. Specialist paranormal equipment manufacturers also produce EVP laser microphones for this purpose.

As a beam of audio-transmitting laser light passes through the air, paranormal researchers theorise that spirits may be able to manipulate or interfere with the light's waveform in order to change the sound being transmitted or even add a sound of their own into the stream, like a voice.

This allows an investigator to call out to any spirits that might be present and encourage them to respond. The investigator can then monitor the audio being carried by the laser in real time, which could include the spirit's responses.

The principle is basically the same as the idea behind a spirit box. However, in theory, it should be much easier for a spirit to manipulate a laser beam. The light is visible as it passes through the air, so if a spirit can see the environment around it, then it will be able to see where it can interact with the laser, whereas radio waves are invisible, presumably even to ghosts.

Secondly, the laser transmission system relies on line of sight; it can't pick up signals from outside the building or even the room. This eliminates the possibility that external broadcasts could be interfering and giving false-positive results.

EVPs via Telephone Calls

This method of EVP research is often called the Phone Experiment. This is a real-time method of listening to EVPs while using a telephone. The idea isn't a new one. One of the early pioneers in EVP, Sarah Estep, once recorded a telephone call from a fellow EVP researcher, Konstantin Raudive, who had died 20 years previously.

The idea of hearing the voices of the dead over a telephone has been adapted by modern-day paranormal investigators using modern technology.

During a paranormal investigation, a mobile phone is used to call the phone of another investigator. It is then put into speakerphone mode and placed in an isolated part of the location being investigated.

The investigators then go to another room with the second phone and call out to the spirits, asking questions and encouraging them to answer while listening for responses through the receiving phone.

Sometimes one investigator remains in the room with the first phone and calls out in the same fashion while the other investigators listen in from the other room.

The exact science of how this process might work is unknown, but it's easier to imagine how it could have worked in the days of Sarah Estep when phone lines carried analogue signals that were susceptible to interference and cross-lines were a common issue. It's conceivable that an intelligent spirit could use its energy to imprint its thoughts on a phone call.

Today, all telecoms, including landline calls, are digitally encoded, which suggests that a spirit would need a degree in computer science to manipulate audio. Since the advent of digital telecoms, interference and cross-lines are a thing of the past.

However, since it seems that spirits are able to communicate using other digital devices, such as handheld audio recorders, there must be a way that they can do so with modern phones too. Presumably the spirit is able to imprint its voice using the analogue component of the device - its microphone. Microphones work using electromagnetic induction created when a diaphragm is vibrated by sound waves. Ghosts are said to be intrinsically linked with electromagnetism, so the theory might fit.

It shouldn't be forgotten that when you make a call on your phone, the signal is sent to a nearby mobile phone tower, bounced around your mobile phone provider's network infrastructure, passed over to the receiving phone's provider, sent to a cell tower, and then received by the second phone. So, if you are monitoring audio from a phone in the next room, that signal is actually travelling a very long way before you hear it.

So why not cut out the middleman? A cheap pair of walkie-talkies placed in different rooms would give you exactly the same result. One walkie-talkie transmits audio, while the walkie-talkie in the room you are in receives that signal. A direct line of communication.

Walkie-talkies are a little more prone to external interference, but because they are locked to one frequency and have limited power, distant transmissions wouldn't carry far enough to interfere in most cases.

You could also experiment with transmitting trigger sounds through the walkie-talkies and the phone line. This would mean that not only does the trigger sound play aloud in the room, but it would also permeate the entire room and beyond in the form of electromagnetic waves. Trigger sounds could be anything from the sound of a battle when investigating a former battlefield to the sound of prison guards jangling their keys in a former jail. These triggers are another way to encourage spirits to respond.

How to Capture EVPs

Today, EVP experiments are more commonly associated with ghost hunts in the field, but at the beginning of the 20th century, the early pioneers of EVP research proved that you can conduct EVP experiments just about anywhere. Much of their research was carried out as part of early séances, which would take place at the medium's home or performance space. The medium's job was to pull the spirits through and communicate with them.

For more than a century, EVP was a field of research that was conducted in homes, laboratories, offices, and workshops. It was only in the early 2000s, when television ghost hunting programmes started using the technique during their investigations, that it switched to being something that is more commonly done at a haunted location.

For example, the 100,000 audio tapes of EVPs recorded by Konstantin Raudive were made without the need to visit a haunted location. Raudive used several methods of recording EVPs, each method was carried out in strict laboratory conditions, which included screening from external radio interference. The same is true of Marcello Bacci, who worked out of a small performance space in Grosseto, Italy. Sarah Estep conducted her EVP research at home, where she had a dedicated space that housed various types of recording equipment.

One of the advantages of practicing EVP recording at home or a controlled location is that you're able to experiment with various types of equipment without having to lug kit around to haunted locations, where you might not be able to plug electrical equipment in and can't always guarantee silence. It's a great way to start experimenting with older, less portable devices like vintage reel-to-reel tape recorders or radio receivers. Remember, both Raudive and Bacci received their voices through unmodified vacuum radios tuned to a part of the frequency band where there was no station, so that it just produced white noise.

Where do the voices come from if you're not in a haunted location? In the case of Sarah Estep, it was often the voices of deceased friends and family members that came through in her recordings. Similarly, in Marcello Bacci's performances, it was the deceased loved ones of audience members who made contact.

So, even if your home isn't haunted, you can still invite spirits to communicate with you there, including those of a particular person, such as a deceased loved one, with whom you wish to make contact. If recording EVPs at home, you should try to conduct your sessions at a regular time in the hopes that spirits may learn that there will be an opportunity to come back and communicate again.

Wherever you are recording, it's a good idea to make a recording of the ambient sounds at the location before you begin your investigation. While recording this, make sure the building is empty if possible and quiet, and record for around half an hour. This will give you a baseline or reference audio recording, which you can refer to later when analysing your session audio.

Setting Up Your Equipment

The first and most important thing to do is read your device's instruction manual and familiarise yourself with the recorder's functions and features, especially any that might be detrimental to the device's ability to pick up EVPs.

No matter what make and model of audio device you are using, you should avoid any noise-canceling or low-cut features, as these will automatically boost, alter, and manipulate the audio you are recording. It's a great feature if you're using the device for its intended purpose as a voice recorder, but not so much when researching EVPs.

You may also find that your device has an auto-gain feature turned on by default. This feature will automatically adjust the sensitivity of the microphone. If you shout into the recorder, it will dip the microphone to accommodate, but when recording in a silent situation, it will boost the gain on the microphone, pushing it to its most sensitive setting.

This is great as it means you will hear really quiet sounds, but it will also mean that something that sounds very loud might have actually been very quiet if the audio hadn't been automatically boosted. So if you keep this feature turned on, you shouldn't assume that sounds in the recording are as loud as they appear to be.

Automatic gain can also mean that the struggling microphone amplifies the ambient sound so much that the recording consists of a lot of background noise in the form of hiss or low-end rumbling. In the same way that unwanted visual artefacts in a photograph or video can cause us to see things that aren't really there, unwanted noise in an audio recording can also lead to audio pareidolia. This is when the human brain tries to find patterns and familiar sounds in the chaos and misinterprets random sounds as voices.

Be sure to set your device to record in the highest possible recording quality; this is usually a WAV PCM format rather than the heavily compressed MP3 format. If you can change the sample rate, then use at least 44,100 Hz. Always choose the high-quality (HQ) or "lossless" setting, or if available on your device, extra high-quality (XHQ) or super high (SHQ). Avoid long play (LP), as this mode extends the recorder's storage by drastically reducing the audio quality so that the file size is smaller.

Some recorders will have a setting for the microphone's sensitivity level. This may give you a sliding scale of sensitivity or the option of low, medium, or high. You may need to experiment with these options to determine which is most suitable for a paranormal investigation. Usually a higher sensitivity is desirable because you'll want to be able to hear everything going on in the room as this adds important context to your recordings, but too high and you might pick up too much background noise.

It might also be a good idea to use a windshield or muffler, which helps reduce unwanted noise from the wind or breeze. A suitable shield can be bought for more professional recorders, like those in Tascam's and Zoom's ranges.

If recording with a mobile device, look for the recording quality settings in the app and set the recording quality to the highest setting, ideally lossless quality. Where possible, switch from MP3 to WAV.

Recording with a computer makes things much easier as you can set the session to a high quality. The settings are defined up front, and the raw audio is recorded as a waveform. It's only when you save the recording that you need to specify a file format, and again, you should save the recording as a WAV file rather than an MP3.

Don't forget the golden rule: always use fresh batteries. Before every investigation, put brand new batteries in your recorder or make sure it is fully charged. Not only do you want to avoid the batteries running out while you're recording, but low batteries may also result in a reduction in the quality of the recording or unwanted noise.

Ensuring High-Quality Recordings

Now that you're ready to start capturing EVPs, you're going to need to make sure they're of the best possible quality; this will make it much easier to analyse them later.

The first step towards achieving crystal-clear EVPs is to ensure the environment is free of background noise. So turn off the heating, air conditioning, fans, and any other loud mechanical devices that could spring into action. Make sure that windows and internal and external doors are closed to reduce noise bleeding through from other parts of the building or from outside.

Place your recorder away from other electrical devices to avoid unwanted interference, especially any device that transmits a radio signal of any kind.

Limit the number of people in the building or room during the EVP session. For every additional person present, there's the added possibility that a strange noise captured isn't paranormal and is just a human moving; this can be very hard to debunk retrospectively during playback and analysis.

Place the audio recorder on a flat, solid surface. Holding a device is a common cause of unexpected sounds, as the slightest change in pressure in your grip can cause the plastic housing of the device to flex and make a sound. This is especially true of recorders with in-built microphones. This sound is often inaudible at the time but can sound very loud inside the device where its microphone is housed.

If holding your recorder is unavoidable then use a firm grip and avoid moving your hand while recording.

Avoid placing the recorder on the floor, as any movement could cause vibrations, resulting in the device translating the vibration as a sound or causing the recorder itself to rock slightly, causing a noise.
Do not place the recorder inside of anything, such as a box, pouch, or your pocket, as this will severely limit the device's sensitivity or make sounds muffled and impossible to either debunk or identify as genuine EVPs.

Take a seat, if possible, and get comfortable. You should also try to stay as still as possible during the session to avoid making any unnecessary noise. Where possible, remove any clothing, like heavy jackets that might rustle or heavy, clanging jewellery. Not only could these sounds be misidentified as paranormal contact in the recording later during playback and analysis, but you could also drown out genuine EVPs.

With the basics in place, the next few best-practice tips are essential.

Upon pressing record, leave five to 10 seconds of silence at the beginning to allow the recorder to adjust to the baseline noise level. If you're using a tape recorder, then remember that cassettes have a seven to 10 second buffer at the beginning that can't be recorded on, so allow for this.

Introducing each recording is very important when it comes to analysing your audio later; it means you will know exactly what you are listening to.

At the start of each recording, you should start by speaking out loud the date, time, location, and number of people present. You can also give the recording a number, e.g., "EVP recording number one." This will make it easier to keep track of recordings when you review the audio later. Knowing where the audio was captured and who was present will help you debunk sounds heard in the recording. To help you debunk non-paranormal noises, you should note verbally any sounds that are heard during the session so that you can eliminate them from your investigation when you later review the audio.

For example, if you cough, sneeze, clear your throat, move slightly, or your stomach rumbles, say out loud "that was me" so that there is no doubt later. It's surprising how different some normal noises can sound with no context in a recording and how they can be very hard to identify, which could lead you to a false paranormal conclusion.

Do not whisper during a session. If you have something to say, say it out loud. Whispers can be very hard to identify later when you review the audio.

How long you record for is really up to you, but a good duration for a session would be around 10 to 20 minutes. You want to give the experiment the best chance of success, but recording too much will mean you have a lot of audio to listen back to later.

However, there are a few different methods that determine the recording time. We'll look at these next.

Active vs. Passive EVP Sessions

When it comes to recording, there are a few different tried and tested methods available. We'll look at realtime and burst recordings later in the chapter, but first let's look at the differences between active and passive recording sessions.

Passive EVP Sessions

A passive EVP session is one in which the investigators conducting the experiment are not actively asking questions or encouraging the spirits to interact. The method was pioneered by Konstantin Raudive and involves no human interaction.

In its simplest form, it involves setting up a recording device in a room or enclosed area, leaving the area, and leaving the recorder running in silence. The idea behind this is that a supernatural entity may inadvertently make a sound in the recording.

Passive sessions might be a better option for locations that are said to house a residual haunting where intelligent two-way communication may not be possible.

After 20 minutes, or however long you feel is necessary, you can retrieve the recorder and review the audio to see if you've captured any unexplained sounds or voices during the session.

We previously discussed steps that should be taken to minimise and eliminate external noise. When conducting a passive EVP experiment, this is more important than ever as you won't be in the room and won't be able to note any non-paranormal sounds heard to eliminate them from your investigation when you review the audio.

Care should be taken to ensure all doors and windows are closed and that adjoining rooms are silent too.

In a silent setting, the device may overcompensate with audio gain and amplification, which could mean that even distant voices in other rooms and floors of the building are picked up.

Although the recorder is normally left in a quiet environment, this isn't always necessary. The device could be left recording in an allegedly haunted location during normal daily life to see if anything is captured. This would still be classed as a passive session, as there are no direct or intentional attempts to actively communicate.

Active EVP Sessions

An active EVP session is when investigators are actively making attempts to communicate during the session. This normally involves asking a question out loud, such as "Is there anybody here?" Then leaving a few seconds of silence before the next question in the hopes that a response will be captured in the gap.

You could also sit in the room with the recorder and have a conversation with your fellow investigators to see if this encourages any spirit interaction. Although this isn't a direct attempt at communication, since you are still encouraging the spirits to communicate, it would still be classified as an active session.

Some researchers have found that when this method of attempting to capture EVPs is used, the voices heard will reference the conversation taking place or reply to certain things that were said. Remember not to be too talkative; you still need to give the voices a chance to be heard over your chatter.

Real-time and Burst EVP Sessions

Both the real-time and burst methods can be used as part of an active or passive EVP session; however, they are most often used during an active session as this method allows investigators to be more responsive.

Burst Session

A burst session is almost like a quick-fire EVP session. It involves recording two or three minutes of audio using the same methods described previously. The audio is then reviewed straight away, allowing the investigator to hear any potential voices that have been captured in the recording.

Real-time Session

A real-time, or "listen live," session is where the investigator monitors the audio being captured in real-time. This can be done using some of the methods described previously, such as capturing EVPs via laser beams or by using telephone calls and walkie-talkies.

However, the easiest and most common way to conduct a real-time EVP session is by simply plugging a pair of headphones into your audio recorder and monitoring the sound. You may find that you are able to hear sounds through the headphones that you can't hear with your ear alone, but the effectiveness of this depends on the sensitivity of the microphone, the frequency response of the headphones, and the quality of the onboard microphone preamp and headphone amplifier.

Listening to live EVPs can also be done through devices like a spirit box or modified radios like those used by Konstantīns Raudive and Marcello Bacci.

With both burst and realtime sessions, the idea is to listen to EVPs as they occur, or in the case of burst recordings, a couple of minutes later, while the investigator is still in the same location and conditions.

This allows investigators to follow up on any words or phrases they hear in order to continue the conversation.

While these methods, especially burst recordings, tend to get good results, you should remember that listening to audio via headphones while on an investigation might not be ideal when it comes to picking up quieter, more subtle voices. Therefore, you should always fully review and analyse your full recordings after the investigation to uncover anything you might have missed. There will be more on analysing EVP recordings later.

Calling Out During EVP Sessions

Unless you are conducting a passive EVP session, you'll need to ask any spirits that might be present questions; this is called "calling out" or "asking out."

We've covered the the concept of calling out in the previous section, Practical Ghost Hunting. You can revisit this section for a refresh on best practices and tips for effectively calling out. The techniques that apply to ghost hunting are also relevant to EVP sessions.

White Noise Generators

Based on the theory that spirits can reorganise radio noise to form words, some EVP researchers use a white noise source to give spirits a base of raw sound to use to form words. This is done by playing back a pre-recorded sample of white noise, by recording near a source of static noise like a television or radio, or by using a white noise signal generator to artificially produce random and constant white noise.

The drawback to using this technique is that the white noise contaminates the recording, making it hard to analyse the audio. However, some EVP experts use audio editing software like Adobe Audition and Audacity or bespoke audio filtering software to remove the white noise, leaving only the more sustained sound in the recording, which could include spirit voices.

If using a source of white noise during an EVP session, be sure not to have the volume too high as it might flood your recording. Because white noise, by its very nature, covers the whole spectrum of sound, it will mask all other frequencies if it is too loud, including human speech and EVPs.

When it comes to filtering out the white noise from your recording, this can't be totally removed for the same reason. Again, because white noise, by definition, lives all across the frequency spectrum, audio filters can't distinguish it from the sounds you want to keep in your recording.

However, the good news is that you don't have to completely remove it. For the most part, your brain can't hear noise when it is masked by a real sound in the same frequency range. So the noise reduction techniques mentioned later in the book also apply to recordings where white noise is present.

The Ghost Frequency

In 1980, Vic Tandy was an experimental officer and part-time lecturer in the school of international studies and law at Coventry University in the UK. He was working alone late one night in a lab, which has a reputation for being haunted. He reported feeling anxious and claimed he could see dark objects out of the corner of his eye, but when he turned to face the greyish blob, there was nothing there.

The next day, the researcher noticed what some might describe as poltergeist activity. He was working on his fencing sword, which is made of a lightweight, flexible metal. He had the handle of the foil held in a vice on his desk when he noticed that the blade started vibrating, even though nothing was touching it.

Tandy realised that it was a specific frequency of infrasound in his lab that was being produced by a fan that was causing his discomfort and even the movement of the foil.

In 2003, an experiment using infrasound was carried out in London. Infrasound was played during a concert in the Purcell Room. Afterwards, the audience was interviewed and their responses were analysed by psychologists. On average, infrasound boosted the number of strange experiences by around 22% and caused the concertgoers to report feelings of sorrow, coldness, and anxiety.

The specific frequency of sound that Tandy detected in his lab was 18.98 Hz, and it is known to paranormal investigators as the "ghost frequency" or "ghost tone." The tone is impossible to hear as it falls just outside the range that the human ear can pick up.

While some parapsychologists think that the ghost tone tricks your senses into seeing, hearing, and feeling the type of unusual things that are commonly associated with hauntings, some EVP researchers believe that playing the ghost tone during an investigation increases the chances of capturing EVPs as the sound acts as a carrier wave or effective source of sound for transformation to occur.

If you'd like to experiment with playing the ghost tone during an investigation, you'll need to first use an audio tone generator website, which will allow you to play a clean tone at exactly 18.98 Hz. The problem is that most speakers can't actually reproduce this tone. Laptop speakers aren't very good at reproducing sounds under 300 Hz, and smartphone speakers are even worse.

There's no way to know if a sound you can't hear is playing, but the best way to ensure you are exposing yourself or your investigation to the frequency is to use a subwoofer with a large amplifier, the type you use as part of a home cinema system.

Regular speakers are optimised to reproduce sound waves at the peak of the human ear's frequency range; tones that are much higher or lower than this tend to be much weaker. However, subwoofers are designed specifically to play very low-frequency sounds, known in the movie industry as LFE, or low-frequency effects. The LFE sounds are amplified much higher to compensate for the low frequency.

You still won't be able to actually hear 18.98 Hz, but if you place your hand in front of the subwoofer, you will almost certainly be able to feel it, and that's exactly what is required for this experiment. It doesn't matter that you can't hear the sound; the vibration of the sound waves is said to affect your whole body and even your visual system.

Analysing EVPs

When it comes to EVP research, playback is arguably the most important and time-consuming task. It can also be quite tedious, but without a proper review of your audio, the whole EVP session is pointless.

Even if you were conducting a "quick fire" burst session or a "listen live" session and you reviewed the audio as you went during the session, you should still review all of the audio in full after the session.

The built-in speakers on audio recorders are often inadequate for a proper review, and while at a location, you may find it hard to find somewhere quiet enough to properly review the audio.

The simplest approach for reviewing and analysing your recordings is to plug your audio recorder directly into a good-quality external speaker or connect a pair of good-quality over-ear headphones. Either of these methods is really the minimum required effort; they're not ideal, but they're a good place to start.

A better approach is to transfer the audio to your computer; this allows you to review the audio in greater detail. Once on your computer, it then becomes easier to turn up the volume, pause, and go back to re-listen to specific parts of the recording again. Transferring audio is normally done via a USB lead, and audio files are compatible with Windows or Apple devices. You should refer to the specific instructions in your audio recorder's instruction manual for more details on this.

There are some cases where the process of transferring audio may be a little different and require a little more effort. If you're using an analogue recording device, such as an old tape recorder or an early dictaphone, then there won't be a USB port on the device. You may need some special audio leads and a USB audio interface in order to capture the audio. The downside of this is that the audio isn't transferred instantly like it is over USB; it is captured by the computer in real time, and poor-quality audio connections might lead to unwanted noise in the transferred audio.

Unfortunately, this is unavoidable and is the nature of analogue recordings. To ensure you obtain the best audio possible when transferring from analogue device, practice the transfer process in order to familiarise yourself with the ideal settings and levels required on both the recording device and the computer.

Once the audio is on your computer, you should again ensure you are listening to it through high-quality speakers, or better yet, a good pair of over-ear headphones.

MP3 and WAV files can be played easily on computers, either using Windows Media Player on a Windows machine or QuickTime Player on an Apple Mac. You can also use a free audio player such as VLC, which is available for both operating systems.

Listen to the audio from start to finish, from the moment you press record to the moment you press stop. EVPs don't always happen on demand, so you might hear unexpected voices in parts of the recording where you weren't actively asking for responses.

You should listen carefully for anything that sounds like a voice in the audio. If you hear anything, either make a note of the time in the recording or what you think the voice is saying. Or better still, isolate the specific piece of audio and save it as a separate file. This can be done using free audio editing software like Audacity or the more professional Adobe Audition.

When saving a highlight, be sure to leave a few seconds before and after the sound, as this provides important context should you wish to play these highlights to someone.

Be sure to set up a method of saving your sessions and recordings so that you can easily refer back to the raw session and find examples of the EVPs you captured. Of course, how you do this is up to you, but a good way to manage this is to create a folder with a meaningful name that includes a date code, such as "2021-10-31 - Hampton Castle." Save the raw audio recordings from your recording in this folder. Don't edit your raw recording files; this is your evidence. Editing the file could remove vital context, making later analysis impossible.

If you are logging the EVPs, then save a text-based log file document in the same folder and note anything you hear. So for example, if you hear a voice at 5:12 in the recording that sounds like it's saying "help me", then in the document type "05:12 - Help me".

You should use the same naming approach if you are isolating and saving the individual EVP clips. Again save the clips in the same folder and call the file "05-12 - help me.wav". This will allow you to easily find a specific EVP you captured and also tell you where you can find that EVP in the original recording.

The trickiest part can be hearing the voices, figuring out what they're saying, and recognising when something that sounds like a voice isn't a voice at all but has another explanation.

The problem is that when you listen back to audio alone, you don't have any real record of the causes of background noises and other sources of sounds other than your recollection of events. Your memory alone simply isn't reliable enough. You won't remember every sound that was heard at the time of recording; you may not have even picked up on the sound or been consciously aware of it.

Normally we are able to see the things around us in order to add context to help us understand what we're hearing, this is of course not the case with an audio recording.

If you are finding it hard to distinguish a sound from background noise, then your baseline recording might help. As mentioned previously, it's a good idea to make a recording of the ambient sounds at the location before you begin your investigation there. This is where that baseline reference recording might come in handy. If you hear a sound in your session recording, but you're not sure what's causing it, you can refer back to your baseline recording to see if it naturally occurred prior to the investigation during your baseline recording.

However, don't be too quick to rule out sounds heard in your baseline recording either, as the idea of creating a clean baseline recording as a reference contradicts the passive EVP session method, where researchers intentionally try to capture EVPs in silent environments. Both approaches are valid and should be researched.

While you're trying to pick out a sound from the background, don't ignore the background noise all together, as it provides important context and clues that may help you explain an unexplained sound in the recording. For example, if you hear a strange sound moments after someone takes a piece of electronic equipment out of their bag, that could be the piece of equipment being switched on.

Comparing the suspected EVP to the background noise can also give you an idea of how loud the sound was. Was it louder or quieter than the investigators' voices? Are there any other similarly pitched sounds heard before or after?

The quality of EVPs varies, and researchers need a certain amount of patience and concentration to distinguish them from background noise. Some words are difficult to understand, while others can be very clear.

Some EVP researchers liken understanding the voices in EVPs to learning a new language, but this isn't a good approach as it suggests that the words are unclear and the researcher is inventing ways to hear what isn't really there.

Auditory Pareidolia

As a paranormal investigator, you've probably come across the term "pareidolia" before. This is the tendency for the human brain to perceive a familiar or meaningful image in an object or pattern where, in fact, there is none. This becomes most relevant in ghost hunting when investigators see what looks like phantom faces in a blurry photo, which in reality aren't paranormal at all; it's just our minds seeing something that's not really there.

Pareidolia is a form of apophenia, which is a more general term for the human tendency to seek patterns in random information, and this applies to audio too. Just like with vision, we are all susceptible to hearing words that are not actually in the sounds we are hearing. This can occur by misinterpreting words that are being said or by hearing words in random noise.

Auditory pareidolia isn't the only thing that might cause you to misidentify an EVP. The truth is, understanding or interpreting what an EVP is saying is subjective. You will find that people often disagree with your interpretation of a word or phrase and hear something completely different. As the listener, you may be influenced by the question that was asked prior to the EVP or by your knowledge of the location you were investigating. You are likely to simply hear what you expect to hear.

Auditory pareidolia is by far the biggest and strongest argument against the credibility of EVPs. Skeptics maintain that the majority of EVP recordings are sounds that are misinterpreted; most often, they are caused by natural phenomena, including ambient sounds, atmospheric electrical interference, radio interference, faulty equipment, sounds caused by the recording device being moved or handled, or the sounds of the inner workings of the recorder itself. Because of this, you should do all that you can to validate your recordings.

Luckily, there are ways to remove subjectivity and validate your EVPs. First off, if you hear something anomalous, isolate the clip and remove all context by removing anything said around it or any questions asked. Then forget about it for a day or two. After this time, listen to the clip out-of-context and decide whether the sound still sounds like the word you thought it did previously, a different word, or nothing at all.

The next step is to get other people to listen to it, ideally a group who are not interested in the paranormal or familiar with EVP research. Again, make sure there is no context, and do not tell them what you believe the voice is saying. Don't tell the listener where the clip was recorded or what was being asked; just play them the sound and ask them to tell you what they hear.

If their interpretation matches yours, then this is good validation of the EVP. However, after asking several people you may find that the majority hear a different word or phrase to you. Since all these people heard the same speech without the influence of the context of the recording, this should tell you that your interpretation is wrong.

It's really important to remove the context when you review the audio after some time away from it and when asking others to review it. If a question was asked in the recording, then the listener may try to interpret the sound in a way that fits the question rather than listening objectively.

The Cocktail Party Effect

One of the benefits of using an audio recorder during an investigation is that it gives you another chance to hear something you might have missed at the time. Have you ever been on an investigation and someone has asked, "Did you hear that sound?" As soon as they mention it, you recall it, but at the time you weren't consciously aware of it. This is due to the "cocktail party effect."

The effect describes an ability of the human brain that allows us to focus our auditory attention on one particular stimulus while filtering out a range of other stimuli. This is most obvious at a party when you are able to hold a conversation with a single person while other partygoers chatter all around you.

It's for this reason that you might be listening to someone call out on a vigil and perhaps even waiting for responses through a spirit box or other gadget, and because your auditory attention is focussed on this, you might not notice normal or paranormal sounds coming from around you.

Let's go back to the cocktail party. After your chat, you might wander off and help yourself to a drink, ignoring the buzz of chattering guests, until you hear your name mentioned. Even though you weren't consciously aware of anything else that was being said, clearly you are hearing what's going on around you; your brain just filters it out unless it's relevant.

We may not remember hearing a disembodied voice or an unexplained sound during a vigil, but that's not a reason to assume it wasn't audible at all if the noise is later heard while playing back an audio recording. An audio recorder captures everything it hears within its frequency response, depending on its microphone sensitivity. If a sound is captured in a recording, it's not necessarily paranormal in nature just because you don't remember hearing it at the time.

Should EVP Recordings be Enhanced?

One area of EVP research that is often debated is whether the audio captured should be enhanced and manipulated or not. A researcher may choose to enhance their audio in order to make the words heard clearer or to filter out background noises.

The problem with doing this is that if you are intentionally manipulating the audio to make it sound more like the words you think it sounds like, then what you're left with is your ideal interpretation of your own subjective perception of what that EVP should sound like, not a true representation of what it sounded like at the time it was captured.

It's the audio equivalent of distorting a photo or video until it looks like what you want it to look like. Case in point: you could also manipulate the audio to sound less like words, which would also be an untrue representation of the sound.

EVP recordings often have a lot of hiss due to the nature of how they're recorded in very quiet situations. This hiss is similar to white noise, a cacophony of random sounds spanning across the whole frequency range. When this sound is run through a digital filter to clean it up, normally the high-frequency sounds are taken out. These are the frequencies that our ears are most sensitive to, therefore creating the dominant hiss sound in white noise.

What you're left with is a collection of sounds within a certain frequency range; this can sound very different, and with some of the noise removed, random patterns may present themselves, causing a greater risk of pareidolia.

Some EVP researchers sometimes capture what sounds like words spoken at a slower or faster speed than normal. It's not uncommon to use audio editing software to speed up or slow down recordings for this reason, but again, this should be avoided as changing the speed will cause the audio to become an inaccurate reproduction of the original sound.

Therefore, the filtering or manipulation of clips should be minimised and clips presented as close to their original form as possible. However, if done properly, manipulation can improve the audio. You can filter out just the extraneous sounds, leaving you with a more accurate representation of the captured sound.

There are also types of manipulation and enhancement that are acceptable and can be very useful when reviewing your audio, and that's the simple amplification of the audio in order to enable you to hear any potential EVPs more clearly.

While logic states that a clean recording is always preferable, many prominent investigators have established a trend of manipulating and enhancing their recordings. They often say that it makes it easier for the listener to hear the EVP, but of course, as mentioned previously, what's being heard may not be a true reflection of what was originally recorded.

Although it is generally not advised, there is no right or wrong when it comes to paranormal investigation, and what works for one investigator doesn't necessarily work for another. So, if you strongly feel the need to aggressively enhance your recordings, then do so with the awareness that you might be destructively altering your evidence.

In the spirit of keeping your audio as true to the source recording as possible, if you really must enhance it, then limit yourself to just one or two enhancements.

Of course, recording conditions vary, but try to find filters and enhancements that work for you and stick to them; at least this way, you'll be treating all potential evidence fairly. If you apply different filters to varying degrees on different clips, then you will not be able to make objective comparisons between the audio clips.

If there is a need for different filters or enhancements with different pieces of audio, then this merely highlights the problem with enhancement. It shows that you are intentionally altering a clip in order to make a noise sound more like the voice that you subjectively think it should sound like.

Enhance and Filtering Recordings

Before you do anything to your recordings, make sure you make a copy of the original files and back them up to ensure that you don't unintentionally and irreparably alter the original.

In order to enhance your audio, you'll need some audio editing software. The most commonly used are Audacity, Adobe Audition, both of which are available for Apple Mac and Windows computers, as well as Goldwave on Windows. Audacity isn't quite as good as Audition, but it is completely free to download and use.

Although these and other applications are great for editing audio, they're not really fit for the purpose of enhancing EVPs to the degree that some investigators push them. In the field of audio recording, there is a commonly used term, "signal to noise ratio." The "signal" is the audio you want, the voice, the music, or in this case, the EVP. The "noise" is any unwanted hiss, rumble, or buzz. So a high signal-to-noise ratio means there's lots of what you want to hear without much unwanted noise. This is the type of recording that audio editing software is designed to work with and what most audio industry professionals want to use the software for.

Unfortunately, in the case of EVP recordings, there's often a low or even negative signal-to-noise ratio, which means that the signal power is lower than the noise power. Editing software struggles to deal with this sort of audio because there is often not enough clean signal to successfully be restored. So, enhancing a very faint sound from a recording with significant ambient noise will often be too much of a stretch.

The problem is that the normal noise reduction or hiss removal tools in the software will not be able to tell the difference between the noise and your EVP, so when the filter is applied, it will either mute the whole recording or try to aggressively enhance a certain frequency range while softening the surrounding frequencies that it judges to be unwanted.

For their intended purpose, these filters work well. If you're trying to remove an unwanted hiss from a clean and loud recording of a speech, then the software will take away this hiss and leave the speaker's voice relatively untouched. However, when used to try to enhance faint sounds within a lot of noise, it may change them so significantly that the results are of no use as evidence.

Due to the nature of software, settings options and tools often change, so it would be impractical to offer step-by-step guides to enhancing audio in this book. Instead, we will take a look at the tools you can use, which should be similar to some extent across all audio editing software.

Some audio editing software allows you to switch to a "spectral frequency display" view rather than the standard waveform. This view can be very useful for identifying and removing or enhancing noise in your recordings. Don't worry if you're not familiar with working with audio frequencies and waveforms; there will be more on this later.

Amplification

Perhaps the most useful tool is amplify, which is normally found in the effects tools. This allows you to basically increase the volume of your clip. Be sure not to amplify your clip too heavily, as over-amplification will cause it to become distorted.

Start with a 1 to 3 dB (decibel) boost and play the audio to ensure it's not too loud. You will know if it is because the volume metre will be going into the red. If it's too loud, then press undo and try a lower level. If the audio is still too loud, don't simply apply another amplification on top; again, press undo to take you back to the original level and start with a slightly higher amplification. This will ensure your audio stays as clean and true to its original state as possible.

Although amplification is the best option for enhancing your clips and the least aggressive, it might not help in this case. The problem is, by trying to increase the volume of the EVP, what you're actually doing is increasing the volume of the whole clip, including the background noise. Since both elements get a boost, the EVP does not become any clearer. So another approach is to try to remove that background noise.

If you are using a spectral view of your recording, then after playing the sound through a few times, it may be easy to see where the sound is in the spectrum, not just in terms of when the sound starts and its duration, but also where it appears in the frequency range. If you are able to see the sound in the spectral view, then you can highlight and amplify it. This will more or less amplify just the selected sound without any of the unwanted noise.

Noise Reduction and Restoration

Most software has some basic noise reduction tool. This might be called simply "noise reduction," but also look out for restoration, hiss removal, hum removal, and vocal enhancers.

If you want to reduce the background noise, then noise reduction or restoration is your best option, but you could also try hiss removal. Vocal enhancer should be a last resort, as it is an automated tool that may struggle with clips with a lot of noise and apply filters too aggressively.

Experiment with the different settings, but, like with amplification, don't jump in with very harsh enhancements straight away. Try a less intense filter once, one with a low level of noise reduction. If this doesn't have much of an impact, or if you've applied too much, then again press undo to return to your un-enhanced audio and start again with a different setting.

Capturing a Noise Print

In some applications, the noise reduction tool requires you to select a sample of noise for best results. The tool then subtracts this noise sample from the rest of the recording. If you made a baseline recording in this same environment, then you could use a portion of that recording as your noise print, or alternatively, use a quiet period in the recording before or after the suspected EVP appears.

You should try to pick a part of the recording where the noise is similar to the background sounds heard throughout the clip and at the point where the sound of interest is heard. Unfortunately, making the judgement is subjective. No two investigators would select the exact same area and this will cause results to vary.

Once you have highlighted the area of noise - ideally at least five seconds of audio, press the "capture noise print" option followed by the "process" button.

Understanding Frequencies and Waveforms

A major part of EVP research requires you to be able to analyse audio recorded during investigations. Knowledge of frequencies and waveforms will help you determine if a captured sound is a genuine EVP or just unwanted noise in your recording. The main terms you'll need to understand are frequency, amplitude, wavelength, and pitch. Knowledge of these key terms is vital when examining a waveform. We have covered waveforms in-depth in the previous section, Scientific Theory.

For a refresh you can revisit the chapter on Instrumental Transcommunication or keep reading to find out how to progress from waveforms into analysing the full audio spectrum.

Spectral Frequency Display

We know that the height of a waveform tells us the amplitude, or how loud or quiet the sound is. We also know that the horizontal axis of a waveform tells us the duration of the sound, but one thing that cannot be immediately determined from a waveform is the sound's frequency.

However, there is another way to analyse audio that gives you a better understanding of which frequencies are present in a recording, and that's the spectrogram view, sometimes called the spectral frequency display. This is a tool built into Adobe Audition, Audacity, and some other audio software.

In the view, rather than being presented with a waveform, you will see what looks like a heat map, an overview of the audio from which you can determine the volume and different frequencies present in a recording.

Whereas in a waveform view the vertical axis represents the amplitude of the sound, in a spectral frequency display the vertical axis represents the frequency range while the horizontal axis still represents time.

The lighter areas on the display represent louder sounds, and the sound's vertical placement in the graph shows us the frequency of the sound.

If there is a higher density of light patches at the top of the display, then this represents a high-pitched sound. A similarly dense area at the bottom of the display represents a low-pitched sound. This view can make it easier to pick out human voices or low or high-pitched sounds at a glance - something you can't do with a waveform view.

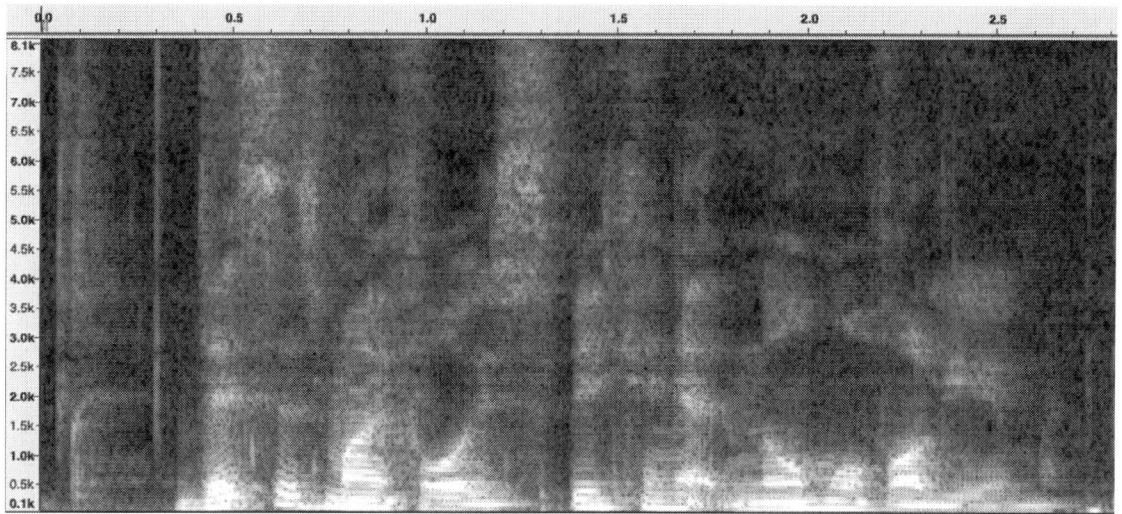

The spectrogram above represents a human voice. Speech has a characteristic look, which you will be able to recognise with a bit of practice, as it always falls within a certain frequency range and therefore has roughly the same vertical placement on a spectrogram.

A male voice has an average frequency of 125 Hz, while a female voice is around 200 Hz. However, we don't speak in a monotone; the pitch of our voices fluctuates, and the voice spans a frequency range up to as high as 8 kHz. In the example above, you can see that the speech is mostly concentrated below the 500 Hz mark, but there are elements of the speech that reach as high as 6 kHz.

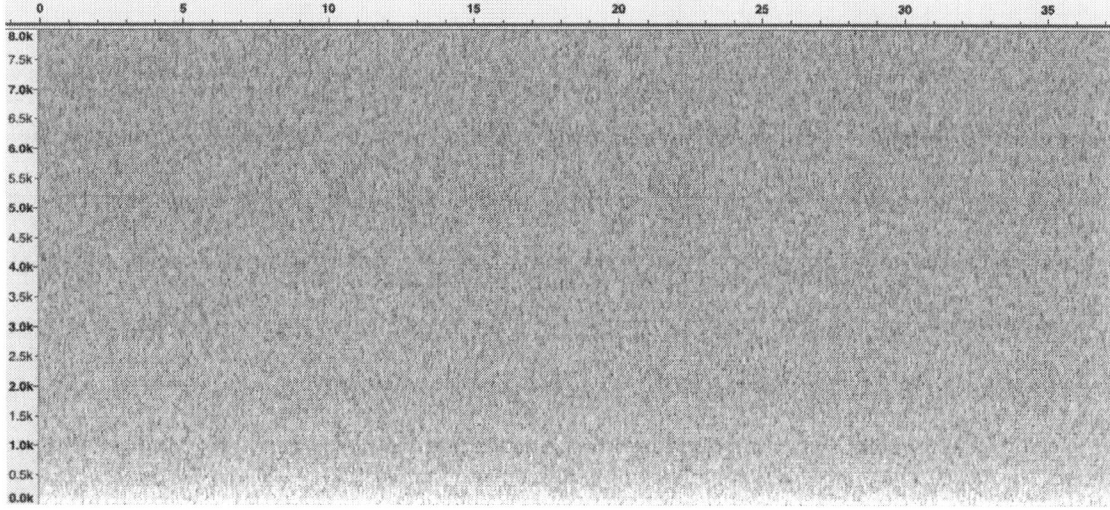

This spectrogram shows pure white noise. It is made up of random sounds across the whole spectrum of frequencies, which gives the spectral frequency display a very uniform look across both the frequency and time axes.

If we mix the previous two examples together so that the voice is playing over the white noise, we get a spectrogram that looks like the example below.

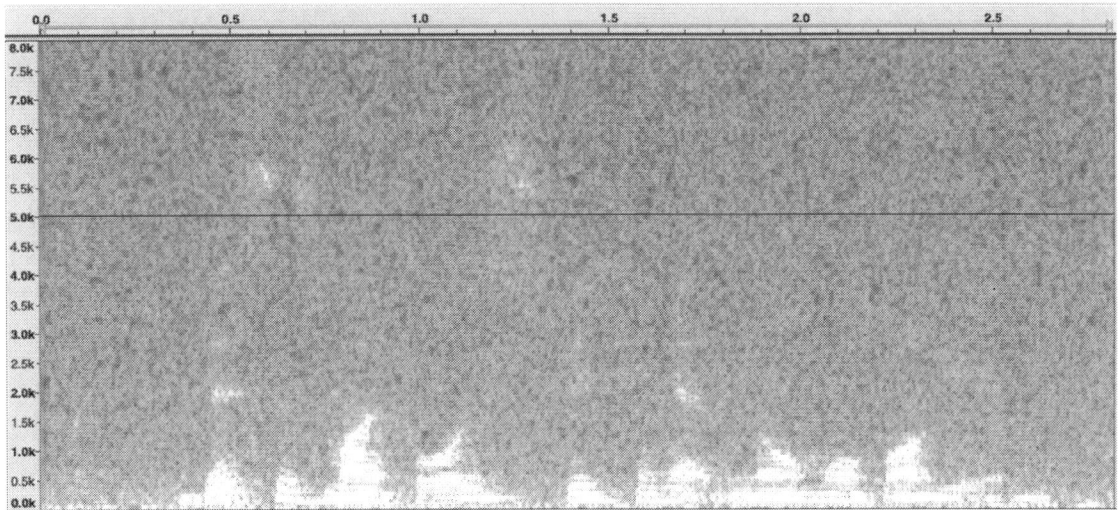

Although there is the same amount of white noise in the example above, it is still clear to see where the voice lies in the recording. Understanding the parts of the spectrogram can be very useful for isolating voices and removing background noise.

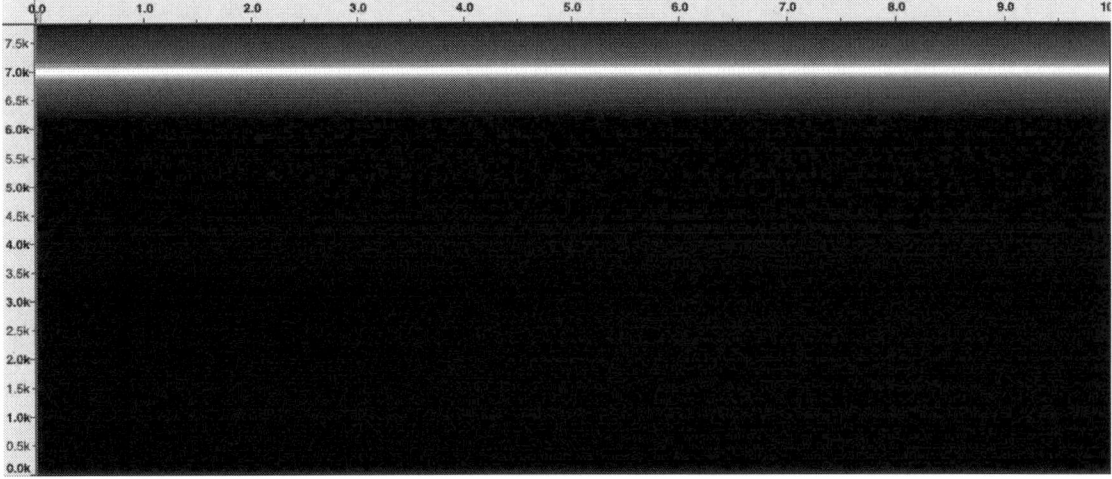

To create the spectrogram above, a pure, high-frequency tone was generated. You can see that the only sound in the recording is the tone, which sits around the 7 kHz mark and lasts for the full duration of the recording. The black portions of the display show that there are no sounds at all within these other frequency ranges.

The spectrogram below was created in the same way but with a 400 Hz tone, which you can see towards the bottom of the spectral display. Again, the large black portions show there are no high-frequency sounds present.

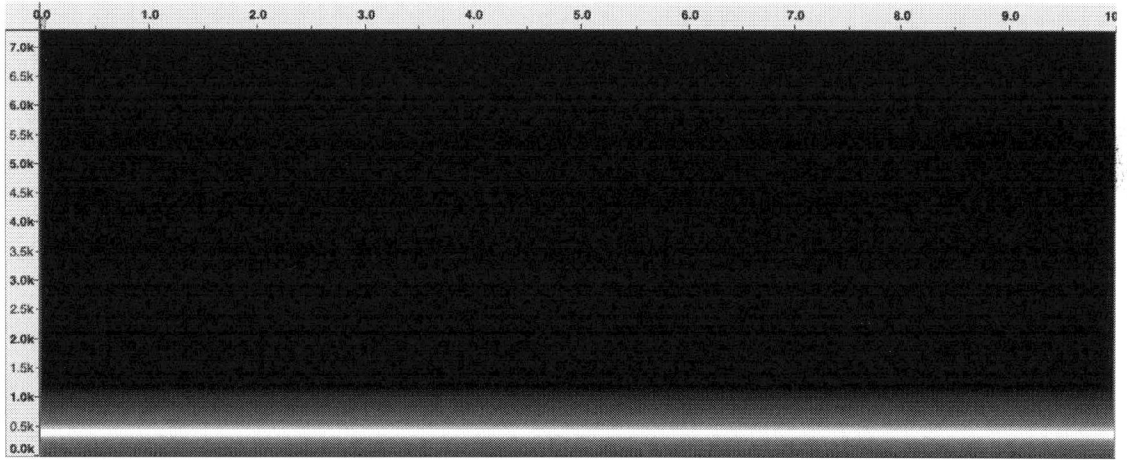

Often, unwanted noise in recordings will be high-pitched hisses or low-end rumbles, so understanding how to identify noises across the frequency ranges will enable you to isolate those sounds and remove them from the recording without affecting the speech you're trying to preserve.

You can remove or reduce these unwanted sounds by highlighting the specific frequency range in the recording and either removing it by pressing delete or cut, or by reducing the volume to zero. Tools like the spot healing brush can also help you to seamlessly remove unwanted sounds with as little disruption to the rest of the recording as possible.

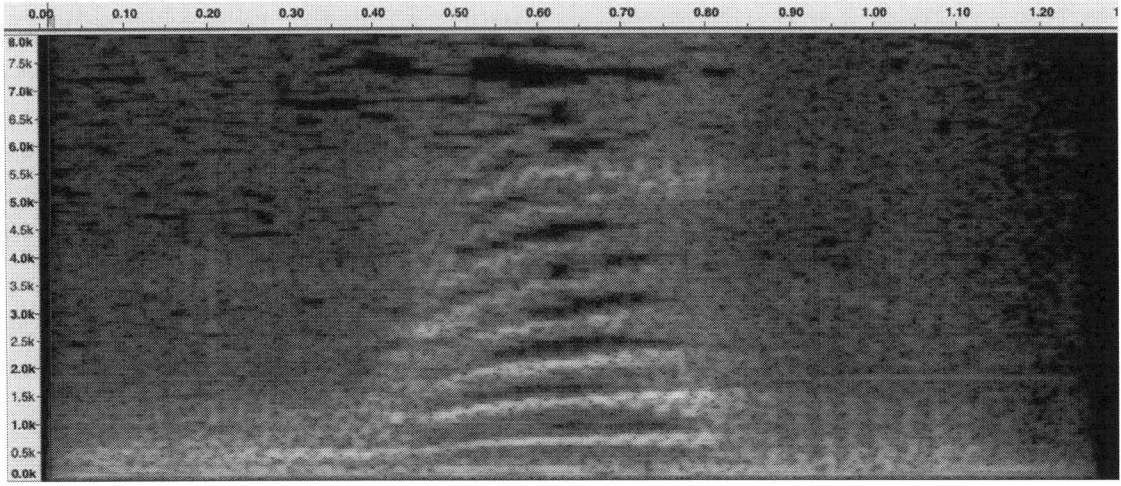

The spectrogram above doesn't show a human voice; it actually represents a cat's meow. You can see that the shapes of the sounds are quite different; they are more uniform in the case of the meow, and the sound is made up of more high-frequency sounds.

Understanding the frequency that sounds are made up of can be very helpful when analysing EVPs. If you capture a voice in your recording, a spectrogram will tell you one of two things: either the voice falls within the normal frequency range of human speech or the voice does not match the tone of a normal human voice.

Since so little is known about the nature of EVPs, where the voices come from, and how they are captured, this information can be interpreted in several different ways.

If a suspected EVP has the signature of a normal human voice, then this could tell you that you have captured the voice of a spirit as they may have sounded in life. It could also tell you that the EVP is the result of radio interference, a real human's voice bleeding through the recording, or the voice of someone present at the investigation.

It may be that the voice is made up of background noise or ambient sounds that have been transformed by having their pitch changed to form words.

If you hear a voice in your recording and then upon inspection in a spectral view determine that it is higher or lower pitched than a normal human voice, then this tells you that it is not the voice of a living person on the investigation.

This leaves you with a few possibilities. The first is that it isn't a voice at all and that this is an example of auditory pareidolia. The second possibility is that spirits don't communicate using the voice they had when they were alive or that, through some strange quirk of recording, the voice's pitch has been shifted.

The other possibility is that sounds from non-human voice ranges have been manipulated to form words. This could have been done in a way that the original pitch of the sound has been preserved but the sounds have been altered to form words or sentences.

Although there's no clear way to tell exactly what is going on in these situations, as a good researcher, you should be aware of the frequency ranges of EVPs, not only to help you debunk or validate evidence but also to look for trends in the evidence captured in order to help further the field of EVP research.

Depending on which software you use, sometimes the spectral view will be a 3D representation of the sound, with frequency, amplitude, and time along the three axes. More commonly, it is a two-dimensional representation as described above, with time along the horizontal axis and frequency on the vertical.

Capturing EVPs Outside the Audible Range

There's often talk in the field of EVP research about capturing voices that are outside the human hearing range, but this is not something that is easily done. It requires specialised equipment and is impractical as part of a paranormal investigation.

The human hearing range, or audible range, is the frequency range that the human ear can detect. The cochlea in the ear is only stimulated by a limited range of frequencies. This means that we can only hear certain frequencies. The range of normal human hearing is 20 Hz–20,000 Hz.

If a voice were outside of this range, it would be speaking at a pitch so low that we can't imagine how that would even sound. On the other hand, if a voice is at a frequency higher than the human audible range, then it would be beyond any piercing high-pitch sound we've ever heard.

There are many cases where an EVP has been captured, and the person playing it back and reviewing the audio has recognised the voice as someone they know. One factor that makes our individual voices recognisable is the frequency we speak at, it determines how low or high pitched our voice is.

When a voice is recorded using an audio capture device and played back, the tone and pitch of the voice remain unchanged in the recording. This tells us that a recording device perfectly preserves the frequency of any voice it records. Therefore, if any recording device were able to capture a voice outside of the audible range, when it was played back, it would be unchanged and would still be beyond the frequency range of the ear - it would remain inaudible.

This means that if an EVP is heard in a recording, it isn't and never has been outside of the human hearing range. If the sound wasn't heard at the time the audio was being recorded but appeared in the recording via some supernatural means, then this is exactly what an EVP is: a mysterious voice captured on a recording that was not heard at the time. The exact mechanism of how the sound is recorded is not understood, but since the recording device would not alter the pitch in anyway, we know that it couldn't have been outside of the human hearing range; it was just unheard at the time.

This doesn't mean that the idea of capturing sounds we can't hear is a ridiculous one; it just means it's not an easy thing to do. Microphones, like the ones you'd find in a smartphone, camera, or digital audio recorder, are designed to capture what the human ear can hear; anything beyond this is just unnecessary data that won't be audible to us in the playback of the recording. Some dictaphones, the type often used on ghost hunts, are even optimised just to capture sounds within the audio range of a human voice; this helps them eliminate extraneous sounds and background noise.

Even if a microphone did have a wider frequency range, the recording device would ignore any sounds outside of the human audible range because it too doesn't want unnecessary data, especially in the case of digital audio where keeping file sizes low is important.

One of the most popular recording formats, and the one used in digital audio recorders that are commonly used to capture EVPs, is the WAV file. It's called a "lossless format," which means that the audio that is stored is an accurate representation of the original sound with no loss of audio quality.

An audio recorder captures packets of audio, usually at 44,100 bits per second; this amount of detail gives it the capacity to capture the entire audible frequency range of 20 Hz to 20 kHz. It will not waste resources capturing any sounds beyond this, as they would be inaudible anyway and would only make the file size bigger unnecessarily.

This means that if you are using a digital audio recorder to try to capture EVPs, you know that the device isn't going to pick up any sounds that you can't hear with your own ears. So, if there is an EVP in your audio recording, then you know it must have been created in one of three ways:

1. The sound was audible at the time of recording and was extremely quiet. It must have been either very close to the

microphone or nearer to the microphone than you were, so it picked up the sound but you didn't. Or the device is more sensitive to low-level noise than your ear.

2. The sound was not audible at the time but has made its way into the recording via a form of electrical interference, which affects either the device's circuitry or storage medium.

3. The sound was somehow imprinted onto the recording via some kind of currently not-understood supernatural method.

The first two possibilities in the list above suggest that the sound might not be an EVP, as in point 3, but this is not strictly the case. In point 1, it could be a spirit making the very quiet sound that the audio recorder picks up, and in point 2, a spirit could be causing the electrical interference.

The very high and very low frequency audio spectrums are an interesting and as yet untapped area of research when it comes to EVPs, perhaps because they come with a high cost of entry due to the need for specialist equipment. Plus, logic dictates that the audible range is where we should focus our attention on capturing EVPs, as this is the frequency range we communicate within in life, so it shouldn't be any different if we can communicate in death.

The equipment needed to investigate the possibility of EVPs outside of our hearing range is different depending on whether you want to capture low-frequency sounds or high-frequency sounds.

Ultra-High Frequency Sound Recording

A very high-frequency sound is called ultrasound; it has a frequency higher than 20,000 Hz, which is outside the upper limit for human hearing.

Ultrasound has several applications in healthcare. It is used to treat kidney stones. The vibrations caused by the ultrasound shake apart kidney stones, breaking them up. It is also used to scan the inside of the body, creating a picture of something that cannot be seen directly, such as an unborn baby in the womb. Ultrasounds are the sounds that bats use to echolocate.

Ultrasound occurs in almost every situation. There is noise around us all the time, but we may not be hearing all of it. Any sort of movement can create a vibration, which in turn creates sound waves; these can be in the ultrasonic range as well as being audible. A lot of the electrical equipment we use on a daily basis emits ultrasound.

Microphones, including those in smartphones and digital audio recorders, are designed specifically to pick up the frequency range that roughly matches the range that the human ear can hear, but most microphones aren't quite as sensitive and fall within this range at about 50 Hz to 18 kHz. Some very expensive specialist microphones are able to pick up audio outside of this range, but you wouldn't find this sort of microphone in any consumer device.

This means that if you want to capture ultrasound, you will need some specialist equipment rather than standard, off-the-shelf recording devices.

There is one tool that might allow you to hear high-frequency sounds without spending a lot of money, and that's a bat detector. These gadgets can be tuned to pick up frequencies from 15,000 Hz to 130,000 Hz, which is far beyond what our ears can hear. These types of detectors are mainly used to pick up ultrasound signals emitted by bats, insects, or other animals.

These devices are capable of translating high frequencies into audible sounds we can hear in real-time. They convert the ultrasound into lower frequencies, which are in the range of human hearing. A headphone output on the device can be used for monitoring the converted sounds in real-time, and some models can also record the sounds onto a memory card.

A bat detector could be used during paranormal investigations to obtain a baseline reading of ultrasound at the location, but also as a means of capturing EVPs at a higher frequency than we can normally hear or capture using a recording device, should they exist in the first place.

Ultra-Low Frequency Sound Recording

Very low-frequency sounds are called infrasound; they have a frequency ranging from 0.1 to 20 Hz. These sounds are below the human range of hearing. While infrasound isn't commonly linked to EVPs, how these sounds affect us is a common area of research for parapsychologists because these low frequency vibrations have been known to cause people to report discomfort in the form of disorientation, feeling panicked, and an increased heart rate and blood pressure. In extreme cases, infrasound has been attributed to feelings of depression, a general feeling of unease, as well as visions of apparitions.

Scientists researching the low frequency noise created by wind turbines and traffic noise discovered the effects of infrasound on humans. They found a link between infrasound and the sensations often described as getting chills down the spine.

As specialist audio equipment is required to detect infrasound, it can be hard to eliminate this from your investigation. However, keeping doors and windows closed will help to keep these frequencies out of the building. It should also be noted that some machinery and even fans can produce the low frequencies associated with infrasound. For this reason, care should be taken to turn off any electrical equipment that could interfere with your investigation.

The link between infrasound and paranormal activity was first researched by some of the early paranormal investigators, including Harry Price, who would make a basic tilt switch using mercury (similar to a modern accelerometer in a phone) in order to detect tremors that could produce infrasound waves. It was the subject of Vic Tandy's 1980 discover relating to a standing wave in his lab being responsible for perceived paranormal activity.

Infrasound is very hard to record; it's not just a case of buying an expensive microphone, as even the best microphone is designed to only capture audible sounds. Although there are purpose-built infrasound mics available, like those manufactured by Bruel & Kjaer, they will set you back around $500. You'll also need a preamp and specialised recording equipment. There's also specialist infrasound monitoring equipment, like the Earthworks QTC-1, which will set you back around $1,000.

It might be possible to construct your own infrasound monitor in a similar way to Harry Price by using a large membrane or diaphragm with a diameter of at least 60 cm or by using a long hollow pipe that could be compressed when the sound hits it. You'd then need to attach a sensitive accelerometer to measure the vibration of either apparatus. Although this approach might work, it wouldn't give you a recording as such, but you'd be able to monitor the amplitude of the infrasound waves using an oscilloscope.

EVP Classification

Unlike a lot of evidence of the paranormal, it's common practise to grade voices captured as EVPs. There is one commonly agreed upon classification scale with defined requirements to help investigators determine which category of EVP they've captured.

According to the Association TransCommunication (ATransC), any form of ITC, including EVP, can be split into two types:

Type 1: Transformative - manipulation of dissimilar sounds

Type 2: Opportunistic - selective use of existing voices

These two types of EVP actually have more to do with the environment the EVP was captured in than the voice recording itself.

Type 1 EVPs are transient sounds of a pitch matching a human voice that spontaneously appear amongst background noise or sounds of a differing pitch. This could be the sound of a voice coming through amongst the hiss or hum that is the ambient sound of the room, or a voice with a similar tone to a human voice heard amongst white noise.
In Type 1 EVPs, the voice is made up of background noise that has been transformed. Random and chaotic background noise is manipulated; its pitch is changed, and words are formed from the ambient sounds. This would cover most EVPs captured during a paranormal investigation, including those captured on audio recorders, whether additional noise was generated or not.

Type 2 EVPs appear within persistent or constant sounds that are already human voices. The EVP is made up opportunistically by using existing words or word parts to form new words or sentences.

For an EVP to be classified as Type 2, it must have been captured using a device that has voices being inputted into it. This could either be via the device's microphone or another audio input, or via a radio modulator (AM or FM) in the case of a spirit box.

The input sound that is being used to form the EVP could include a conversation taking place in the room or someone talking on the radio. It could also be pre-recorded voices that are being played in. It's a fairly common technique for EVP researchers to use audio tracks featuring chanting, foreign languages, or abstract voices during EVP sessions. The same method is also employed by electronic speech synthesis systems like the Ovilus and Echovox, which spew out the random phonics that make up words.

Each of these two types of EVP is divided into subclasses, and it is these that are most commonly referred to by paranormal investigators. You may have heard someone say that a capture is a "Class A EVP," for example. There are a few different scales used to classify EVPs.

All of these scales categorise EVPs as A, B, or C. With class A being the best quality or less objective. Class A EVPs are much stronger evidence than classes B or C. Class C EVPs are generally not easily heard or understood; therefore, it's difficult to determine whether the voice is of paranormal origin or not.

Generally, class A EVPs are clear to hear without explanation, while class B EVPs may require directions. Class C EVPs are vague and mostly obscured by noise.

The Raudive Scale

Konstantin Raudive was the first prominent EVP researcher to attempt to categorise the voices he captured into three classes of audibility. He described the scale he used in his 1968 book, 'Breakthrough: An Amazing Experiment in Electronic

Communication with the Dead,' which was printed in English in 1971.

He wrote, "This grading and my comments are but a rough guide in the present stage of our approach to the psycho-acoustic aspect of the investigation."

Raudive's scale was not widely adopted but is a forerunner to more popular EVP classification methods. Raudive ranked EVPs based on the ease of hearing the voice; later classification systems would take into account the context of the words spoken by the voice.

The Raudive Scale	
Class A	Voices can be heard and identified by anyone with normal hearing and knowledge of the language spoken; no special training of the ear is needed to detect them.
Class B	Voices speak more rapidly and more softly, but are still quite plainly audible to a trained and attentive ear.
Class C	Voices give us a great deal of information and much paranormal data.

Unfortunately, these can be heard only in fragments, even by a trained ear, but with improved technical aids, it may eventually become possible to hear and demonstrate these voices, which lie beyond our range of hearing, without trouble.

Raudive wrote that most of his recordings fell into Class A; he noted that "it is easy to make tape copies of 'A' voices, and they can be repeated as often as desired. Thus, I have analysed roughly

25,000 voices according to speech content, language and rhythm. By this method of repetition, the acoustic reality of the voices can be established beyond doubt, and hallucinations of the ear are excluded."

As Raudive points out, Class B voices can be harder to identify and he suggests that practising analysing EVPs might help; "the ability to differentiate increases with practice, but this is a slow and wearisome process. For this reason it is difficult to use non-regular participants for experimental purposes with class 'B' voices."

The Estep System

The Raudive Scale was soon replaced by a classification system that was clearer and took into account filtering and amplification where needed. The first iteration of this system was first popularised in Sarah Estep's 1988 book, 'Voices of Eternity'. The scale became a global standard for EVP classification.

The Estep System	
Class A	Voices are loud and clear, they can be duplicated onto other tapes. Can be heard without headphones.
Class B	Voices aren't as loud and clear, and can often be heard without headphones.
Class C	Voices are faint or whispery. Headphones must be worn to hear them, and rarely can all the words be interpreted.

Contrary to Raudive's scale, the majority of the voices that Estep captured fell into the Class C category. However, like Raudive's scale, Estep's system soon became outdated and was updated by the AA-EVP. The Association's system of classification was based on the quality and clarity of the EVP, and it also aimed to remove subjectivity, something previous classification scales hadn't attempted to tackle.

The AA-EVP System	
Class A	EVP is a message that can be heard without headphones and that people can generally agree on its content.
Class B	EVP requires headphones to distinguish message content and not everyone will agree on the message.
Class C	EVP requires headphones, often needs amplification and filtering and will seldom even be heard by others.

The KM System

Although the AA-EVP's classification are commonly used still, today the most widely used and accepted classification system is the KM EVP system. It is named after EVP researchers, Doug Kelley and Jari Mikkola.

Kelley and Mikkola's system is more useful when it comes to rating not only the quality of the EVP recording, but also the message contained within it, as this is where any evidence to support paranormal contact will lie. Their scale takes things a step further than the previous classification methods by taking into account the context of the message, how meaningful it is, and how easy it is to comprehend.

The KM System	
Class 1 *Interactive*	Spirit voice is a direct response to a human statement, question, action, activity, or spirit voices respond to each other: • Most or all of the words are clear and intelligible, with or without headphones • Spirit voice communicates comprehensible and existentially meaningful expressions of thoughts, feelings, emotions, opinions, actions, or intentions
Class 2 *Non Interactive*	Voice is a general statement and not a direct response to a statement, question, action, or activity, by humans: • Most or all of the words are generally clear and understandable, with or without headphones • Spirit voice communication is comprehensible and existentially a meaningful expression of thoughts, feelings, emotions, opinions, actions, or intentions

The KM System	
Class 3 *Non Speech*	Spirit voice is a sound other than the spoken word: • Growls, screams, humming, etc • Musical instruments, TV, radio, concerts, footsteps, rapping, banging, barking, etc
Class 4 *Null*	The EVP contains nothing of value in understanding the spirit realm or spirit psychology: • Words are unintelligible, with or without headphones • Spirit voice does not communicate comprehensible and existentially meaningful expressions of thoughts, feelings, emotions, opinions, actions, or intentions, although the word(s) may be intelligible

Event Planning and Management

The key to hosting a successful paranormal event is to meticulously plan how the event should unfold. The benefits of having such a plan include:

• Efficient movement of people and equipment

• Reduction to the likelihood of issues which could result in additional costs due to damage and cleaning activities

• The ability to respond to unexpected occurrences

• Securing long-term loyalty from clients and staff and generating repeat bookings

• Reduction in liability arising from accidents and injuries and related insurance costs

In order to ensure your event delivers, you'll need to put together a plan for the event, including a running order. You'll need to ensure you have the tools, equipment, and staff necessary to make the event successful.

In order to plan your event, you'll need to develop a few essential skills that every event planner relies upon, including the following:

• Ability to work in a team or independently

• Interpersonal and social skills

• Analytical ability

• Communication skills

• High organisational skills

• Good time management

• Ability to work to deadlines

- Able to pay attention to details
- Negotiating skills
- Ability to deal with pressure situations
- Problem-solving skills
- Creativity
- Marketing and public relations

To get into the mindset of an event manager, there is one basic principle that you should follow, which event planners call 'the five Ws'. When planning an event, you should always ask why, who, when, where, and what. Throughout the following chapters, we will attempt to answer these questions in relation to a paranormal event, but here's a quick overview of those five important questions.

Why am I putting on the event?

This is the first and most important question you need to ask when planning an event. You need to have a clear purpose for staging the event in the first place. In the case of a ghost hunting event, it is to give the public a taste of what a professional paranormal investigation is like.

Who do I want to come to the event?

Knowledge of your target audience is essential information. You should build a picture of the types of people who are likely to attend. This will form the basis of your marketing plan. Most ghost hunting events are targeted at adults over the age of 18, but they are more popular with those in their late 20s to early 50s, a demographic with enough disposable income to spend on a night of paranormal entertainment.

When is the best time to stage the event?

This is very important to determine to avoid conflicts with other events. In the case of ghost hunting, you will be limited by venue availability. Paranormal events can be held on any day of the week. People are always willing to take time off work, and those who work shifts will be able to come even on a weeknight. The most popular days tend to be Friday and Saturday nights, as this is when most people are free.

Where is the best place to stage the event?

Traditional event planners try to find the most suitable and convenient venue to facilitate easy access and also create an enjoyable atmosphere. While this is still important with paranormal events, there's also the added complication of finding a venue with a haunted reputation and one that will allow you to host an event late into the night. Most ghost hunting events start late in the evening and finish between 1 and 3am. Some even allow sleepovers. We will look into location scouting in more depth in the next chapter.

What concept or idea will best serve the purposes of the event?

This is quite a simple question for paranormal events. We already have a fairly good idea of the type of event we want to run. However, events can vary depending on the venue and the number of attendees. It is generally recommended for event planners to engage in brainstorming sessions to come up with a concept for the event if one has not been developed or proposed already.

Types of Events

Not all paranormal events are the same, and customers will be looking for different things. The most common types of events include ghost walks, either at a private venue or on public land, or ghost hunts.

Ghost Walks on Public Land

Ghost walks are becoming more and more popular. In some cities in the United Kingdom multiple tour guides compete for the business of tourists every night of the week. Walks on public land means a guided ghost tour around the streets, usually the guests don't venture into locations but the guide will tell them about the haunted history of the buildings on the tour.

Ghost Walks at a Private Venue

This option works well in a larger haunted location, such as a castle and its grounds or a large manor house. Guests can take part in a guided walk around the venue, stopping at the paranormal hotspots where a guide can tell them about the haunted history and spooky stories associated with that location.

As well as walking tours of a property, you may also want to consider a ghost stories night. This is perfect for a small location where guests might be contained in one room of the venue. An experienced and engaging storyteller will be more than capable of holding attendees' attention with some tales of ghostly goings-on. For this type of event to work, it is important to set the mood, perhaps with low lighting and a roaring fire in an atmospheric venue.

Ghost Hunts

Ghost hunts are the most popular type of event and the type we will be focussing on in the most detail. They are almost always conducted in privately owned properties. The number of guests depends on the size of the property, but can be anywhere from a handful to 60 or more. Often the guests are split into smaller groups and are guided through paranormal activities such as séances and vigils at various paranormal hotspots around the location.

There are a few approaches to ghost hunts. They can be either scientific or spiritual in nature, or include elements of both. In a scientific ghost hunt, guests might use ghost hunting gadgets such as EMF meters and thermometers to try to collect quantitative evidence of the paranormal. In a more spiritual ghost hunt, a medium might facilitate the event and attempt to or encourage guests to try to make contact with ghosts through methods such as a Ouija board or calling out to spirits.

Locations

One of the most important things to consider when planning a paranormal event is the location. Unlike regular events, you have a bit more to think about, as you won't only need to find a venue that you can hire that is of a suitable size and is safe for the general public, but you'll also need to make sure there are ghost stories and hauntings associated with the location.

If you are planning a walking tour, then your job is a little easier, as you can simply research the haunted locations in the area where you plan to run the tour and then plot a route between them. You won't need permission from the venues, as you will simply lead your guests to the location and talk about the haunted history from the outside. However, you will need to consider the route, is it safe? Are there pavements? And most importantly, can your guests safely stand outside the location in a group without being at risk of being hit by passing traffic or causing an obstruction to pedestrians or customers of the location?

However, if you're planning a tour or a ghost hunt in a privately owned haunted location, then you'll need to first find a location and ensure it is sufficiently haunted to make it an entertaining evening. Although ghosts can be found in almost any location, the stories vary depending on the specific venue. You may encounter properties that house the lost souls of murder victims, playful spirits, or even poltergeists.

But remember, a ghost hunting event where you tell customers you are on the hunt for a famous serial killer may be deemed to be in poor taste and could become a PR disaster.

If you are planning on having 20 or more people attend, then you will have to consider your venue carefully.

Before choosing the location for the event, you should carefully consider the exact specification of space required for the particular event, taking the following into consideration:

• The size of the venue

• The location of toilets

• Ease of access

• Where to put signs to direct people to specific locations throughout the venue

• How would rooms be accessed, at all times or at specific times only?

• Providing information about the rules for using facilities at the venue

• The number of reports of ghost sightings or paranormal activity

Based on these factors, you'll need to create a shortlist and evaluate each location based on the following:

• Permission to display branding and signage

• Physical state

• Capacity

• Control of lighting

• Available amenities

• Accessibility

• Out-of-hours access

The venue will usually be able to provide you with guidelines in regards to promotional activities that can be carried out at the venue, including the provision for displaying banners, branding, and directional signs and information on restrictions concerning the display of event information.

You should take the physical state of the venue and its capacity into account. It should be atmospheric, safe, and well-maintained. Remember that ghost hunts are often carried out in the dark, which can greatly increase risk. With this in mind, you should check that you have adequate control of the lighting in the venue. Can all the lights be turned off without emergency lighting coming on? You should also check that there is a means to control the amount of natural light entering the building.

How will people get to the event? Make sure your publicity includes details about public transportation and parking. Will you need to put up signs in the surrounding streets to make the event easier to find? The venue should have good transportation links or adequate parking. Guests' cars should not cause obstructions to local residents or businesses or limit access to the venue itself.

As disused or abandoned buildings are popular locations for paranormal events, you should check the availability of restrooms and other amenities. The general rule is to provide one toilet for every 75 people of each gender, which can be increased for VIP events. Portable toilets, for example, can be hired in blocks.

Another thing to consider, which is very specific to paranormal events, is the time the venue is accessible. Most locations are open during standard business hours or evenings, but ghost hunts often take place at unusual hours. They usually start late in the evening and finish at around midnight or the early hours of the morning.

An important part of selecting a location is accessibility. Disability laws make it a requirement for planners to create adequate accessibility and support for guests who have need of these facilities. You should ensure that locations have provisions for wheelchair accessibility.

You should do what you can to ensure that disabled people can take part in your event. For example, if possible, choose a venue that is accessible for wheelchair users and provide a sign language interpreter for speeches and talks, if needed. You may want to include information about how accessible your event will be on your event's website so that people will know in advance if their needs are going to be catered for. You could also invite people to contact you in advance if they have a particular access need so that you can adjust your plans to make the event accessible for them.

Once you have decided on a location and researched its haunted history, you should always try to obtain written evidence of the venue's availability to avoid booking conflicts.

Researching a Location

Finding a suitable venue is only half the battle. Once you've chosen your location, do your research. You need to make sure that it has a suitable haunted history and that your guests are likely to experience some kind of paranormal activity, although this can never be guaranteed due to the nature of the paranormal.

The more you know about the location, the better. Find out as much as possible about the ghosts you may encounter. When do they appear? Where have they been spotted? How do they make their presence known? Do they communicate, and how?

Details about the hauntings of a building can be found in several places. You should ask the venue owner for information about ghost sightings and paranormal activity and, if possible, contact previous owners. Local interest books on ghost stories may also include details of hauntings. And of course the internet is a great place to do research.

You should cross-reference these ghost stories in order to establish which ghosts, spirits, and activities are the most prevalent.

As well as getting the facts on hauntings, you should also research the history of the location, including details such as:

• When it was built

• What it's been used for over the years

• Notable residents

• Events of interest such as fires, murders, or ancient battles

It's recommended to put together a document with the full history and information of hauntings. This is not for the guests' use but should be used as a consistent reference document when putting together marketing materials, writing scripts, planning tour routes, and deciding which parts of the building to focus on during ghost hunts.

Staging Event

When holding your first event at a new location, you should always hold a staging night. This should be done with a group of staff, friends, or volunteers of approximately the same size as the group that will attend the real event.

We'll cover exactly what activities should be included in your event in a later chapter, and it's these activities that you should run through at the location during the staging event. This gives you a chance to check that the activities you have planned are practical for the locations within the building and that there will likely be some paranormal activity for your guests.

Guidance on putting together an actual event comes later in the book, but it's also important to remember the need for a staging event during the early planning stages when you are first searching for and booking a venue for your event.

This step is equally important for ghost walks, as you'll need to be very familiar with your route and know exactly how long the route will take when you have guests in tow. It's likely to be much slower than when walking the route alone.

If you're already well known in the paranormal field or have a following, then a good way to recruit volunteers would be to run a competition to give your followers the chance to go ghost hunting with you. This way, you get volunteer ghost hunters for free, but it also allows you to start publicising the event, gauge interest, and offer those that didn't win the chance to book a night at a discounted rate.

You'll need to learn all you can from the staging event, such as how smoothly it ran, what worked well, and what could be improved. To help you evaluate the night, it may be a good idea to use a video camera or audio recorder to capture the event so that you can review it later, or ask a volunteer to take notes throughout the night.

It's also a good idea to ask your volunteer guests for feedback at the end of the evening.

Risk Assessment

An important part of planning any event is doing all you can to avoid accidents and injuries, and with paranormal events, there are significantly more risks than with other events, such as darkness and the dangers of derelict buildings. These dangers should be taken into consideration when planning an event, and as many risks as possible should be eliminated.

No matter how much you plan, a few unexpected problems may arise and you might discover that you have a few last minute details to resolve. The only thing you can do is prepare for the unexpected. Make sure you have at your fingertips the tools to solve any problems that may occur.

Whatever the scale of the event, make sure there is a clear understanding within the organising team of who will be responsible for safety matters. For organisations with five or more employees, this is likely to be driven by the company's health and safety policy.

Advice on carrying out a risk assessment could be an entire book of its own. It would be impractical to cover this topic in full, especially when there are plenty of existing books that deal with this subject specifically, but I have included some useful information and some general principles that should be followed.

A risk assessment is a document that lists in detail anything that could cause harm to people, so that you can weigh up whether you have taken enough precautions or should do more to prevent harm. Its main objective is to determine the measures required to avoid incidents and accidents.

There are no fixed rules on how a risk assessment should be carried out, but if you are unsure, it may be wise to ask the owner of the property to help you out or consult a health and safety professional to conduct an inspection of the property for you.

The aspects of assessing risks that can be challenging for someone without training are the abilities to identify hazards, categorise risks, and evaluate them. These abilities will allow a suitable and sufficient risk assessment to be conducted as part of your event plan.

The four main steps to ensure that your risk assessment is carried out correctly are:

- Identify the hazards

- Decide who might be harmed and how

- Evaluate the risks and decide on control measures
- Record your findings and implement them

Identify the Hazards

In order to identify hazards, you need to understand the difference between a 'hazard' and a 'risk'. A hazard is something with the potential to cause harm, and the risk is the likelihood of that potential harm being realised. Hazards can be identified by using a number of different techniques, such as walking around the location or asking the property owner.

Decide Who Might be Harmed and How Likely It Is

Once you have identified the hazards, you need to understand who might be harmed and how, such as guests, other members of the public, event staff, or volunteers.

The likelihood of a specific risk causing injury is usually rated on a scale of A to E. These ratings mean:

A - Almost certain: Is expected to occur in most circumstances

B - Likely: Will probably occur in most circumstances

C - Possible: Might occur at some time

D - Unlikely: Could occur at some time

E - Rare: May occur but only in exceptional circumstances

Evaluate the risks and decide on control measures

After identifying the hazards and deciding who might be harmed and how, you are then required to protect people from harm. The hazards can either be removed completely or the risks controlled so that the injury is unlikely.

In order to control the risk, you need to work out the best method of handling it. The following methods, which are referred to as the 'hierarchy of controls', guide you on how to eliminate or reduce the risk:

• Elimination – by removing the hazard entirely through new design or implementing a new process

• Substitution – by replacing hazardous materials or methods with less hazardous alternatives

• Engineering – by isolating, enclosing, or containing the hazard or through design improvements

• Administrative – by ensuring guests are familiar with safety guidelines and that staff and volunteers are trained effectively

• Personal protective equipment (PPE) – by making sure that appropriate safety equipment, such as gloves, hats, sunscreen, etc. are available

Record your findings

Your findings should be written down. By recording the findings, it shows that you have identified the hazards, determined who could be harmed and how, and also shows how you plan to eliminate the risks and hazards.

Remember that even if you've held an event at a location previously, few locations stay the same, and as a result, this risk assessment should be reviewed and updated when required.

Due to the varying nature of events and venues, it is impossible to foresee all potential hazards. Below are some examples of common hazards:

• Trip hazards such as cables running across a floor, loose flooring, or carpet

• Falls and drops, check for any sheer drops, steps that aren't clearly visible

• Collision risk with vehicles and guests/staff on the event site
• Certain activities cannot be offered due to weather conditions

• Extreme weather effects on guests and personnel such as heat exhaustion, heat stroke, fainting and sunburn

If you allow guests time to explore the property on their own, be very clear when highlighting any area that the public is not allowed to enter. This is especially relevant for disused properties where there may be unsafe floors, trips, and other hazards.

If areas of the property are cordoned off, it probably means they are structurally unsafe and could be hiding hazards that could hurt or even kill you or your guests. Putting together a risk assessment document will help you avoid mishaps.

Another important consideration is the guest evacuation procedure in the event of an emergency, bearing in mind that not all properties will have a working fire alarm system.

You should be prepared for all eventualities. Think about the worst-case scenario. What provision needs to be made for the emergency services? What will be the procedure for summoning assistance, and how will they get into and out of the site?

Ensure you have vehicles close by to deal with incidents. Planners also need to identify the nearest hospital and have knowledge of all local emergency phone numbers.

Decide who will be responsible for first aid on the day. For large events, you could ask a first-aid organisation to attend. Even if you are just using your own volunteers, it's reassuring for guests to have a visible first aid point at the event and people who are taking the role of first aiders. Remember, some of your staff or volunteers may already have first aid training.

Logistics

Staffing

The key to successfully staffing an event is assigning the right person to the right job. Be crystal clear about who is qualified to set up the event, run the event, and pack up when the event is done. The best approach to staffing is to prepare a list of activities from your plan and assign each of these activities to the most qualified person.

Of course, when it comes to paranormal events, the more experience the staff members have with ghost hunting, the better, as this will allow them to inject their own personality and experience into the event.

The ratio of staff to guests at an event should be identified early in the planning process based on the risk assessment. Every event is different, and as such, we would not recommend applying a formula to assess the numbers of personnel needed.

However, you should work on the basis of approximately one member of staff for every ten members of the public. Additional requirements may also be needed at events that are spread out over a large area to help guests find their way around.

In general, security personnel (guards, door supervisors, etc.) are not needed for paranormal events, but they should be considered for larger events and certain locations. The venue owner should be able to advise you on this.

Budgeting

Budgeting for an event can be tricky, especially as the majority of ticket sellers don't release the funds until after the event. Luckily, a lot of businesses within the events industry work in a similar way and don't require payment until after the event, so this shouldn't make cash flow too much of an issue.

One of the biggest costs you'll need to budget for to put on a ghost hunting event is paranormal kit and gadgets. Of course, this is a cost that is unique to paranormal events. Most people attending your event won't have their own equipment, but using the gadgets of the trade is something they will expect to experience.

The upfront cost for these devices can be fairly high, as you will need to buy a significant amount of equipment and multiples of some items to ensure that people can investigate properly. For a group of around ten people, you will probably need to spend around £1500. The bigger your events, the more equipment you will need to make available to your guests. There are ways to pick up equipment a bit cheaper. There is always a huge variety of both new and secondhand ghost hunting equipment on eBay, which can mean you can get a full setup for much less. We'll take a look at the specific types of equipment you'll need in a later chapter.

When preparing your event budget, you should consider the following:

• Balance sheet showing a list of all expenses relating to accommodation, transportation, catering services, marketing, etc.

• Sufficient funds must be available to pay for all expenses and a separate account opened for accrued expenses during the event.

• Estimate costs using records of budgets for similar events held previously

• Make budget provisions for licences and insurance for all potential liabilities such as cancellation/postponing the event or a fire.

• Have some emergency funds available to take care of unexpected expenses.

A document containing details of all expenses should be prepared. Take into account all your costs so that you don't end up with nasty surprises along the way. This may include:

• Creating a website

• Venue hire

• Publicity and promotion

• Purchase of ghost hunting equipment

• Spare batteries

• Decorations/branding

• Audio-visual equipment hire

• Refreshments

• Transport

• Phone bills, postage, and other admin

• Insurance

• First aid equipment

• Fees for licences and permissions
• Hire of a photographer or videographer

Public Liability

However well prepared you are, accidents do happen. For this reason, if you're running an event for members of the public, then you must have public liability insurance and should consider professional indemnity insurance. There are plenty of insurance companies that will provide you with annual or single-event public liability insurance. There are even insurance companies that specialise in paranormal investigation and public liability.

Public liability insurance is very important, as it can protect you if someone is injured, loses their life, or their property is damaged because of your event. Policies tend to offer between £1 million and £5 million of cover to protect you against these costs.

For example, if a client or guest tripped over a cable to one of your cameras and broke their arm, then decided to make a claim against you for compensation, the policy would help you defend it and cover the cost of compensation claims and legal expenses.

Public liability insurance also covers accidental damage to the venue where your event is being held. Venue managers will often require evidence of your public liability insurance before the booking is confirmed, usually up to a value of £5 million.

The cost of a policy is specific to your requirements and will depend on how many people are involved in your business, the limit of indemnity you require, and whether you have previously had any claims made against you, but a typical insurance policy as of 2018 costs less than £200 per year, which gives you £1 million worth of protection. A single-event policy with the same level of cover costs around £50.

Public liability insurance only covers injury or damage to third parties, not to any of your staff or volunteers. To ensure that your team is covered, you may also want to investigate employers' liability insurance, which protects staff, short-term staff, casual workers, contractors, and volunteers. If you employ people, you are legally obliged to take out employers' liability insurance. Failure to do so could result in heavy fines.

Professional indemnity insurance, also known as "malpractice" insurance, is a vital consideration for all businesses. It covers you against claims from clients who allege that the advice or services you provided them have caused them loss, damage, or suffering.

This can be the result of anything from giving bad advice or causing psychological harm or upset to a breach of confidentiality, defamation of character, or damage to their reputation.

When buying event insurance, be sure to read your policy documents carefully in order to understand any exclusions.

Dates, Times and Availability

Due to the nature of paranormal events of this type, they almost always take place in the evening, whether it's a ghost hunt, tour or ghost walk. This is mainly due to the fact that it is dark in the evening, which adds to the atmosphere.

This is especially important when planning a ghost hunt, as you will need to eliminate the amount of light from the outside world entering the property. It's not always possible to black out every window. It's equally important for ghost walks, as these types of events just wouldn't be the same in the day.

Most ghost hunting events start late in the evening and finish between 1 and 3am, but when planning a start time, be aware of the time of year as summer days may be much longer and daylight will last much longer into the evening.

Paranormal events can be held on any day of the week, and in general, people are always willing to take time off work or come to the event after work. There are also those who work shifts and will be able to come even on a weeknight. Having said that, the most popular days for any public event tend to be Friday and Saturday nights, as this is when most people are free.

You should start planning your event well in advance. This will ensure you have enough time to organise everything in time and will give your guests plenty of notice to check dates, arrange babysitters, arrange transportation, and do anything else they need to do to ensure they can make the event. Producing early publicity for the event also serves as a good opportunity to appeal for volunteers.

Promotion and Sales

Promoting Your Event

If you are considering selling tickets to a public event, then you probably already have a following online, whether that be through YouTube, Facebook, TikTok, Twitter, or other social media platforms. This existing audience is crucial when it comes to marketing your event. Without it, you may have to spend a lot of money, time, and effort promoting your event.

Even if you are already established on social media, you will need a website if you don't already have one. But don't let this scare you off. It can be very cheap and easy to set up a basic website. If you are looking to turn this into a business and run multiple events, then a website is the best way to list upcoming events. It's also a place that you can direct potential customers to in order to buy tickets. There will be more on ticket sales in the next section.

Paying to promote your event on social media can be effective if the ads are targeted to a niche group of people in the local area. However, you may find it's more effective to manually target those who you think might be interested for the first few events by setting up an event on Facebook and inviting people to it. You could also use Twitter to send out reminders about your event in the weeks and days leading up to it.
Who do you want your publicity to reach? Think about where those people are most likely to see your publicity and what will attract them to the event. This could be groups associated with the location who'd like to learn more about its haunted history. Can the venue help promote the event?

It is best to get publicity out early, even if this means that it can't include all the final details of the event. You might want to do one piece of publicity as early as possible, which includes the date of the event and some basic information about it, and another closer to the time, which includes more detailed information.

Once you have a few well-run events under your belt, you will often find that many choose to rebook or that you gain a large number of new attendees through word of mouth.

A few tried and tested ways to promote your event include:

• Offer early bird tickets

• Run a competition

• Offer group discounts

Early bird tickets are discounted tickets, which are made available for a limited time long before the event. Offering a special price will encourage those who are interested to book early, giving you a better idea of numbers in advance.

Competitions can be a very effective way of promoting an event, especially when run through Facebook. By offering one pair of tickets as a prize to your Facebook followers if they comment, like, or share your post on Facebook, you have the potential to reach many more people, as this post will become visible to the friends of all those who have engaged with it.

Offering group discounts can also be beneficial as it will encourage large groups to book in bulk, but use this option with caution and only when needed as it will decrease your revenue. You need to do the maths to implement a group-buying campaign.

Sales

In order to sell tickets for your event, you'll also need to not only find a suitable site to sell them through, but you'll have to decide on the price for your event tickets. Will you sell the same ticket to everyone or offer discounted early bird tickets and VIP tickets with extra perks? How many of each type of ticket will you sell? And, of course, you'll need to think of ways to process payments, monitor your ticket sales, and stay connected to the buyers.

For small and medium-sized event organisers, self-service ticketing sites are the most efficient and affordable way to sell tickets for an event. These sites let you create events and sell event tickets on your own. It's easy to register, create your event, and start selling tickets.

The benefit of using a service like this is that it handles the payment processing and issues the tickets (either physically via the post or eTickets via email). It also manages a guest list for you and gives you realtime stats for tracking sales and guest numbers.

Self-service ticketing sites have different pricing models. Some charge you a flat fee to use their services. Others charge no upfront fees. Instead, whenever someone buys a ticket, a small booking fee is added to the price. Most sites let organisers decide whether to absorb this fee, which means the buyer only pays the original ticket's face value, or pass the costs on to the guests, in which case the buyers pay both the ticket price and the booking fee.

Using a self-service ticketing site can be easily combined with whatever event promotion you might already be doing. For example, you might create your event on a self-service ticketing site and then promote it on Facebook or other forums of your choice.

With most ticketing services, you get the option of embedding a ticket widget directly on your website or blog so that people can buy tickets without having to leave your site. This obviously works well if you have an established online presence.

However, you can find tools that enable you to create a website or turn your existing website into an event ticket shop. If you have a Wordpress site, you'll find a number of plugins that enable you to sell event tickets. Other sites, like Shopify, specialise in helping you run an online store and can also work well for selling event tickets.

With this approach, you have more control over your own brand and get to decide on the look and feel of your ticket storefront.

A final option is to sell at the door. It may seem obvious, but with so much attention paid to selling tickets online, it's easy to forget the potential for on-site sales, and this option is particularly popular with guided ghost walks. A lot of ticketing websites have a mobile box office app, which allows you to sell tickets quickly in person from any device.

The downside of on-site sales is that you don't have a clear idea of the number of guests in advance, and things like inclement weather might affect the turnout if guests don't have tickets in advance.

On the Day

When the big day arrives, it is vitally important that you are ready to receive guests, that the location is safe, that paying customers have a good experience, and that the event runs as smoothly as possible.

This process starts in the days leading up to the event. You'll need to run through the day in detail:

Where will everybody be on the day?

What will each person be responsible for doing?

Are all the jobs covered, or do you need to do a last-minute ring round to fill some gaps?

Have you set up all the admin (forms and paperwork) that will be needed on the day? e.g., guest lists, photo consent forms, etc.

How will equipment and volunteers get to and from the venue?

Will you be able to take hired equipment directly to and from the event, or will it need to be stored?

What will happen if it rains?
Do you have enough time, materials, and people for setting up and clearing away?

On the day of the event, most event organisers use a 'schedule of events' to ensure the event runs smoothly. This is a document that you should prepare when planning your event. This important document breaks down activities into individual tasks and highlights the time for performing activities, the details of activities, and the person responsible for ensuring the objectives of a particular activity are achieved.

This cue-to-cue document takes into account activities such as the arrival of guests, transportation plans, hospitality arrangements, security, information about the venue, clean-up, and equipment set-up procedures.

Having adequate, detailed information in this document makes for a smooth and organised overall event experience for all concerned.

The ideal approach to putting together an effective event schedule is to engage all stakeholders in the planning process, encompassing all activities from the start of the event to its completion, especially the guests. You can get a better perspective by viewing all aspects of the event through the eyes of the guests. Consider how things will appear to them, how they will feel about the atmosphere, and what the overall experience will be like.

Remember that if you are using an event photographer or videographer, you should put up signs informing people that their image may be captured in photographic or video form.

Welcoming Your Guests

The welcome or orientation is an important part of the event to help guests feel at ease, to let them know what they can expect over the evening, and to run through important safety information in order to keep them safe. It's a time to introduce the team and run through the history of the property.

Although it's a good idea to tell guests about the history of the location, the organisers of many ghost events avoid telling guests too much about its haunted past, the spirits that have been encountered, and what guests at previous events have picked up. This means that if a guest does unearth some information like a name or date during a vigil, it's less likely that they've been influenced by what they've heard.

You should assure guests that the event is a genuine investigation of the paranormal and that nothing will be faked or staged by you or your staff. However, you should make it clear that you cannot guarantee any activity and that it's up to guests to decide whether anything they do experience is paranormal or not.

Guests should be encouraged to mention anything they see, hear, feel, or experience at the time. Some guests may feel silly doing this, but by talking about it, they may find others in the group experienced the same thing. Mentioning it later means it cannot be investigated.

You should encourage guests to respect each other's beliefs. Public ghost hunting events are usually attended by a mix of people, from firm believers in the paranormal to the harshest skeptics, plus the open-minded, undecided few in between. Guests should be reminded that everyone picks up on different things and experiences things in different ways. One guest may feel a cold draught on their face, but the person standing next to them may feel nothing. This shouldn't become a point of contention or debate.

As ghost hunting events are always conducted in the dark, guests are usually asked to bring along their own torch. The welcome briefing is a good time to check that everyone has access to a torch. You may need a few to loan out. Ensure there is at least one torch with every party of guests.

You'll also need to encourage guests to take photos. This not only gives the guests some kind of evidence to take home with them, but can also act as excellent social marketing for you. Remember to ask guests to tag your event or company when they share them on social media.

You could also offer guests some advice on how to take photographs during a ghost hunt. One of the most important things for them to remember is that ghost hunts are conducted in the dark, so guests should say "flash" before taking a photo so that other guests know to look away.

The best piece of advice you can give guests is to stand still and take three photos as quickly as their camera will allow you to. This way if you spot something in one photo you can use the other photos to corroborate it.

You should ask guests if they are planning on using audio or video recording equipment. If anyone is, then you should make the rest of the group aware and check that this isn't a problem in order to respect their privacy. You may need to ask a guest not to record at certain times or make sure that guests who don't want to be recorded are in different groups from those with the recording equipment.

In terms of health and safety and venue rules, you'll probably need to mention:

• Fire and evacuation procedures

• No smoking policy

• Acceptable behaviour

Before the paranormal activities get underway, you'll need to go through the running order of the event. Give guests a breakdown of what they can expect, when there will be breaks and free time, and what time the event comes to an end.

This welcome briefing may also include individual and group photographs, which are taken by a professional photographer or a member of the team.

Some events also include a chance to have your photograph taken with the known or celebrity ghost hunters at the event. These celebrity photo opportunities are sometimes sold for a small additional fee as an extra source of income for the event or as a sweetener for the celeb expert.

Ghost Hunting Activities

You will not be able to run a ghost hunt with more than a few people without having a few extra expert helpers. These facilitators will teach guests the way of paranormal investigations, guide guests through the venue, and help guests interpret their findings.

It's important to remember that, even if you don't believe in the effectiveness of some of the activities that are usually carried out at paranormal events, your guests will probably expect to partake in them, so you and your team will need to conduct these activities in a positive and engaging way.

Other guests may not believe in certain activities either, so it is also the job of the event's facilitators to encourage the guests to get involved in all activities with an open mind.

At most events, the activity starts by taking the group to a location on the property where a group vigil is held. This may not be possible in larger groups, in which case guests will begin with team vigils.

For team vigils, the guests are split into small teams and sent to two or three paranormal hotspots around the property, where a facilitator will guide them through a series of paranormal experiments, often using specialist equipment. The teams will swap around throughout the night so that everyone gets to experience everything the event has to offer.

The vigils usually consist of a few staple paranormal activities, which make up the group and team vigils:

• Calling out to spirits

- Ouija boards

- EMF meters and other gadgets

- Table tipping

- Lone vigils

Equipment

The number of individual pieces of equipment you need at an event depends on the number of guests. As a very rough guide, you'll need at least one gadget for every five people. If the group is to be split into smaller teams, then you'll need a piece of equipment for each of those teams.

When it comes to equipment for events, rule number one is to make sure all your batteries are charged and you have plenty of spares.

You might consider using Ouija boards, thermometers, EMF meters, electronic speech synthesis (EchoVox, Ovilus etc.), spirit boxes, or trigger objects.

There's no rules as to what equipment you can and can't use on a public ghost hunting, but to ensure the satisfaction of your guests pick equipment that everyone present can enjoy. By this we me a device that triggers audibly or with lights, so all guests will know when it has triggered rather than a single user or a small group huddle around the device.

"calling out," something we have covered in-depth in the section on Ghost Hunting.

Post event

Near the end of the event, after the vigils have taken place, the group should come back together to talk about their experiences. At this point, you might want to tell guests if any of the information they've collected through séances matches the haunted history of the location.

This point in the evening is also a good opportunity to ask guests for feedback on the event, which of course should be noted by a member of the team to draw lessons for future events.

Once the event is over and the guests have left, it is your responsibility to return the location to its original condition. Make certain that you return all spaces used to the state you found them in.

It's a good idea to gather your staff and volunteers before they leave for a brief discussion about the event, to talk through what went well and badly. Remember to thank your staff and volunteers.

Vigils

Many events start out with a group vigil before breaking out into smaller teams for individual vigils. They should ideally be conducted in silence, so you should make sure there is a good separation between groups.

It's best to perform these vigils or séances in darkness. Not only does this help set the mood, but it's also said to help the spirits around you manifest. Many paranormal investigators believe that in order for a spirit to manifest, it needs to draw on all of its energy to take on a physical, or at least visible, form. When light is present in the room, surrounding energy drowns the spirit out. Occasionally, a spirit will be strong enough to overcome this barrier and manifest during the day, but generally, it is considered to be more difficult.

The effect is similar to the principle that a radio has better reception at night. You'll find that you're able to pick up radio stations from further away. This is because during the day, solar radiation from the sun ionises our atmosphere. This heavy ionisation in the atmosphere is known to drown out certain forms of electrical activity, such as radio and television broadcasts, and it is this same energy that is preventing ghosts from manifesting.

The participants of the séance should either stand or sit around a table. You should make sure your guests are comfortable, as movement or fidgeting may be wrongly attributed to paranormal activity in the dark. The guests should then hold hands to form a circle. This is done for protection and to focus the energy of the participants, allowing spirits to draw on it and use it to communicate. Knowing everyone is holding hands also means your guests know that no one at the séance is creating any tapping noises or moving anything themselves in the dark.

At this point, you should start asking the spirits questions and looking for responses through either a ghost hunting gadget, an ouija board, tapping, or by using a trigger object. This is called

Printed in Great Britain
by Amazon

33b03d00-b15c-4212-baf9-f1c566fce26fR01